PENGUIN BOOKS

THE CLASSIC AMERICAN CHILDREN'S STORY

Jerry Griswold is the author of two books, *The Children's Books of Randall Jarrell* and *The Classic American Children's Story*, which won the Outstanding Book of the Year Award from the Children's Literature Association. He has also written more than one hundred essays in *The Nation*, *The New Republic*, *The Paris Review*, *The New York Times Book Review*, and elsewhere. Griswold's work also appears frequently in the *Los Angeles Times*. Professor of English and Comparative Literature at San Diego University (where students honored him as Outstanding Professor in 1991), Griswold has also taught at Northeastern University and the University of Connecticut and has been a visiting professor at UCLA and the University of California at San Diego.

THE CLASSIC AMERICAN CHILDREN'S STORY

❖ ❖ ❖ ❖ ❖ ❖ ❖

Novels of the Golden Age

Jerry Griswold

PENGUIN BOOKS

PENGUIN BOOKS
Published by the Penguin Group
Penguin Books USA Inc., 375 Hudson Street, New York, New York 10014, U.S.A.
Penguin Books Ltd, 27 Wrights Lane, London W8 5TZ, England
Penguin Books Australia Ltd, Ringwood, Victoria, Australia
Penguin Books Canada Ltd, 10 Alcorn Avenue, Toronto, Ontario, Canada M4V 3B2
Penguin Books (N.Z.) Ltd, 182–190 Wairau Road, Auckland 10, New Zealand

Penguin Books Ltd, Registered Offices: Harmondsworth, Middlesex, England

First published in the United States of America as *Audacious Kids:
Coming of Age in America's Classic Children's Books* by Oxford University Press, Inc. 1992
Published in Penguin Books 1996

1 3 5 7 9 10 8 6 4 2

THE LIBRARY OF CONGRESS HAS CATALOGUED THE HARDCOVER AS FOLLOWS:
Griswold, Jerome.
Audacious kids: coming of age in America's classic children's books/Jerry Griswold.
p. cm.
Includes bibliographical references and index.
ISBN 0-19-505888-7 (hc.)
ISBN 0 14 02.5639 3 (pbk.)
1. Children's stories. American History and criticism.
2. Children—United States—Books and reading. I. Title.
PS374.C454G75   1992
813.009'9282—dc20   91–31115

Printed in the United States of America
Set in Garamond #3

There is no past without the sense of play that keeps it fresh.

Carlos Fuentes, *Distant Relations*

Preface

Compare the best-selling fiction of our own era—for example, James Michener's *Hawaii* and *Texas,* William Peter Blatty's *The Exorcist,* Stephen King's *The Dead Zone,* Danielle Steel's *Daddy* and *Star,* Tom Clancy's *The Hunt for Red October* and *Clear and Present Danger*—with the most popular novels of a hundred years ago:

- 1865–1869: *Our Mutual Friend, Hans Brinker, Alice's Adventures in Wonderland, Ragged Dick, Little Women, Innocents Abroad*

- 1870–1879: *The Rubaiyat of Omar Khayyam, The Luck of Roaring Camp, Little Men, Around the World in Eighty Days, Twenty Thousand Leagues Under the Sea, The Adventures of Tom Sawyer*

- 1880–1889: *Uncle Remus, Ben-Hur, Madame Bovary, Heidi, Treasure Island, A Child's Garden of Verses, Adventures of Huckleberry Finn, Little Lord Fauntleroy, King Solomon's Mines, War and Peace*

- 1890–1899: *Black Beauty, The Adventures of Sherlock Holmes, Dr. Jekyll and Mr. Hyde, The Prisoner of Zenda, The Red Badge of Courage, Quo Vadis*

- 1900–1914: *Mrs. Wiggs of the Cabbage Patch, The Virginian,*

The Call of the Wild, Rebecca of Sunnybrook Farm, Penrod, Anne of Green Gables, Pollyanna, Tarzan of the Apes

Whatever point might be made about these lists,[1] one thing is notable: many of the top-selling books in the United States during the last century were children's books. What may be equally obvious is that, since children weren't the only ones who bought and read books, these works must also have been unusually popular among adults.

The Golden Age of Children's Books, from 1865 to 1914, was a remarkable time. It was an era when "the majors wrote for minors"; when the very best authors on both sides of the Atlantic, writers with worldwide reputations, addressed themselves to juveniles— Mark Twain, for example, and Robert Louis Stevenson and Rudyard Kipling. It was a time when Children's Books was not some satellite department, but the very center of publishing houses. And it was an age in America that produced such timeless childhood classics as *Little Women, The Adventures of Tom Sawyer, The Wizard of Oz, Tarzan of the Apes, The Secret Garden,* and *Hans Brinker*.

What is equally remarkable is that these books are still important. When surveys are taken and people are asked to name their favorite book, they frequently mention a children's book. Graham Greene suggests a reason for this: "It is only in childhood that books have any deep influence on our lives. . . . What do we ever get nowadays from reading to equal the excitement and the revelation of those first fourteen years?"[2]

Noting that, I and others have made surveys in which we asked various individuals (Ronald Reagan, Carol Burnett, Jack Anderson, Gore Vidal, bricklayers in the South, librarians in the Midwest, and hundreds of others), "What was your favorite children's book?" Mentioned most often are the enduring classics of the Golden Age—those stories about Tom Sawyer, Huckleberry Finn, Dorothy of Kansas and Oz, Rebecca of Sunnybrook Farm, Meg and Jo and Beth and Amy, and their contemporaries.[3]

Like childhood itself, America's children's classics are what we have in common. They are part of the fabric of our culture—the way Tom Sawyer gets a fence whitewashed, the desire to run away (like Toby Tyler) and join the circus, the description of someone as a "Pollyanna."

One measure of their influence is the way these books have

leaped from the printed page and been incarnated in a thousand different forms. *The Wizard of Oz* is an example. There are gift stores filled with Oz coffee cups and ashtrays and *objets* of all kinds—even a postcard from Seattle showing the Tinman sunbathing on a beach while the rain pours down (the caption reads "Oil!"). "There's no place like home" and "Toto, I have a feeling we're not in Kansas anymore" are references nearly everyone comprehends. Judy Garland's and Frank Baum's story provides a kind of shared conversational shorthand that, in another era, might have come from the Bible or Greek mythology.

Other such incarnations must include Johnny Weismuller's famous yell in Tarzan matinees and the Little Lord Fauntleroy suit. There are countless others. Taken together, they do more than suggest how immensely popular children's classics are; they suggest how much these books have made American culture itself. Henry Steele Commager once quoted Paul Hazard's statement that if England were destroyed, the country "could be entirely reconstructed from its children's books." Commager went on to suggest that this is even more true of the United States and its children's books.[4]

It seems that foreigners agree. Go into bookstores abroad and you will see the United States represented by two kinds of books: translations of contemporary best sellers by American authors—Sidney Sheldon, Judith Krantz, Irving Wallace, and others—and children's books—*Huckleberry Finns aventyr, El mago de Oz, Tarzan melekh ha-kofim,* and the adventures of a memorable American youth by the name of Toms Soiers (Latvian), Tom Soyer (Yiddish), Tam Saiyara (Bengali), Tomsayar (Malayalan), Toma Sawyera (Czechoslovakian), and Tomu Soya (Japanese). As Leslie Fiedler has observed, "There is a real sense in which our prose fiction is immediately distinguishable from that of Europe, though this is a fact difficult for Americans to confess. The great works of American fiction [e.g., *Adventures of Huckleberry Finn, The Last of the Mohicans,* the tales of Poe, *The Red Badge of Courage*] are notoriously at home in the children's section of the library."[5]

What is surprising, consequently, is that there has been no systematic study of what must be reckoned America's mainstream literature: its children's classics. In an article titled "Themes in Search of an Author," a writer in a 1965 *Times Literary Supplement* lamented: "Alas! This must be a review of a book yet to be written: *the* book about children's books." Several years later, Canadians

G. T. Stubbs and L. F. Ashley would say, "We still do not have "*the* book about children's books."[6] Closer to home, Russel Nye would observe, "There is no adequate study of juvenile literature in the United States."[7]

This book means to begin that enterprise. It is an examination of twelve American childhood classics published during the Golden Age. In the course of these explorations, a number of questions are addressed: What makes these particularly "American" children's books, and what is the American conception of the child? What accounted for these books' vast appeal in their own time, and what explains their enduring popularity? What stories do they tell, and what meanings do they reveal?

In writing a book of this kind, I have learned how lists of favorite children's books are hotly contested. The literary works we remember from our childhoods are special favorites, and on their behalf otherwise kindly friends and readers turn into insinuating supplicants, then (if disappointed) into vicious partisans. When it appeared that their favorite might not be included, literate lobbyists stood ready to attack my principles of selection or begrudged the choices I had made.

In choosing American children's works published during the Golden Age, I excluded (to the chagrin of some) works on either side of that era: Longfellow's *Evangeline* and Dana's *Two Years Before the Mast,* for example, as well as *Charlotte's Web* and *Little House on the Prairie.* Even within the Golden Age, there are other works I might have included but didn't: Sidney's *Five Little Peppers* and Aldrich's *The Story of a Bad Boy,* to mention just two.

Because part of my concern in this work has been to identify American conceptions of the child, I have focused my discussion on novels that feature child heroes; I have excluded, consequently, high fantasy (Palmer Cox's *The Brownies,* for example) and animal stories (notably, Jack London's *The Call of the Wild* and *White Fang*). At the same time, while I have been concerned to see America's childhood classics within their cultural context, I have not written a social history. I chose, consequently, books that seem to me to have lasting literary value; this has meant omitting certain volumes that are important not so much as art, but as artifacts or cultural indicators—most notably the novels of Horatio Alger, Jr. Nonetheless, I realize that some of my choices are sure to be controversial, especially in the case of books that I reckon as distinguished but that others would consider important only for historical reasons—*Little Lord Fauntleroy*, *Rebecca of Sunnybrook Farm*, and *Pollyanna*, for example.

Because I am discussing twelve books, I have always been mindful of the Grimm Brothers' story "The Sleeping Beauty" and the problems that arise from the uninvited thirteenth guest. Let me apologize beforehand, then, if someone's favorite is absent.

Let me also say something about my methodology. The major conviction reflected in this study (and detailed in the Introduction) is that each of these books tells essentially the same story: that of a child who "overthrows" its parents and becomes independent. In the first two sections, I identify the pattern of this "ur-story" (the remarkably similar plot that these works share) and suggest that many American readers, as Americans, were particularly drawn to this story because of our political history (because our national identity began with a similar struggle for independence from Old World "parents"). In the last two sections, I turn from plot to theme and examine what are especially American obsessions: an interest in the emotional lives of children and an advocacy of positive thinking. Because my primary concerns are structural and thematic, then, I have arranged my discussions not in a chronological fashion, but in terms of a progressively more sophisticated apprehension of these books' essential unanimity—their shared story.

In completing this study, I have had the assistance of numerous institutions and individuals. I wish to acknowledge with gratitude the assistance I have received from the American Philosophical Society for my research in early American Children's Literature, from the American Council of Learned Societies for funding the planning stages of this work, and from the National Endowment for the Humanities for subsidizing its completion. At the same time, I want to express my thanks to San Diego State University for its generous provisions of that kind of time which *is* money.

Any genuine teacher also owes a debt to bright students who, in the give-and-take of classroom discussion, amend ideas and point to new directions. I wish to thank my students and the universities that provided these fruitful occasions: San Diego State University, the University of California—San Diego, the University of Connecticut, and the University of California—Los Angeles.

I also wish to express my gratitude to various individuals for their encouragement and advice and help: scholars—John Seelye, Francelia Butler, Hamida Bosmajian, Peter Neumeyer, Lois Kuznets, Clare Colquitt; librarians—Nancy Asaaf, Karen Hogarth, Bonnie Biggs and her staff; editors—William Sisler, Elizabeth Maguire, Cele Gardner, and Irene Pavitt; and agent—Sandra Dijkstra. Throughout this study and for much of my life, I have also had the patient support and tolerance, the sharp eye and tongue, of my helpmate and first editor, Linda Rodríguez.

Some of my work here has appeared elsewhere in different form, and I have also profited from the discussion these earlier publications engendered: "Hans Brinker: Sunny World, Angry Waters," *Children's Literature* 12 (1984); "There's No Place but Home: *The Wizard of Oz*," *Antioch Review* 45, no. 4 (Fall 1987); "Pollyanna, Ex-Bubblehead," *New York Times Book Review*, 25 October 1987; and "Shooting the Monkey: Oral Greed in *Toby Tyler*," *Lion and Unicorn* 12, no. 1 (1988).

San Diego, Calif.   J.G.
September 1991

Contents

✣ ✣ ✣ ✣ ✣ ✣ ✣

THE CLASSIC AMERICAN
CHILDREN'S STORY

✤ ✤ ✤ ✤ ✤ ✤ ✤
Introduction:
Fundamental Similarities Among
Twelve American Children's Books

This study began when a student asked me, "Why are the children, in so many American childhood classics, orphans?" The question arose in a class I had decided to offer on the Golden Age of American children's books (1865–1914). I had, for the most part, chosen the books statistically, identifying (from various reference books and surveys) what had been and remained some of the most popular literary works of the period: *The Wizard of Oz, Adventures of Huckleberry Finn, Rebecca of Sunnybrook Farm, Little Lord Fauntleroy, Tarzan of the Apes, The Prince and the Pauper, The Adventures of Tom Sawyer, Little Women, Toby Tyler, Hans Brinker, The Secret Garden,* and *Pollyanna.*

Looking back at the books we were studying, I saw that it was so: many of these literary juveniles were orphans. But I also began to notice numerous other similarities among them.

Some of these resemblances can be explained by "intertextuality," that kind of "conversation" which happens between authors and books. Mark Twain's *Tom Sawyer* (1876), for example, clearly inspired the story of Rebecca Sawyer when Kate Douglas Wiggin decided to write about a tomboy in *Rebecca of Sunnybrook Farm* (1903). In the same way, the subplot of Laurie and his grandfather in Louisa May Alcott's *Little Women* (1868) seems to me to have been enlarged and become the story of Cedric and his grandfather in Frances Hodgson Burnett's *Little Lord Fauntleroy* (1885)—a novel that served, in turn, as the basis for Eleanor Porter's *Pollyanna* (1913). Such "borrowing" was, in fact, so common during this period that authors grew suspicious: though Twain himself had borrowed from Charlotte Yonge's *The Prince and the Page* (1866) to create *The Prince and the Pauper* (1881), he was so miffed when he felt Burnett had borrowed from his book to create her *Fauntleroy* that he contemplated a lawsuit.[1] Edgar Rice Burroughs mentioned that these last two were among his favorite childhood books, and the evidence of that is clear throughout his *Tarzan of the Apes* (1914).[2]

Intertextuality, however, provides only a partial explanation for the resemblances among these books. The similarities are, in fact, so extensive and so remarkable that it seems possible to say that each of them tells the same story over and over again, that each of them plays a variation on this basic plot: A child is born to parents who married despite the objections of others. For a time, the family is well-to-do, members of the nobility or otherwise happy and prosperous. Then the child's parents die, or the child is separated from its parents and effectively orphaned. Without their protection, the child suffers from poverty and neglect and (if nobly born) is dispossessed. The hero or heroine then makes a journey to another place and is adopted into a second family. In these new circumstances the child is treated harshly by an adult guardian of the same sex but sometimes has help from an adult of the opposite sex. Eventually, however, the child triumphs over its antagonist and is acknowledged. Finally, some accommodation is reached between the two discordant phases of the child's past: life in the original or biological family and life in the second or adoptive family.

Does this mean that there is a single story on which many American children's books work their permutations? I can speak with complete assurance only about the dozen books that are the subject of this study, leaving it for others to trace the presence or absence of this ur-story in other American works for children. What I can say with confidence is that, among the childhood classics discussed here, their resemblances go even beyond what is suggested by this plot summary. Even in the smallest of details, the magnitude of their similarities and the unanimity of their plots are extensive and striking.

We can begin to glimpse those resemblances as our discussion becomes more complex, when we examine the books themselves in greater detail. What we discover then is their shared story, a recurrent structure that I have called "The Three Lives of the Child-Hero." It might be outlined in this fashion:

The First Life: Exposure

The Story of an Orphan. The American childhood story is almost always the story of an orphan; think of Tom Sawyer, Dorothy Gale, Pollyanna, Toby Tyler, and Tarzan. Even when this is not quite so, the hero is a "virtual orphan" who has only one living parent and is soon separated from that guardian (Little Lord Fauntleroy, Huckleberry Finn, Rebecca of Sunnybrook Farm). In *Little Women*, too, Father is away and Marmee soon departs.

Poverty and Neglect. Besides the loss of parents, the child-hero suffers from exposure to other hardships—notably, poverty and neglect. For a vision of poverty, consider the opening pages of *The Wizard of Oz,* in which Dorothy lives on a drought-stricken farm in Kansas. For a vision of neglect, consider the opening pages of *The Secret Garden,* in which Mary Lennox is referred to as the child whom nobody wanted. In other books, notably *Adventures of Huckleberry Finn,* both motifs are present.

Dispossessed Royalty and the Vanished Happy Time. The themes of exposure are made more acute in stories that portray the child as dispossessed royalty: *Tarzan of the Apes, The Prince and the Pauper, Little Lord Fauntleroy.* Other child-heroes, while not of royal birth, are the rightful heirs to a "vanished happy time" that existed before the novel's opening: when, for example, Rebecca's father was alive and the family was wealthy, when Hans Brinker's father wasn't mentally impaired and the family was prosperous, when the March family was well-to-do before Father lost all their money.

Parents' Violation of a Marriage Prohibition. The child-hero is often the offspring of a marriage others disapproved of: in *Pollyanna* the girl's mother married a minister whom her family found unacceptable because of his poverty. In *Little Women* Marmee, too, weds an unacceptably poor minister, and in the subplot of Alcott's novel we're told that Laurie's Yankee grandparents disapproved of his father's marriage to an Italian artist. In *Rebecca of Sunnybrook Farm* the girl's Yankee relatives found repugnant her mother's nuptials with another Italian artist. In *Little Lord Fauntleroy* the boy's British father entered into a union with his American mother over the nationalistic objections of her new in-laws.

The Journey. The death of parents, poverty and neglect, vanished happy times, dispossession, and disapproval—these characterize the First Life of the child-hero. At this point, travel enters the story. On the one hand, the journey is the apex of the various forms of exposure that the child encounters; on the other hand, it marks a transition to a new life. The journey can take a variety of forms: Rebecca boarding a stagecoach, Toby Tyler boarding the circus wagon, Pollyanna boarding a train, Fauntleroy boarding a steamship, or Huck Finn boarding his raft. Not to be outdone, Dorothy whirls away from Kansas in her mobile home.

The Second Life: Social Problems

Destination: The Big House and the Great Outdoors. The destination of all these journeys is remarkably similar and two-fold: the Big House and the Great Outdoors. Perhaps this dual locale is best represented in *The Secret Garden,* with its mysterious mansion (Misselthwaite Manor) and the garden itself (a zone of taboo adventures). The Big House is a recurring locale: the earl's castle in *Fauntleroy,* the aunt's mansion in *Pollyanna,* Mr. Laurence's and Aunt March's palatial homes in *Little Women,* the Brick House in *Rebecca.* Opposite these are equivalents of the Secret Garden: the outdoors where Tom Sawyer eludes the rules enforced in Aunt Polly's house, the jungle where Tarzan is free from civilization, the rough-and-tumble world of the *sans-culottes* so different from the world of the court in *The Prince and the Pauper,* the river to which Huck escapes when he has had enough of "smothery" homes ashore.

Adoption by a Second Family. At this new location, the child-hero is always adopted into a second family. Perhaps the most dramatic example occurs in Burroughs's novel, with the infant Tarzan's adoption into a family of apes. But other examples abound: Tom Sawyer and Pollyanna are adopted by their respective aunts Polly; Rebecca is taken in by her aunts; Mary Lennox is adopted by her uncle; Fauntleroy is raised by his grandfather.

Surrogate Parents of Different Social Rank. The new guardians are often of a noticeably different social rank from the child-hero. Impoverished children are often adopted by adults who are wealthy or of a higher social station: Pollyanna's aunt owns the town of Beldingsville; Huck is cared for by the aristocratic Grangerfords; Rebecca's aunts are well-to-do; Fauntleroy's grandfather is an earl. In some cases, the hero is adopted by surrrogate parents who are lower on the social ladder: circus folks take Toby Tyler in; apes care for Tarzan. In any event, there is often a reversal of the character's fortunes, in the manner of *The Prince and the Pauper*.

The Same-sex Antagonist. If the First Life is marked by various forms of exposure, the Second Life is marked by social problems. In particular, the child-hero is frequently persecuted by an adult antagonist of the same sex. Tom Sawyer, for example, is harassed by Injun Joe, Tarzan by his ape stepfather Tublat, and Fauntleroy by his grandfather. The case of heroines is similar: Dorothy is persecuted by witches, Rebecca and Pollyanna and the March sisters by their aunts.

Opposite-sex Helpers or Outsiders. The child-hero doesn't have to face these persecutions alone. Frequently, he or she has a helper in an adult of the opposite sex: the motherly females who aid Tom Sawyer, Fauntleroy, and Tarzan; the helpful males who assist the March sisters, Rebecca, and Pollyanna. In a few cases, the helper is an adult of the same sex as the child-hero, but in these cases this character is a social outsider: Nigger Jim is a friend to Huck, the disenfranchised Miles Hendon to the prince mistaken for a pauper.

Triumph over the Antagonist. These social problems eventually reach a crisis, and the child-hero triumphs over his or her antagonist. In some cases, the victory is marked by the death of the antagonist, for which the child is responsible in some way, either directly (Tarzan kills Tublat) or indirectly (Tom Sawyer and Huck Finn are inadvertently responsible for the deaths of Injun Joe and Pap, respectively). In other cases, the triumph is signaled by the humbling of the antagonist: the earl apologizes to Fauntleroy, and Aunt Polly admits she has been wrong to Pollyanna. Other books seem a mixture of these resolutions: the last chapter of *Rebecca,* for example, is titled "Aunt Miranda's Apology" and speaks of that woman's death.

The Child Emerges as Savior. Having overcome their antagonists, these literary children now emerge as saviors: Tom Sawyer thwarts Injun Joe and saves Muff Potter and Becky Thatcher; Dorothy slays the witches and frees her friends and the people the witches have enslaved. In other stories, the hero rescues a hardhearted adult from his or her worst self, by melting the curmudgeon's heart: Pollyanna does this with Mr. Pendleton, Beth March with Mr. Laurence, Colin Craven with his father.

The Third Life: Return

Issues of Identity Are Resolved. The denouement of the story is, in some sense, a return to or an acknowledgment of the First Life. The child-hero is recognized as someone who has led two lives. As a result, issues of identity are resolved: at Phelps Farm, after impersonating so many others, a certain boy is finally revealed to be Huckleberry Finn; once the false claimants are disposed of, the true Little Lord Fauntleroy is recognized; events lead aunts Polly and Miranda to finally acknowledge Pollyanna's and Rebecca's paternity when they abandon grudges against the girls' fathers and admit that their nieces share their bloodline; results of fingerprint tests arrive, and Tarzan is identified as heir to the title Lord Greystoke; and, after a series of elaborate tests at the coronation ceremony, it is finally made clear who is the prince and who is the pauper.

Recognition Ceremonies. Once issues of identity are cleared up, the child-hero is publicly recognized, and with this recognition comes a host of cognate themes—wealth, inheritances, the return of the Vanished Happy Time. Tom Sawyer, Hans Brinker, and Tarzan become wealthy. Edward, who had seemed a pauper, is crowned king. Cedric is designated Lord Fauntleroy. Archibald Craven acknowledges his son and heir in an embrace in the Secret Garden. Father returns home, notes how much his daughters have changed, and salutes them as "little women."

Accommodation of Two Lives. In the conclusion of the novel, some accommodation must be made between the child-hero's two lives. Some characters choose between the two: some opt for the First Life (Dorothy leaves Oz and returns to Kansas; Toby Tyler leaves the circus and returns to Guilford), while others choose the Second Life (between the Widow Douglas in St. Petersburg and freewheeling adventure on the river, Huck chooses the latter and lights out for the territories). Other characters integrate their two lives: Little Lord Fauntleroy brings his American friends to England; Rebecca brings the inhabitants of Sunnybrook Farm to the Brick House; and the pauper who was once a prince is given a royal office, while the prince becomes a better ruler by not forgetting what he learned when he was a pauper. Still other stories conclude on the tragic note of their child-heroes' inability to integrate their two lives: *Little Women* ends with Jo in limbo, unable to freeze her family in the snug bliss she knew in childhood and unwilling to accept the new stage implied by Meg's imminent marriage; *Tarzan,* likewise, closes with a hero at home neither in the jungle nor with Jane in the civilized world.

Psychological Explanations

How are we to account for these extensive and fundamental similarities between these American children's books? Alison Lurie—looking at a wide variety of Children's Literature, but predominantly British and American works of the nineteenth and twentieth centuries—has argued that they share a subversive attitude toward the world of adults.[3] Perry Nodelman, examining a number of girls' books published between 1881 and 1913 (some of which are discussed in this study), suggests that their commonality resides in a romantic and pastoral notion of childhood.[4] Nina Baym, in her study of American women's fiction between 1820 and 1870, has identified a pattern analogous to the one I have outlined above; her concern, however, was not to trace the relation between women's and children's literature, but to explain how women's fiction articulated a nineteenth-century vision of rational and liberal females, of "enlightened domesticity."[5]

Each of these studies suggests fruitful ways to explore the essential uniformity between American childhood classics of the Golden Age. There are, no doubt, other possible approaches. My own means of explaining these similarities is psychological, and, for the most part, I employ that methodology throughout this study. I realize that some readers, hearing that, may be wondering whether to reach for their hats. I must admit that, initially, I shared in that reluctance. But over several years of study, it became clear that a psychological approach to the ur-story discoverable in these works quite simply yielded more than other approaches did: it made more sense of more of the books' shared particulars and, at the same time, offered explanations for the consistent arrangement of these components, for their shared "syntax."

The effort to identify large-scale resemblances and ur-stories and to discuss their meanings has largely been the activity of the folklorist-cum-psychologist—notably, Otto Rank, Joseph Campbell, and Vladmir Propp.[6] If we adapt their ideas, it is possible to see that the above outline of "The Three Lives of the Child-Hero" essentially presents a developmental vision of childhood.

In "The Myth of the Birth of the Hero," Rank argues that maturation should be seen primarily as a process of the child's separation from its parents to achieve autonomy. The impetus for this process arises partly from a child's own wish for independence and partly from the parents' encouragement and expectation of the child's becoming independent and assuming responsibility. The transition from infancy (when needs are largely met and demands are few) to childhood causes emotional upheaval. From this come exaggerated feelings of being neglected. And from these arise familiar childhood fantasies of being *orphaned, hungry, impoverished,* *mistreated, exposed*—fantasies echoed in the opening motifs of many American childhood classics. Likewise, the shift from the bliss of infancy to the more demanding time of childhood is symbolized by themes of being *dispossessed* or by references to a *vanished happy time.*

The *journey* in these children's books is an extravagant symbol of separation from the parents. It is the apex of the traumas of exposure. But it also marks a second birth, or a transition to a second life—a "leaving of the nest" and a "cutting of the apron strings."

This new life, the destination of the journey, is both exciting and frightening. At various times, the *Big House* seems to Amer- ica's literary juveniles to be either a refuge or a prison. Similarly, the *Great Outdoors* appears as either an attractive arena of adventure or a mysterious region of danger. These dualities seem to represent the competing emotions of separation anxiety: the child's simul- taneous desire to be independent and fear of separation from the parents. At the same time, this twofold setting, the Great Out- doors and the Big House, symbolizes conflicts involved in the transition to maturity: the pleasures of uninhibited behavior versus the need to repress impulsive desires in order to become more responsible.

The recurring situation in which the child-hero undergoes *adoption into a second or surrogate family* is a further symbol of a child's separation from its biological parents. This theme echoes a familiar fantasy known as the "Family Romance," in which the child is convinced that "these people are not my real parents. I was adopted. Someday my real parents will come and get me."

Another recurring motif is that these surrogate parents are of a noticeably *different social rank* from the child. This is a common situation in American children's books. Tarzan, for example, is the offspring of English nobility but is raised by apes. Little Lord Fauntleroy entered life as a poor boy living in the alleys of New York but is raised by his grandfather, the Earl of Dorincourt. The conspicuous difference in the social rank of these surrogate parents provides one more way of exaggerating the child's separation from its real parents.

The *social problems* with the *same-sex antagonist* that the child- hero encounters in the Second Life can generally be described as oedipal. This is made clear because the antagonist is an adult and a parent figure. Because the child loves its same-sex parent, guilt arises when the child harbors oedipal hostility toward that parent. To accommodate that guilt, the antagonist is disguised through symbolic mitigation: the villain is not a parent, but a parent figure—a grandfather, for example, or an aunt or uncle, or a persecutor completely outside the family. Even before that, to alleviate guilt, the child disguises this hostility by projection and attributes it to the other. Then, as in the children's books, the child is not antagonistic; it is the adult who is antagonistic toward the child.

Oedipal emotions are a normal part of every child's life. They involve not only an antagonistic relation with the same-sex parent, but also a special affection for the opposite-sex parent. It is not surprising, consequently, that the child-heroes of American children's books often find a special *helper in an adult of the opposite sex,* in parent figures like the "motherly" characters who aid Tom Sawyer, Little Lord Fauntleroy, and Tarzan, and in the "fatherly" characters who assist the March sisters, Rebecca, and Pollyanna.[7]

The second or surrogate family of the child-heroes, then, provides a means for them to work through their complex emotions in a remote fashion with parental substitutes. And the child's *triumph over the antagonist* (signaled by the death or humbling of that same-sex parent figure) is a salutary symbol of the child's resolution of these oedipal problems and the achievement of independence.

Once these problems are resolved, the fantasy structure of the second or surrogate family is no longer needed; once the child has achieved a definition of itself as an independent person, the original family can be reconstituted. With this comes the last of the "Three Lives of the Child-Hero," which is, in a sense, a return to the First Life. This return is marked by a host of cognate themes: *the return of the vanished happy times,* the discovery of lost or buried wealth, the bestowing of inheritances, the celebration of *recognition ceremonies.*

But while the "lost child" returns, it does so in some changed way—as someone now on the threshold of maturity. For this reason, it is not surprising that these events are often accompanied by *identity tests* and the resolution of questions regarding paternity. Likewise, it is not surprising that in the conclusion the child-heroes must strike some *accommodation between their two lives*—between what they were and what they have become.

National Considerations

This psychological interpretation of the fundamentally similar story discoverable in American childhood classics suggests the presence of a nearly universal account of childhood development. Since this pattern can be found in other national literatures, what makes it particularly American?

To view it correctly, "The Three Lives of the Child-Hero" should be seen as only one paradigm within a platonic panoply of archetypes available to writers for children. For example, its pattern is different from that of didactic tales (from Aesop to *Pinocchio*) in which the foolish are humbled and the lowly triumph, or the Good and the Bad merit rewards and punishments. It is different, too, from the pattern found in the tales of Hans Andersen and Oscar Wilde, for example, with their atmospheres of *Weltschmerz* in which society seems more to blame than parents. Moreover, in its emphasis on the story of a child resolving family problems, the pattern at work in "The Three Lives of the Child-Hero" is also distinguishable, from identifiable formulae in works that aim to tell different stories—be they Robinsonades (e.g., *Swiss Family Robinson*), Christian allegories (e.g., C. S. Lewis's Narnia books), or pastoral fantasies (e.g., *Winnie-the-Pooh*). There are, in other words, dozens of ur-stories or patterns to be found in works for children.

The question, then, is not how "The Three Lives of the Child-Hero" is an American paradigm; as we have acknowledged, it is found in other national literatures. Instead, the question is why, given the plenitude of other possibilities, American authors and readers were so consistently drawn to this particular pattern when such a wide field of alternatives was open to them.

To answer that is to begin to recognize how much America's sense of national identity is intimately connected to its children's books. Historians have pointed out that, from the beginning of American history through the nineteenth century, Americans consistently saw their political history in terms of the development of a child. In fact, by 1849, the *Southern Literary Messenger* would say, somewhat wearily, "There is no similitude more trite and familiar, certainly there is none more striking and true, than that which likens the origin and progress of nations to the growth and development of children."[8]

14   *Introduction*

This pervasive notion of "America-as-Child" shaped the way Americans saw themselves and their history. In its colonial days, America was an infant in a macrocosmic family headed by the English monarch. The American Revolution marked a different phase in the growth of this macrocosmic youngster. As scores of scholars have shown in examinations of hundreds of diverse documents (from Franklin's *Autobiography* to the political writings of Thomas Paine and Patrick Henry), America's writers and thinkers consistently understood and presented the Revolution as the story of a child who had grown older and entered into a period of oedipal rebellion.[9] The argument between George III and his colonists was constantly portrayed as a family squabble between an intractable father and deserving sons. Declaring themselves independent, the Sons of Liberty came together in a fraternal struggle against the tyranny and despotism of the patriarch. Indeed, Christopher Looby has argued, this vision of America-as-Child engaged in oedipal rebellion remained the "quintessential motif" of American political thought well into the nineteenth century.[10]

This metaphor did not work in only one direction, however. Instead, domestic and political language was commonly used in a reciprocal and interchangeable fashion. Examining hundreds of political documents, George Forgie and others have concluded that it was not only "a convention of American political language" to speak of government in terms of "an idealized family," but also common to refer to the family as "a miniaturized version of the state."[11]

The extent of this metaphoric reciprocity becomes even more evident when we turn our attention from political documents to pediatric literature. Near the end of the Civil War, for example, Samuel Osgood would address the subject "Books for Our Children" in the *Atlantic Monthly* and offer the conceit not of America-as-Child, but of the Child-as-America:

> The war is over, yet our fight is not through. . . . We shall settle the Reconstruction problem, the Negro, the Debt, John Bull, and Louis Napoleon, all in due time. . . . But there is a question to be settled which comes nearer home to each family . . . —What shall we do with our children? . . . The Slaveholder's Rebellion is put down; but how shall we deal

with the never-ceasing revolt of the new generation against the old? and how keep our Young America under the thumb of his father and mother without breaking his spirit? . . . and how does our legion of juvenile infantry compare with the young legions of England, France, Germany, Russia, or Italy?[12]

If American political writing presented the nation as a family writ large, we should not be surprised (given the reciprocity between domestic and political tropes) that America's domestic novels addressed political issues and presented the family as a nation writ small. As we will see, this was in fact the method of Burnett's *Little Lord Fauntleroy*, in which the story of a boy's resolution of troubled relations among his family members presents, simultaneously, an emblem of America's new relations with Europe. When William Gladstone, then prime minister of England, told *Fauntleroy's* American author that he believed the novel would lead to an improved understanding between the two countries,[13] he was doing more than offering what we now might think an unusual compliment for a children's book; he was also acknowledging how much this American children's book is a political allegory.

When William Dean Howells called *The Prince and the Pauper* a "manual of republicanism,"[14] he, too, indicated the partisan nature of another American childhood classic. As we will see, in Clemens's story (where, for a time, a commoner rules wisely because he is a commoner) can be found an American advocacy of "natural nobility" and an implicit critique of monarchal government—apparent also in the unflattering portraits of the Duke and the King in *Adventures of Huckleberry Finn* and in the comic exposure of the ruling Wizard in *The Wizard of Oz*. And when Darwin wrote that "the wonderful progress of the United States and the character of its people are the results of natural selection,"[15] Edgar Rice Burroughs apparently found a reason to end his exemplary account of Tarzan's evolution there. Equating natural nobility with natural selection, Burroughs offered his own jingoistic argument for American supremacy and legitimacy.

As this evidence begins to suggest, many American children's books must be seen as nationalistic tracts. Following a long tradition of metaphoric reciprocity, we glimpse in them incarnations of

America-as-Child. Given that, it is not surprising that, among a variety of other options, the pervasive pattern that emerged was one of an orphan, estranged and engaged in oedipal rebellion against its parents, making its Declaration of Independence and achieving autonomy. In it we hear an echo of our own national endeavors.

American Motifs

If what is "American" in our country's children's books is revealed, then, in its choice of ur-structures, this distinct national character is even more evident in the variations played on that plot. Certainly this country's children's classics have much in common with Children's Literature of other cultures, but it takes little to recognize that there is much that is uniquely American about them. While the Germans have Grimms' fairy tales (those timeless stories about Cinderella, Rapunzel, Snow White, and the like), when L. Frank Baum announced his intention to write an American fairy tale, the result was *The Wizard of Oz.* The French have Saint-Exupéry's cosmic and quizzical *The Little Prince,* whose best friend is a flower on an asteroid, and Americans have *Little Lord Fauntleroy,* whose best friend is a grocer in New York. The English have *Alice in Wonderland,* and Americans have *Rebecca of Sunnybrook Farm.* In Italy, the character who runs away and ends up working for a circus is a marionette named Pinocchio; in the United States, the character who does the same is a boy named Toby Tyler. If *Swiss Family Robinson* and *Heidi* have their counterparts in the United States, they are probably *Little Women* and *The Secret Garden.* And while winged-monkey warriors appear in both India's epic *The Ramayana* and *The Wizard of Oz,* in one they attack a Hindu prince and his soldiers, and in the other they attack a little girl from Kansas and her companions (who include a scarecrow and a tin man).

One way to make these national differences more apparent is to eliminate the variable of time. If we compare America's childhood classics of the Golden Age with those appearing in, for example, England during the same period, we see a panoply of differences. In *Secret Gardens,* Humphrey Carpenter has examined, for the most part, English Children's Literature of this era (1860–1930) and identified what is most characteristic about these works: misgivings about Christianity and the wish to create imaginary paradises as alternatives. In the aquatic sexuality of Charles Kingley's *The Water Babies*, the fundamental negativity of Lewis Carroll's nonsense, and the constant searching of George MacDonald's "phantasies," Carpenter discovers authors whose disillusionment with Christianity manifests itself in a desire to destroy the old order. In contrast, in the tales of Beatrix Potter and E. Nesbit, Richard Jeffries' *Bevis*, A. A. Milne's *Winnie-the-Pooh*, J. M. Barrie's *Peter Pan*, and Kenneth Grahame's *Wind in the Willows*, Carpenter finds authors whose disenchantment with religion led not to destruction, but to the construction of green alternatives—enchanted places, arcadias, never-never lands.[16]

If these are the characteristics of British children's classics of the Golden Age, it must be said that American juvenile books of the same period have different emphases. Among the more conspicuous of these motifs are the following.

A PREOCCUPATION WITH HEALTH

English children's books of the same period offer no comprehensive equivalent of the concern in so many American childhood classics with the subject of physical health. While he is a pauper, Twain's prince sees the state of his kingdom and it presents him with a prospect of disease and hunger. This vision of the world as a sick ward is also apparent in *Little Women*, not only in Beth's long bout with scarlet fever but also in the frequent role the March family takes on as nurses to diseased immigrants or the injured of the Civil War. Like Beth March, Pollyanna plays nurse to an infirm community and finally needs to be nursed herself. Even robust heroes like Tom Sawyer and Huck Finn participate in this obsession when they con others with elaborate lies about terminal toothaches and families ravaged by smallpox. But there is, perhaps, no other novel to compare with *The Secret Garden* in its preoccupation with matters of health; the account of the transformation of the jaundiced Mary Lennox and the bedridden Colin Craven, the abundant details regarding their diet and regimens of exercise, make the book seem one long convalescence.

AN ADVOCACY OF POSITIVE THINKING

If English books of the period expressed misgivings about Christianity and posited as an alternative a kind of geography of imaginary paradises, in a growingly secular America the alternative to religion was something more like a psychological program of positive thinking. This substitution of psychology for religion is evident in the way lessons about avoiding sin and fostering virtue were replaced by instructions about controlling untoward emotions and encouraging a confident optimism. If *Little Women* had been written a hundred years ago before it actually was, the March sisters might have wrestled in their souls against the wiles of Satan; in 1868, however, their shortcomings (vanity, envy, anger, shyness) seem personal faults rather than sins, and Marmee's instructions to her daughters concern personality development rather than religious salvation. *Hans Brinker,* too, is about the control of emotions (those oceanic feelings that threaten to break through the dykes of self-control) and the need to be always cheerful. Pollyanna (the daughter of a minister and something of a secular evangelist herself) encourages others to avoid negative thinking and preaches that optimism with which her name has become synonymous. The main means to health in *The Secret Garden* is also positive thinking; in fact, the book may be reckoned a secularized version of the doctrine of right thinking found in Christian Science. "Believe in yourself!" "Have confidence!"—these are the lessons learned in *Pollyanna, The Secret Garden,* and *The Wizard of Oz* (when the Wizard finally speaks to Dorothy's companions about what they seek).

REDEMPTION THROUGH NAIVETÉ

Although America's childhood classics are not without their tricksters, what sets many of these books apart is the conviction that Adamic innocence alone is redemptive. Little Lord Fauntleroy is different from others because of his wide-eyed optimism, his ignorance of evil, and his naive belief that, for example, his conniving grandfather is a paragon of virtue. In this he is something of a fool, but this foolishness remakes the world, since every adult finally wishes to live up to the boy's estimation of them and no one wishes to see him disillusioned. Dorothy is likewise an innocent abroad when she comes to Oz; she is a rather ordinary and slow girl and something of a lamb among wolves (in a realm presided over by tricksters and a humbug whose kingdom is built on his ability to fool others), but she emerges as a savior. Perhaps the paragon of this figure is Pollyanna, whose comprehensive optimism is often mistaken for empty-headedness but whose naiveté turns out to have a contagious and redemptive effect in her community.

Historical Considerations

To identify native motifs in the preceding discussion, we eliminated the variable of time and sketched differences between British and American Children's Literature published during the same era. When that variable is restored, other issues arise: What accounts for the great flowering of Children's Literature in the United States a hundred years ago? Why is it that, among adult and juvenile readers alike, the best sellers of the era were children's books? And why were so many of America's major authors of the period drawn to this genre?

In beginning to answer the last question, it is worth noting that an interest in Children's Literature by all kinds of authors was not uncommon then; the ghettoization of children's writers is a relatively modern phenomenon. As Jason Epstein has observed, "The great children's books of the past . . . were commonly written by authors who, in contrast to the situation today, were not primarily writers for children, . . . Defoe, Swift, Blake, . . . Hawthorne, Mark Twain, Kipling, etc."[17]

There were certainly commercial reasons for this. Many of America's most popular periodicals of the era were directed at children—*Our Young Folks* (1865–1873), *The Riverside Magazine for Young People* (1867–1870), *Harper's Young People* (1879–1899), and *St. Nicholas* (1873–1943). These publications paid well, and this fact may explain why their contributors included such noted writers as Charles Dickens, Jack London, Henry Wadsworth Longfellow, William Cullen Bryant, Helen Hunt Jackson, Robert Louis Stevenson, Louisa May Alcott, Joel Chandler Harris, Frances Hodgson Burnett, Edna St. Vincent Millay, and Howard Pyle. Still, this explanation begs the question and leaves it unanswered:

Why were children's books best sellers and children's publications among the most popular and best-paying?

One answer: the popularity of Children's Literature during the Golden Age was a reflection of the era's unusual fascination with the figure of the Child and the subject of childhood. To a great degree, the period between 1865 and 1914 might be reckoned the Era of the Child. Several intellectual trends account for this.

NOSTALGIA

The second half of the nineteenth century was dramatically different from the first half, when American Rip Van Winkles slumbered in a long Jeffersonian dream of pastoral tranquility and agrarian self-sufficiency. The horrors of the Civil War changed all that, and Americans awoke to find a country already being reshaped by forces of accelerating change: by rapid industrialization (as commercial interests supplanted the preeminence of agriculture) and massive urbanization (as families moved from country to city and waves of immigrants settled in municipal centers). In the latter half of the nineteenth century, many writers and readers felt displaced by this rapid growth and longed to recapture the past; and they did so along the lines of the English Romantic poets in their celebrations of childhood. Following such horrors as Antietam and Gettysburg, Americans wished to recall the prewar bliss of their own agrarian childhoods. This may explain why the children's books of the period had such wide appeal, and why so many are memoirs (e.g., *The Adventures of Tom Sawyer, Rebecca of Sunnybrook Farm*) or in large part autobiographical (e.g., *Pollyanna, Little Women*) and have settings that are essentially rural or pastoral (e.g., *The Secret Garden, The Wizard of Oz*).

FASCINATION WITH THE FUTURE

While some people were made uneasy by rapid change, others were filled with dazzling visions of progress. Between 1865 and 1914, Americans were facing what seemed a wonderful new world marked by such events as the laying of the transatlantic cable, the completion of the Union Pacific Railroad, the invention of the telephone and electric light, and the first flight by the Wright brothers. Some historians have seized on symbols of the great hope of the era in events like the Chicago World's Fair in 1893 (with its attractive prospects of what the future held), in images of the Virgin Land (as settlers traveled westward to create new lives in newly opened lands), and in figures like the Immigrants (with their visions of opportunity, social ladders to climb, and streets paved with gold). Just as important as these—more important, perhaps—was the figure of the Child. Writers would often portray the Child as a symbol of the hopeful future, enjoying a better life than its parents and more ready to accept the fruits of progress than recalcitrant seniors. The opening words of the first issue of the *Youth's Companion* would say, "The human mind is becoming emanicipated from the bondage of ignorance and superstition. Our children are born to higher destinies than their fathers; they will be actors in a far advanced period."[18] These circumstances, too, may explain the unusual popularity of children's books during the era—with their stories of optimistic juveniles (*Pollyanna, Little Lord Fauntleroy, Rebecca of Sunnybrook Farm*) redeeming curmudgeonly adults.

PROGRESS THROUGH RECAPITULATION

Nostalgia and an enthusiastic interest in the future might seem contradictory impulses, but they were inextricably mixed within authors who wrote for children during the Golden Age. To be sure, such writers as Twain, Alcott, and Burnett wrote books that were memoirs and had rural and idyllic settings; but these writers were not simply reactionaries enamored with a pastoral past and reluctant to embrace what others saw as a glorious future. Nearly all of them were regular passengers on transatlantic steamships; Burnett alone made thirty-three such crossings. Twain installed in his home the first telephone in Hartford, and his fascination with the potential of new technologies like typesetting machines is well known. Baum and Burnett were eager visitors who eyed and wrote about the future on display at the Chicago World's Fair (where teenager Edgar Rice Burroughs was employed driving guests around in an electric car). And Alcott, among others, was involved in forward-looking political movements meant to improve the lots of blacks and women.

One way to comprehend these apparently contradictory impulses is in terms of Lloyd deMause's theory that "the central force for change in history [is] the ability of successive generations of parents to regress to the psychic age of their children and work through the anxieties of that age in a better manner the second time they encounter them than when they did in their own childhood."[19] If, as deMause suggests, in times of rapid change a recapitulation of childhood can be a means of summoning the energy necessary for genuine progress, this may explain why so many of the children's books of the Golden Age are memoirs (in which childhood is lived again) or historical novels like *The Prince and the Pauper* (in which history is relived) or elaborate Darwinian fantasies like *Tarzan of the Apes* (in which the evolution of the race is recapitulated in the evolution of the hero).

CHANGING ATTITUDES TOWARD AND ATTENTION TO CHILDHOOD

While it cannot be said that childhood was ignored before the nineteenth century, nevertheless children were less indulged in these earlier times and childhood was not the primary locus of attention. Because of the labor-intensive demands of an agrarian culture, childhood was a brief interval through which children were encouraged to pass quickly so that they might become mature providers. Religion, too, in this earlier era, seemed to argue for a speedy transit through childhood. From a religious perspective, children were evil incarnate, tainted by original sin. As Benjamin Wadsworth said in 1721, "As sharers in the guilt of Adam's first Sin, they're *Children of Wrath by Nature*. . . . Their Hearts . . . are unspeakably wicked, estranged from God."[20] This also seemed an argument for individuals to put childhood, like Satan, quickly behind them.

The nineteenth century brought changes in this attitude. The rise of a middle class meant more leisure time to devote to children and childhood. In religious circles, challenges were being made to the Calvinistic view of children: in the early part of the century, progressive ministers like William Ellery Channing questioned the idea of infant damnation; and in the latter part of the century, theorists like Granville Stanley Hall asserted that "childhood as it comes fresh from the hand of God is not corrupt . . . but illustrates the survival of the most consummate thing in the world."[21] Moreover, by the nineteenth century, the ideas of Jean-Jacques Rousseau and John Locke had gained currency and altered attitudes toward childhood; instead of a predisposition to evil because of an inheritance of original sin, Rousseau had argued that childhood exhibits original innocence and Locke had spoken of the child as a tabula rasa. Finally, by the late nineteenth century, scientific developments in embryology and genetics, along with the rise of Darwinian theory and psychology, had led to the conviction that, to a great extent, the child really *was* father to the man. Together, these attitudes reoriented public attention toward beginnings, from the mature to the nascent, from adults to juveniles.

A NEW INTEREST IN CHILD-RAISING PRACTICES

These new notions of childhood required a new attention to the "formative" years of children. If the child was father to the man, then parents had to be particularly careful not to sully a child's original innocence and had to be cautious about what they wrote on that tabula rasa. Countless books and magazines appeared that answered parents' questions and recommended certain child-raising practices. In these and other public forums, opinions were now offered about child nature, and "experts" (educators, psychologists, journalists, advertisers) suddenly became visible. By 1862 the first pediatric clinic was established in New York City, and by the 1880s pediatric medicine had become a specialty taught at Harvard University and accepted by the American Medical Association. Eighteenth-century parents would have been startled not only by the amount of public attention being given to child raising, but also by the notions that it was *parents* who had to be responsible and that they must be concerned with a child's "needs." One can only imagine how astonished parents of this earlier era would have been by books published a hundred years later with titles like Jacob Abbott's *Gentle Measures in the Management and Training of the Young* (1871) and Kate Douglas Wiggin's *Children's Rights* (1892).

INSTITUTIONAL CONCERN WITH CHILD WELFARE

As the discussion of methods and theories of child rearing became more prominent and complex, a conviction began to arise in some quarters that this task was too important to be trusted to families alone. To reformers, the era was anything but a Golden Age for children. What they saw instead was the erosion of family life in urban centers and among the working poor, waves of immigrants who left their offspring unattended in the streets, and scores of young children being sent out to work long hours in mills and sweatshops. For them, this decline in traditional mores constituted a threat not only to the family but also to a democratic society like America's, which depended on good citizens who had started off life on the right foot.

Accordingly, a number of reformers (many of them women, ministers, physicians, and humanitarians) developed institutions whose purpose was to serve children *in loco parentis*. The Golden Age witnessed the widespread creation of orphanages, reform schools, and foster-care agencies; the enactment of child-labor laws; the spread of public schools and compulsory attendance; the rise of the kindergarten and playground movements; and countless other, similar enterprises. The Child had become the concern of government and society at large.

THE CHILD AS PUBLIC FIGURE

Through the early nineteenth century, the majority of America's children lived in rural areas and were raised in the sinecure of the family. By mid-century, children had lost that invisibility. As Jay Martin has observed, "Beginning in the 1870's, the child rapidly became the center of American cultural life."[22] The child became a public figure, seized on as a vehicle for nostalgia or as a symbol of the future's promise, brought from the shadows as original sinner and put on center stage as original innocent, ministered to by educators, health professionals, humanitarians, and politicians. Given this milieu and these obsessions, it may not be so surprising after all that many of the best sellers of the period were children's books. These works reflected the era's fascination with the figure of the Child and the subject of childhood. But the complement of that idea also has to be considered: how these children's books functioned not only as a mirror but also as a lamp; how they not only reflected American culture but also were a force in creating that culture. To consider that subject, we must turn from the times to the books themselves and discern the stories they tell.

ONE

✦ ✦ ✦ ✦ ✦ ✦ ✦

Oedipal Patterns

H·M·G

1

✤ ✤ ✤ ✤ ✤ ✤ ✤

There's No Place but Home
The Wizard of Oz

Landscape is one of the most memorable features of *The Wonderful Wizard of Oz* (1900). When readers demanded more from L. Frank Baum, they did not ask for more "Dorothy books," but more books about the land of Oz. This central importance of place in Baum's book is also indicated in the titles he considered before he arrived at the final one: *The City of Oz, The City of the Great Oz, The Emerald City, From Kansas to Fairyland, The Land of Oz*. Indeed, after the book appeared, children wrote Baum to ask how they might buy tickets to travel to that marvelous place.

In the 1939 MGM movie, Dorothy is hit on the head during the cyclone and dreams up the magical land. Nothing like this happens in Baum's book. Judy Garland may wish to go "Somewhere over the rainbow," but in the book the cyclone takes Dorothy there against her wishes and while she is wide awake. In the book, Oz is a real place, not a land created by Dorothy's fertile imagination.

Scholars have failed to take this point seriously and, in general, have viewed Oz as a utopian dream. Baum's landscape has been seen, variously, as a Jeffersonian agrarian paradise, evidence of his interest in the Populist movement, and an exemplification of the ideas of such utopian thinkers as William Morris and Edward

Bellamy.[1] Such assertions are, however, difficult to believe, because while a utopian writer might be concerned with such issues as poverty and war, among the greatest problems of Oz are Fighting Trees and Hammerheads. Attention might be better devoted to the question of where Oz actually lies.

The Kingdom Without

What cannot be ignored is how much the land of Oz is a reflection of actual circumstances in the United States at the turn of the century. At that time, America must have appeared a kind of fairyland to foreigners and natives alike.[2] As impossible as it might seem, in America, as in fairyland, any boy could become president of the country. As if by some lucky spell, fortunes could be and were made overnight. Merchant princes of the Gilded Age built or bought castles for their private homes. P. T. Barnum, as much a master of hokum as Baum's Wizard, was a national hero. Immigrants believed that the streets were paved with gold, only to discover, perhaps, that they were really made with yellow bricks. And if Baum's green paradise in the midst of a great desert seemed remarkable, what could be more remarkable than Brigham Young's building the land of milk and honey near the Great Salt Lake?

The map of Oz is recognizably a map of the United States. To the west is the land of the Winkies: a wild, untilled region full of marauding prairie wolves and not unlike South Dakota, where Baum lived for a time as a shopkeeper and newspaperman. To the east is the land of the Munchkins: a place that resembles the Pennsylvania Dutch country where many Germans settled (Baum's ancestors came from Bavaria). To the south is the land of the Quadlings; it is inhabited by hillbilly-like Hammerheads and white-frocked ladies and gentlemen known as the China People (two classes of people with whom Baum became familiar while he was a traveling salesman in the South). To the north (in later Oz books) is Gillikin Country: a place of mountains and lakes, not unlike the Michigan where Baum used to vacation.

Since the Wizard's kingdom is in the very center of Oz, it is hard not to think of Chicago as its counterpart. Baum was living in the Windy City when he wrote his story about his cyclone-transported girl (named, significantly, Dorothy Gale). And like other writers,[3] he was very impressed by the Columbian Exposition, held in Chicago in 1893. It was, according to observers, a very Oz-like affair "with streets thronged with characters straight out of the Arabian Nights, 'hootchy kootchy' dancers, a cyclorama of the Swiss Alps, a full-size knight in armor on a full-size horse (both made out of dried California prunes), a Ferris Wheel, a Lapland village, a collection of nasty-tempered ostriches and a Chinese theater."[4] The Great White City, as the fairgrounds were known, seems to have been the inspiration for the Wizard's Emerald City.

A few intrepid scholars have suggested, however, that more than Middle America, Oz is a portrait of California—or, at least, the dream of California, that verdant vision that haunted many a dirt-farming family in the Dust Bowl even before the publication of *The Grapes of Wrath* and the great westward migration of the 1930s. As Jordan Brotman observes, "The Oz books [have] a kind of California extravagance about them, and I [can] remember the time when California with its sunshine and its golden oranges and movies was an earthly paradise hankered after by people all over the country, certainly in the midwest."[5]

Midwesterner Frank Baum apparently shared this dream. A few years after his success with *The Wizard of Oz* ("wonderful" was dropped from the title after the first edition),[6] he began to spend the winter on Coronado Island in San Diego. In an interview in the *San Diego Tribune* in 1904, he said: "Those who do not find Coronado a paradise have doubtless brought with them the same conditions that would render heaven unpleasant to them did they chance to gain admittance."[7] In the books that followed, Baum deliberately included California locales in his paradisaical geography, and in 1909 he moved permanently to the Golden State.

Besides noting geographical correspondences, we can also see that Oz is an American place by considering its particular imaginative design and observing its resemblances to another California dreamscape. Baum lived in Hollywood, in a home he named Ozcot; just south of there, in Anaheim, is another magical kingdom—Disneyland. In both places the homespun facts of America are made dreamlike, and dreams are made palpable facts. In Oz, turn-of-the-century America (be it Chicago or California) becomes a visionary landscape, and at the same time the visionary is made commonplace. In Oz, a familiar thing like a scarecrow is magically a person, and at the same time a magical person like the Wizard is actually a balloonist from Omaha. Oz is an eclectic place like Disneyland— which visitors enter through an idealized version of an American small town at the turn of the century, and then can meet (in the flesh) Snow White or Alice (from Wonderland), pass by castles or under futuristic skyways, travel through Frontierland and Tomorrowland. In Oz, as in Disneyland, ordinary American citizens find themselves actually living in a fairy tale.

A Fairy Tale Aborning

It is difficult, of course, to separate Baum's book from the 1939 movie, generally regarded as the most popular film ever made. But perhaps we need not do so if we take seriously Baum's claim in the Introduction that *The Wizard of Oz* "aspires to being a modernized fairy tale."

As his later essay "Modern Fairy Tales" indicates, Baum was no amateur folklorist. He was intimately familiar with the history of his genre and with the techniques of Perrault, the Grimms, Lang, Andersen, and subsequent writers who set out to write fairy tales. More important, he knew that fairy tales reached their classic status by becoming community property, "told by professional storytellers, and sung by wandering minstrels" who revised and improved the tale over the ages.[8]

Baum would have been pleased to learn, consequently, that his own story has likewise moved into the public domain, become the property of the folk. There are Oz coffee cups and Oz T-shirts and a kind of doughnut called a "munchkin." There are films: the famous MGM movie (which, it is estimated, has been seen more than a billion times), more than a dozen other spinoffs (including the all-black version *The Wiz* and, most recently, Disney Studios' *Return to Oz*), and countless other derivative works (including *Gremlins* and *Star Wars*).[9] And there have been songs, from Judy Garland's "Somewhere over the Rainbow" to Elton John's "Goodbye, Yellow Brick Road." And there are coloring books and postcards and Oz novels written by other authors. Like the classic fairy tale, private dream became public dream.

Today, when people think about such classic fairy tales as "Cinderella," "Sleeping Beauty," and "Little Red Riding Hood," they do not discriminate between versions by Perrault and by the Grimm Brothers. In the same vein, consideration of *The Wizard of Oz* ought to consider its two most famous versions, Baum's book and the MGM movie.

Like the economizing process that occurs when tales are reshaped over the ages by constant retelling, the movie omits a great deal from the book; in general, the film is more straightforward (converting the tale into a linear story by doing away with Baum's fascination with things that come in fours and twos) and shorter (Dorothy's further journey to the south and through the lands of the China People and Hammerheads, for example, is deleted, so that the film ends shortly after the Wizard's balloon departs). Like the reshaping of the classic fairy tales by constant retelling, the movie also adds some things. To be sure, much of this seems unessential and the result of translating a novel into a Technicolor musical extravaganza; much more time is spent in Munchkinland, for example, so that the audience can be dazzled by spectacle, music, and special effects. Still, there are at least two major elements that the movie adds to the tale.

The first is that Dorothy's entire trip occurs as a dream, brought on by being hit over the head during the cyclone. This adds a psychological dimension. The other major addition is a more important role for the Wicked Witch. She makes more frequent appearances in the movie than in the book: issuing her threat ("I'll get you, my pretty"), throwing a ball of fire from the rooftop, skywriting above the Emerald City ("Surrender, Dorothy"), monitoring the progress of Dorothy's expeditionary party through the woods on the way to the castle. Perhaps the most significant addition in this regard—one that adds another psychological dimension to Baum's version and brings the story closer to the classic fairy tale—occurs when Dorothy stares into the crystal ball and sees a distraught Aunt Em searching for her and then watches as the picture changes to that of the cackling Wicked Witch.

This last transformation offers an entrance into *The Wizard of Oz* and suggests how it might be interpreted in the same way as many of the classic fairy tales. It is a commonplace that the stepmothers of fairy tales are often a result of a child's twofold picture of mother: the Good Mother (the fairy godmother) who loves and protects, and the Bad Mother (the witch) who threatens and punishes. The movie provides the slightest hint that Dorothy sees her own stepmother (Aunt Em) in this twofold way—as both Glinda and the Wicked Witch. In fact, *The Wizard of Oz* might, like many other fairy tales—"Snow White," for example, and "Hansel and Gretel"—be seen as the story of a girl who suffers under the domination of a mother figure, who wishes to replace or otherwise be rid of that rival, and who finally achieves independence. At the same time, Dorothy's adventures in Oz, her oedipal dream, resembles the ur-story discoverable in other American childhood classics.

Filling the Witch's Shoes

Like many other juveniles in America's childhood classics, Dorothy is an orphan who is being raised by guardians (her Aunt Em and Uncle Henry) in a cheerless environment. While Huckleberry Finn chafes under the restrictions of Miss Watson and the Widow Douglas, while Pollyanna and Rebecca of Sunnybrook Farm have to suffer from the hardheartedness of their aunts, Dorothy's own circumstances are described in a way that links the desiccated landscape with the cheerlessness of her guardians:

> When Dorothy stood in the doorway and looked around, she could see nothing but the great gray prairie on every side. Not a tree nor a house broke the broad sweep of flat country that reached the edge of the sky in all directions. The sun had baked the plowed land into a gray mass, with little cracks running through it. Even the grass was not green, for the sun had burned the tops of the long blades until they were the same gray color to be seen everywhere. Once the house had been painted, but the sun blistered the paint and the rains washed it away, and now the house was as dull and gray as everything else.
>
> When Aunt Em came to live there she was a young, pretty wife. The sun and wind had changed her, too. They had taken the sparkle from her eyes and left them a sober gray, they had taken the red from her cheeks and lips, and they were gray also. She was thin and gaunt and never smiled now. When Dorothy, who was an orphan, first came to her, Aunt Em had been so startled by the child's laughter that she would scream and press

her hand upon her heart whenever Dorothy's merry voice reached
her ears; and she still looked at the little girl with wonder that
she could find anything to laugh at. [10]

Dorothy's own lively spirits are at odds with this grayness and
graveness. Her pet is a symbol of that spiritedness: "It was Toto
that made Dorothy laugh, and saved her from growing as gray as
her other surroundings. Toto was not gray; he was a little black
dog" (13). Toto is not simply an antidote to Kansas and Aunt Em.
He is (throughout the story) something like Dorothy's animus, or
her spirit of play, which leads her on to further adventures. For
example, when Dorothy is about to return to workaday Kansas in
the Wizard's balloon, Toto leaps from her arms and she has to
pursue him.

While "Toto played all day long," Dorothy's guardians
"worked hard from morning to night and did not know what joy
was" (13). Work, especially housework, comes to be associated
with arid Kansas and the cheerless Aunt Em. In a later Oz book,
Dorothy seems to view herself as dispossessed royalty: she observes
that while she is a princess in Oz, "when I'm back in Kansas I'm
only a country girl, and have to help with the churning and wipe
the dishes while Aunt Em washes them." [11] Indeed, when Dorothy
is captured by the Wicked Witch in *The Wizard of Oz,* she is not
sent to the dungeon. Instead, she is taken "through many beautiful
rooms in [the] castle until they came to the kitchen, where the
Witch bade her clean the pots and kettles and sweep the floor and
keep the fire fed with wood" (150).

These connections between dryness and Aunt Em and between
the Witch and housework become all the more significant in the
events that follow. As if tired of doing housework for Aunt Em,
Dorothy watches as a cyclone, almost in answer to a wish, comes
and uproots the house. Dorothy and Toto and her home are transported to the land of Oz, a green world that is the complete
opposite of anhydrous Kansas. This wish fulfillment goes even
further: the house falls on the Wicked Witch of the East and kills
her, and she dries up and shrivels away. It is a symbolic matricide:
in the book, the equally desiccated Aunt Em is the only one who
takes shelter in the storm cellar under the house. Feeling guilty,
perhaps, for this oedipal hostility, Dorothy protests her innocence;
but as the Munchkins observe, whether the witch was killed by

Dorothy or by her house, "That is the same thing" (22). The Munchkins congratulate and honor the girl, and these childlike creatures (Baum stresses that they are exactly the same size as Dorothy) celebrate the end of their bondage.

Like the destination reached by children who make journeys in the fairy tales (a great forest in which lies, for example, a Gingerbread House or a cottage occupied by seven dwarves), like the twofold settings reached by the traveling juveniles in many American children's books where the Great Outdoors coexists with palatial homes (Huck's river and the Grangerfords' mansion, for example, or the Secret Garden and Misselthwaite Manor), Dorothy arrives in a Green World dotted with castles. In all these works, the Green World seems to be an arena of independence where the child is free from parental authority, but such freedom is both exhilarating and frightening. No matter how carefree Huck's drifting on the river may seem, he often witnesses wanton violence and has occasions to be anxious. As liberating as the jungle is for Tarzan, it is also a region of omnipresent danger. Like a child on its own for the first time, Dorothy finds that her own Green World is wonderful fun, but she must also face the threats of fearsome beasts and attacking trees.

The counterparts of the Green World are special homes associated with parent figures. Like the witch's Gingerbread House in "Hansel and Gretel" or the cottage of the fatherly protectors of "Snow White," the March sisters in *Little Women*, for example, shuttle between the palatial homes of their mean-spirited Aunt March and their fatherly benefactor, Mr. Laurence. A similar geography can be seen in *The Wizard of Oz*. At opposite ends of the quadrant are the castles of the Good Mother and the Bad Mother, the good witches and the bad witches. In the midst of this quadripartite rivalry, at the very center of the land of Oz, is the *axis mundi* of this oedipal dream: the Emerald City, which is ruled over by the paternal figure of the Wizard. It is there that Dorothy goes first, thence outward to kill (again) the Wicked Witch.

Typically, in American childhood classics and in the fairy tales, after arriving in the Green World the child is adopted by parental surrogates, engages in an oedipal struggle with the parent figure of the same sex, and has the limited but not quite sufficient protection of the parent figure of the opposite sex. Tarzan, for example, is adopted into an ape family, struggles with and finally kills his ape stepfather, and enjoys the safety afforded by his ape stepmother until he grows older and she dies. Likewise, Snow White finds another home with the dwarves, struggles with and eventually slays her stepmother the witch, and for a time enjoys the paternal protection of her companions, whose diminutive size suggests that they can be of only limited help. In the same way, Dorothy is adopted by her three traveling companions, vies with her same-sex antagonist the Wicked Witch, and enjoys the help but limited protection of her opposite-sex companions (the Scarecrow and the Tinman and the Lion are males who are all deficient in some way—lacking a brain, a heart, and courage).

The climax is prepared for when (in the book) the Wizard tells Dorothy she must kill the Wicked Witch of the West. The movie presents the oedipal nature of this task in more symbolic terms: Dorothy is told she must acquire the broom of the Wicked Witch—that is, as in the oedipal dream, the child will take over housekeeping, thus replacing her mother or filling her mother's shoes. In fact, the cause of the rivalry between Dorothy and the Wicked Witch of the West is that Dorothy has already put on the shoes of the other Wicked Witch.

When Dorothy and her party depart for the witch's castle, they are attacked by the witch's minions. The Scarecrow is torn apart, and the Tinman is disjointed. At this point, *The Wizard of Oz* comes to resemble "Hansel and Gretel." Like Hansel, the Lion (Dorothy's one remaining companion) is held in a cage in the yard, where he starves. Like Gretel, too, Dorothy is forced by the witch to do housework. Like Gretel, too, Dorothy slays the witch.

But Gretel's act is forthright: she deliberately pushes the witch into the oven. In contrast, Dorothy's action seems more accidental: she splashes the witch with a bucket of water, which makes the witch melt away. As if dimly conscious that this is matricide, as if guilty and defensive, Dorothy protests her innocence (as she had earlier when the Munchkins congratulated her for killing the Wicked Witch of the East with her house) and insists to the dying witch that she had no idea water would have that effect. But as the Munchkins might say in this circumstance, whether Dorothy or her water was the agent of this death, "That is the same thing." Moreover, this girl—whose laughter so troubles her grave aunt that the woman "would scream and press her hand upon her heart whenever Dorothy's merry voice reached her ears" (13), whose wish to be somewhere over the rainbow seems to evoke a home-wrecking cyclone that kills one witch—notably makes use of water to slay this witch. Aunt Em has been associated with an aridity at odds with Dorothy's own fertility, and Dorothy is (Baum says) "a well-grown child for her age" (20).

Once she has killed the Wicked Witch, it is interesting to note that Dorothy becomes, voluntarily, a housekeeper: "Seeing that she [the witch] had really melted away to nothing, Dorothy drew another bucket of water and threw it over the mess. She then swept it out the door. After picking out the silver shoe, which was all that was left of the old woman, she cleaned and dried it with a cloth, and put it on her foot again" (154–55). In a sense, this is the child's oedipal wish fulfilled: she has slain the mother, replaced her as housekeeper, filled her shoes, and now has the father all to herself. Then the triumphant and liberated Dorothy returns to the Emerald City and confronts the Wizard, and the twosome make preparations to return to Kansas in his hot air balloon. But at the moment of departure, Toto (that animated part of Dorothy's personality), as if sensing that this is an oedipally inappropriate solution, hops from the balloon's basket. Dorothy gives chase, and the Wizard ascends without her.

Something equally important occurred when Dorothy and her three companions confronted the Wizard upon their return to the Emerald City. When he had sent them to kill the Wicked Witch, the Wizard had refused to abide Dorothy's protests that she had never killed anything willingly. He had responded simply, "Until the Wicked Witch dies you will not see your Uncle and Aunt again" (129). Read from a psychoanalytical viewpoint, the Wizard's statement amounts to this: until Dorothy works through her oedipal dilemmas, until she does away with the fantasies that every child creates in which parents are seen in hyperbolic terms (as the All-powerful Father and the Weak Father, the Good Mother and the Bad Mother), she cannot see her parents as they are really are, free of her projections.

This suggests the importance of the scene in which Dorothy and her companions confront the Wizard in the Throne Room and discover who he really is. At that time, there is a simultaneous decline and elevation of Dorothy's father figures. On the one hand, the Wizard is exposed and shown to be a balloonist from Omaha whose power really comes from sleight-of-hand magic; as he says, he isn't all-powerful: "I'm just a common man" (184). On the other hand, Dorothy's three companions are elevated to the average and recognized as they truly are; it is made clear that, instead of being deficient males, they have always possessed the qualities they thought they lacked.

Having dispensed with exaggerated notions about the father, the story turns to consider equally hyperbolic notions about the mother. Dorothy has already come to grips with the Bad Mother; that concept is no longer important and has melted away. It remains for her to confront the equally exaggerated concept of the Good Mother, and the last section of both the movie and the book involves Dorothy's meeting with Glinda, the Good Witch.

In the movie, Dorothy is disappointed to discover that Glinda cannot transport her back to Kansas, that this Good Witch is not all-powerful, as Dorothy had thought. But this diminution is followed by something else when Glinda points out that the girl has had the ability to return all along. No longer needing to depend on others, even on the Good Mother Glinda, Dorothy comes into her own and recognizes her own power. With the click of the heels of her shoes (which are lost in the journey), Dorothy's adventures in Oz and her oedipal dream come to a conclusion. Through her own means, she transports herself back to Uncle Henry, Aunt Em, and Kansas—where people and places are, finally, what they are and not what they seem.

The Kingdom Within

The real apocalypse comes, not with a vision of a city or kingdom, which would still be external, but with the identification of the city or kingdom with one's own body.

Northrop Frye, *Fearful Symmetry*

In the film, Dorothy wants to escape to "Somewhere where there isn't any trouble," somewhere where Miss Gulch isn't trying to get her dog Toto, somewhere over the rainbow. Her subconscious answers her desire in the dream—remaking Kansas into Oz, the hired hands (Hunk, Zeke, and Hickory) into her companions (the Scarecrow, Tinman, and Lion), Professor Marvel into the Wizard, and

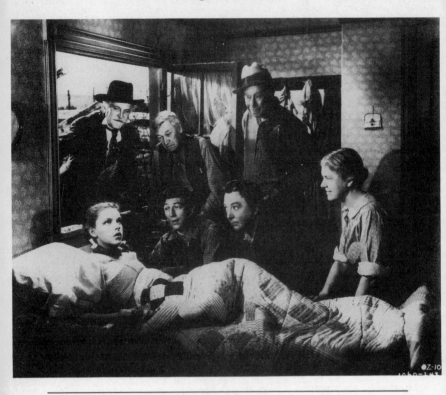

MGM's *The Wizard of Oz*. Copyright © 1939, 1966 Loew's Inc.
Metro-Goldwyn-Mayer, Inc.

Elvira Gulch into the Wicked Witch. All these transformations
make a subtle point: Dorothy cannot escape her troubles by going
elsewhere. The last words of the movie, "There's no place like
home," really amount to "There's no place *but* home."

This is a message that is repeated over and over again in American Children's Literature. Huckleberry Finn's journey is one long
escape from Pap, but all along the river he encounters various
versions of his father. Toby Tyler runs away to join the circus but
finds that the problems he had hoped to leave at home reappear in a
carnival atmosphere, where they are enlarged to freakish dimensions.

The Kingdom Without, America's childhood classics make
clear, is identical with one's own self. The Holland of Mary Mapes

Dodge (that land ever in danger of being flooded if the dikes give way) is the mirror image of Hans Brinker (a stalwart youth who preserves his ego from tidal waves of emotions). The Africa of Tarzan (where tigers found only on the Indian subcontinent are pelted with Hawaiian pineapples) has no objective correlative; it is the Dark Continent of the id, where violent and erotic impulses are unchecked. The quarrels between England and America in *Little Lord Fauntleroy* are coextensive with the domestic squabbles between the boy's paternal and maternal relatives; the two countries are, truly, the fatherland and the motherland. The macro and the micro coincide, so that, in Frances Hodgson Burnett's novel, the Secret Garden comes back to life when the children do, and vice versa.

The Wizard of Oz, then, like other American childhood classics, needs to be understood in a doubled, psychohistorical fashion. The Land of Oz is the Kingdom Without: an imaginative and extravagant version of America. But it is also and simultaneously the Kingdom Within: Dorothy's own circumstances reimagined at large, an extrapolation of her own oedipal or family problems. In the end, however, the Kingdom Without coincides with the Kingdom Within; resemblances finally retreat to their source; and an awakened Dorothy realizes that there really is "no place like home."

2

✣ ✣ ✣ ✣ ✣ ✣ ✣

The Long Parricidal Dream
Adventures of
Huckleberry Finn

Few modern scholars seem to remember, or will only grudgingly acknowledge, that Mark Twain's *Adventures of Huckleberry Finn* (1885) was meant to be a children's book, the second in a series Clemens said (in the Preface to *The Adventures of Tom Sawyer*) was "mainly intended for boys and girls." Embarrassed to find one of their nation's classics so much at home on the shelves of the children's section of the library, these critics also often overlook the fact that Twain's contemporaries and those reviewing the book (Louisa May Alcott among them) were concerned with its suitability for youth. When, however, *Huckleberry Finn* is restored to its place among other children's books of the Golden Age—*Rebecca of Sunnybrook Farm, The Wizard of Oz, Tarzan of the Apes, Little Lord Fauntleroy, Pollyanna, Toby Tyler,* and so on—a largely new and more comprehensive understanding of the novel emerges. At the same time, the novel sheds light on these other books and permits a deeper psychological reading of their recurring story.

With the exception of Leslie Fiedler's notorious theory about Huck and Jim's homoerotic friendship,[1] psychological interpretations of *Huckleberry Finn* have unfortunately been regarded as a minor enterprise, paddling about in a critical backwater while steamboats full of scholarly conventioneers (eager to talk about the structure of the novel, the maturation of Huck, or the *raison* of the conclusion) barge up and down the main channel. Certainly many novels do not seem to call for one particular method of interpretation, but there are several reasons for believing that a psychological approach to Clemens's book would be most productive.

When William Dean Howells tried to articulate the difference between himself and Mark Twain, he explained that, unlike his friend, he always wrote with some thesis in mind: "[I] am anxious to observe some sort of logical order, to discipline such impressions and notions as I have of the subject into a coherent body which shall march columnwise to a conclusion obvious if not inevitable from the start." In contrast, Clemens's technique, Howells says with admiration, is closer to stream-of-consciousness or free association: "So far as I know, Mr. Clemens is the first writer to use in extended writing the fashion we all use in thinking, and to set down the thing that comes into his mind without fear or favor of the thing that went before or the thing that may be about to follow."[2] Clemens would have agreed. In answer to a query, he described his own method of writing as "unconscious or half-conscious, . . . guided and governed by an automatically-working taste—a taste which selects and rejects without asking [me] for any help . . . and [which I don't] even consciously superintend."[3]

What we know about Clemens's compositional habits corroborates this view that he was, largely, a "spontaneous" or "unconscious" writer. In general, Clemens wrote when he was in the mood and shirked when he wasn't. And he was never much interested in his writing after it had passed through him; he was not keen on rewriting or editing or proofreading, and often cajoled others into performing those chores.

As Walter Blair has made clear, *Adventures of Huckleberry Finn* was written in this spontaneous fashion by an author fueled more by inspiration than dedication.[4] It was composed in fits and starts over a seven-year period. When things were going well, the writing passed through Clemens at a speed faster than an amanuensis could take dictation, and he measured his output in miles per hour: "I wrote 4,000 words to-day & I touch 3000 & upwards pretty often, & don't fall below 2600 on a working day."[5] If things weren't going well, he pigeonholed the manuscript and adopted another technique: "When the tank runs dry you've only to leave it alone and it will fill up again, in time, while you are asleep—also while you are at work on other things, and are quite unaware that this unconscious and profitable celebration is going on."[6]

Given this kind of writer and writing, it is not surprising that the novel itself seems dreamlike and "unconscious." *Adventures of Huckleberry Finn* reads like a long dream, like the journal of the somnambulist Clemens was. This is true from the beginning (with Jim's dream of traveling and his inability to separate fact from fancy) to the end (when nearly everyone, black and white, wonders whether they are dreaming or crazy or haunted by witches). And it is true all along the way—when, for example, Huck plays his trick on Jim and passes off his disappearance from the raft as a dream: "de powerfullest dream I ever see," Jim observes.[7]

Add to this the nocturnal floating of the raft (which, for the most part, is tied up during the day), the powerful unconscious flow of the river, Huck's essential passivity as wide-eyed floater and voyeur, an atavistic and irrational world of superstitions and freakish happenstance, a story full of disguises and lies and revelations and childhood memories—and one seems to have a description of the very essence of the dream state. Even the structure of the novel—if it should be called that—seems dreamlike: a scene about a drunkard being shot melts into another in which an apparent drunk is a skilled circus performer; a story about Jim's deaf-and-dumb daughter undergoes metamorphosis and becomes the Duke's deaf-and-dumb act. Scenes follow one another, in other words, by threads of free association; ideas are rehearsed from various points of view, transposed, repeated.

Clemens's predilection for "unconscious" composition, the history of the writing of *Huckleberry Finn,* and the book's dreamlike texture—all would seem to argue for the viability of a psychological approach to interpretation. But where should a psychological investigation of the novel begin? If that is the preferred methodology, what is the subject?

Since Clemens was not the kind of writer who (like Howells) composed with some foreordained thesis in mind, it seems pointless to speculate about what ideas or structures he may have had beforehand and *imposed* on the novel. It would be better to regard the book as prima facie object and search *post factum* for discoverable (rather than imposed) motifs. The place to begin is with the obvious.

In this regard, even relatively simple techniques can be useful. Allan Ellis and André Favat, for example, have employed a computer to examine *Huckleberry Finn* in a lexical fashion and, counting words, have discovered that two concepts appear most frequently and are often linked: "family" and "death."[8] Another researcher, Karol Kelley, has proceeded comparatively, made a "content analysis" of 105 best sellers published between 1850 and 1920, and suggested that *Huckleberry Finn* differs from others in its association of the concept of "family" with "pain and guilt."[9]

Another way of noticing the obvious is to consider the implications that follow from Clemens's choice of genres. In choosing to write a children's book—instead of, say, a travel book or medieval romance—Clemens was opting for a special galaxy of themes. A choice of genre is a choice of vocabulary. If statistical and lexical searches of *Huckleberry Finn* reveal its obsession with the subjects of "family" and "death" or "family" and "pain or guilt," a consideration of the motifs that predominate in other American children's books of the Golden Age might yield similar terms. Unlike English counterparts during the same era, American children's books do not offer Arcadian paradises: the golden kingdoms of Kate Greenaway where children in white pinafores play sweet games by a sparkling river, the comfortable countryside of *The Wind in the Willows* where gentlemanly characters pursue their pastimes with only an occasional interruption by unpleasant events. Instead, the world of America's literary juveniles is clouded over by familial problems: its heroes and heroines are orphans (mistreated, impoverished, neglected, and dispossessed) who come from "broken homes," who are adopted into second families where they are likely to be unloved and encounter parental surrogates who are antagonistic and have to be overcome.

Still another way to decide in which quarter to begin a psychological examination of *Huckleberry Finn* is to put Huck himself on the couch. Consider, for example, the lies he tells: the two he coins for Judith Loftus (in which he is first "Sarah Williams," seeking help for a poor and sick mother, and then an orphan and runaway apprentice); the lie he tells the ferryman whom he persuades to approach the wrecked steamboat (where he has an invented family stranded and in jeopardy); the scenario he invents for the two slave catchers who come near the raft (where, Huck claims, they will find his family, ravaged by smallpox); his handy improvisation when he arrives at the Grangerfords' house (where he is "George Jackson," the last member of a hard-luck family trimmed down by trouble); and his misrepresentation to the Duke and the King (in which Huck is again an orphan from another hard-luck family, once baby Ike and his drunk Pap have drowned.) His lies are surprisingly consistent: they all present families in distress.

Another way to continue this analysis would be to consider the entire novel, with its first-person narration, as Huck's dream. Then what kind of scenes recur, and with whom does Huck identify? The answers to these questions are surprisingly consistent with what is revealed by lexical examinations of the novel and the implications that follow on Clemens's choice of genres. This *is* a novel about families. In his sometimes nightmarish voyage, Huck passes through a variety of them: the Widow Douglas and Judge Thatcher, Pap, the Grangerfords, the Wilkses, and the Phelpses. Even in minor ways, families are often topics in the book: the stories of Moses and Solomon, the separation of the family of slaves at the Wilkses', feuding families, the death of Boggs in the arms of his daughter, and Jim's talk about his little girl. If, then, the dreamlike nature of *Huckleberry Finn* and Clemens's methods of composition seem to require a psychological approach to the novel, these observations suggest where explorations might begin. Lexical statistics, the implications of genre, Huck's unwitting revelations and textual preoccupations—all direct attention to troubled family life.

The few psychological studies that have been made of the novel have sometimes treated this subject. Kenneth Lynn's was among the first of these and shrewdly narrowed attention to the crux of the matter: Huck's troubled relations with his father. Examining both biographical material and various episodes in the book (especially Huck's imprisonment in Pap's cabin and the missing "Raftsmen Chapter"), Lynn advanced a view that is now widely known: that Jim becomes an affectionate father figure, an alternative to both Pap and Clemens's own stern father. [10] Lynn's analysis of the novel is provocative, but now, some thirty years later, its shortcomings should also be acknowledged: his ideas have the convincing force of brilliant and accurate intuitions, but he often sketches them with only cursory references to the text.

Since Lynn's work in the 1950s, a dozen or so other scholars have made this or that psychological observation and annexed it to his.[11] In 1985, however, Jay Martin moved psychological criticism of the novel out of the arena of Lynn's intuitive suggestions and toward a closer, textual examination of the book.[12] Martin's analysis of the paternal issues of the novel is keen, especially as he gauges Jim's replacement of Pap as a father figure and shows the return of ambivalent feelings toward the father when Huck meets Colonel Grangerford. The last third of Martin's essay, however, unfortunately veers off to another topic (biographical speculation about Clemens's identification with his brothers). Finally, while more probing than previous psychological glimpses at the novel, Martin's essay does not go half as far as it might have in its identification and analysis of the novel's familial themes.

The Floating House

Homes play a central role in *Huckleberry Finn,* and Huck's feelings toward them are ambivalent. Both the Widow Douglas's mansion and Pap's shack are, at different times, a prison and a refuge. Judith Loftus's cabin provides the boy with a warm haven until things get too hot for him. The Grangerfords' house is first a welcome port in a storm and then a seat of carnage from which he flees. The Wilkses' home has a thick atmosphere of family life that Huck envies until things become too thick for him. The Phelpses' plantation (including both their home and the shack in which Jim is kept) is both playhouse and jail.

This ambivalence, along with the motifs associated with these locales (captivity and independence, separations and reunions), suggest that these domiciles might be understood in the same way in which psychologists have explained the houses of "Hansel and Gretel." The two homes in the fairy tale can be regarded as the same place: the home of their father and stepmother to which the children are so eager to return whenever they are lost in the woods, and the home of the witch that they are so desperate to escape. "Hansel and Gretel" can be seen as a story about the dual emotions of separation anxiety: on the one hand, the tension a young child feels when apart from its parents; on the other hand, the child's desire to break with the parents and become independent. Because of this ambivalence, the home is envisioned as both a refuge and a prison. These issues are resolved in the fairy tale, however, when Gretel tricks the witch and pushes the old woman into the oven. As the tale makes clear, the witch is a stand-in for her stepmother; and as psychologists say, Gretel's figurative parricide actually symbolizes something quite healthy: a cutting of the apron strings, an end of dependence on parents, a resolution of separation anxiety, a declaration of independence. [13]

"Hansel and Gretel" might be taken as a touchstone for understanding the series of episodes in *Huckleberry Finn* that lead up to the wrecking of the raft by the steamboat—the point at which Clemens laid the manuscript aside for two years. What is interesting is the fact that Clemens is not as straightforward as the fairy tale. He ducks and weaves around the central issue of parricide, and his evasions result in different experiments with the same scene as he searches in a dreamlike fashion for a resolution.

The first of these scenes, Huck's stay with Pap, *does* resemble to a certain extend Hansel and Gretel's interlude with the witch. In both, a threatening adult holds a child captive in a "house in the woods" from which it eventually escapes. But these stories differ, as we have said, because the Grimm tale concludes with Gretel's murder of her same-sex antagonist, while Twain's episode does not include parricide—as least, not overtly.

The possibility of parricide is hinted at earlier in the book. There is the apparently lighthearted mention of a condition of membership in Tom Sawyer's pirate gang: the parents of boys who tell the gang's secrets will be killed. There is the time when Huck feels "comfortable" for a while when he thinks that Pap has drowned (14). There is the moment when Pap is suffering from delirium tremens and believes (or intuits) that Huck wishes to kill him; then Pap threatens the boy: "He chased me round and round the place, with a clasp-knife, calling me the Angel of Death and saying he would kill me and then I couldn't come for him no more" (36). And there is Huck's readiness to shoot his drunken father if he is provoked to self-defense, as he sits in the cabin in a posture of armed neutrality with a gun aimed at his sleeping parent.

Parricide does appear, however, in a concealed and symbolic fashion when, in the course of arranging his escape, Huck drags a pig into the cabin and cuts its throat. Throughout the early pages of the book, Pap has been associated with animals and particularly with pigs; this prodigal father, for example, often sleeps with swine in the tanyard (25). As Lynn and Martin suggest, Huck's ritualistic slaughter of the pig can be seen as a desire "to slay his father and the sordid animality of his ways."[14] That is certainly the case, but it is also possible to trace these parricidal motifs a great deal further.

This house scene is followed by another that is, in fact, the same scene, but this time Twain substitutes a corpse for the slaughtered pig. When Huck and Jim travel the river at floodtime and encounter a floating house with a body inside, what lies at the bottom of Huck's narrated nightmare becomes clearer.

The floating house is, in a sense, the extremities of the unconscious. It is excremental: conspicuously dirty, offal, and awful. It is sexual: some sort of brothel where obscenities are scrawled on the walls, where there is a naked dead man, where women's underclothes are thrown about. It is criminal: scattered about are robbers' masks, cards, whiskey, and a man who has been shot. And it is also, strangely, juvenile and infantile: there is a boy's straw hat and "a bottle that had had milk in it; and it had a rag stopper for a baby to suck" (62).

The last of these items, it should be noted, provides a verbal clue to the identity of the dead man. In this extreme plunge into the unconscious, we encounter the naked truth, the naked wish, a naked and murdered Pap.

A little farther down the river, Huck and Jim come across a third house, another "floating house," the wrecked steamboat *Walter Scott*. This episode amounts to a dreamlike reenactment of the events that led to Pap's murder, but this time Clemens uncovers even more of that primordial scene. As before, he depicts a robbers' lair, a dirty and disordered place reeking of whiskey and filled with loot. There, two robbers are arranging to kill another man—presumably in circumstances like those that led to Pap's murder in the floating house at the hands of the two hard-looking strangers with whom he had disappeared. But of greater importance is the fact that the two murderers are also stand-ins for Huck.

Their nature becomes clear when Huck later arranges to have the stranded murderers rescued from the wrecked steamboat, which is in danger of breaking up. This act is one that Huck feels obliged to explain, and the explanation is simple and revealing. Huck identifies with the two killers, those two men who are about to slay another in circumstances so similar to those that resulted in the death of Pap: "I begun to think how dreadful it was, even for a murderer to be in such a fix," Huck says to himself; then he adds, "There ain't no telling but I might become a murderer myself" (87).

Concealing Guilt

> *Dorothy said with hesitation, "There must be some mistake. I have not killed anything."*
>
> *"Your house did, anyway," replied the little old [Munchkin] woman, ". . . and that is the same thing. See!" she continued, pointing to the corner of the house; "there are her two toes, still sticking out from under a block of wood."*
>
> L. Frank Baum, *The Wizard of Oz*

If the three house scenes slowly bring into focus the parricidal desires of Huckleberry Finn, the energy expended to conceal matters reveals his guilt about these desires. When Jim and Huck come upon Pap's body in the floating house, Jim throws some rags over the man and tells Huck not to look. Why Huck—otherwise such an inquisitive youth—so readily complies on this occasion is not clear. Likewise, Huck's inability to recognize his father from other clues (his discarded clothes and other personal effects) and at close quarters seems strange, especially when this noticing lad had earlier been able to identify Pap by even tiny wardrobe items (crossed nails on the heel of his left boot) and to recognize his father in a distant skiff on the darkest of nights.

This energetic concealing is also evident at a different level. The image of the naked and murdered father lies at some depth in the unconscious and is deeply repressed and concealed in Huck's narrative. This is suggested by the appearance of the corpse within a distracting swirl of *in extremis* imagery—the equivalent, say, of Dorothy's cyclone and uprooted house in *The Wizard of Oz*. Pap's body is found after a cataclysmic thunderstorm and twelve days of rain, at floodtime when snakes and rabbits are clinging to the trees, inside a house that has floated free of its foundation and is "tilted over considerable," in a brothel where obscenities have been scrawled on the wall, where scattered about are women's underclothes, a priapic wooden leg separated from its owner, robbers' masks, and a baby bottle. Likewise, Huck (in telling us his story retrospectively in the novel) continues this pattern of concealment, since he does not reveal until the last paragraphs of the book that the dead man in the floating house was Pap.

The opening paragraph of the next chapter, then, takes on a special significance if recognized as part of this pattern of concealment. Back at the island, Huck and Jim sort through the loot they have taken from the floating house. Among all the things they might talk about, Huck is preoccupied with the question *"Who killed* the man whose body they found?" He is not concerned with *"Who died?"*—which is, perhaps, the more pressing question or, at least, an anterior one to Huck's own. Instead, Huck is obsessed: "I couldn't help studying over it and wishing I knowed who shot the man, and what they done it for" (63).

This peculiar preoccupation may be the result of Clemens's original conception of the book as a detective novel with a plot arranged to answer the question "Who killed Pap?"[15] Looked at psychologically, however, Huck's misdirected obsessions (and the vestigial whodunit trappings of his narration) are both revealing and symptomatic. Huck's dumb fixations seem a contrived form of innocence meant to conceal (even from himself) his responsibility and guilt, as is his referring to the murder victim as "the man."

These evasions are also evident at the narrative level. When Huck decides to go ashore to reconnoiter, he encounters the farm woman, Judith Loftus. When she relates the news of St. Petersburg, it becomes evident that Huck bears some responsibility for his father's death: Pap fell for the trick in the cabin and believed that his son had been murdered; to search for the killer, Pap borrowed some of his son's funds from Judge Thatcher and with that money got drunk and disappeared with two hard-looking strangers. In this way—Huck's readers learn retrospectively—Pap came to the floating house, where he was murdered and robbed.

To readers who already know the book's conclusion, this information creates a problem for Clemens if he wishes to portray our narrator in a sympathetic fashion. Huck's clever trick led to his father's death, and his funds paid for it. Coming fresh from the floating house and dressed in the clothes he was taken from there, Huck is left looking like a homicidal prankster and Pap like a hapless victim. To make Huck more sympathetic and to diminish his responsibility, the narrative forcibly transposes the role of culprit and victim. First, attention is shifted away from the murder of Pap and toward the "murder" of Huck when the voluble Mrs. Loftus feels obliged to report that the talk of the town is "who 'twas that killed Huck Finn" (69). Next, Pap is converted from victim to villain when Mrs. Loftus supplies an answer to the question: "People thinks now that [Finn] killed his boy." Next, as if filicide wasn't enough, Pap is tarred by public opinion: "People do say he weren't any too good" (69–70). Finally, Huck is acquitted by analogy when Mrs. Loftus thinks he is a runaway apprentice whose behavior is justified because he is bound out to a mean master; by extrapolation, Huck's criminal behavior can be excused because of Pap's harsh treatment of him.

If the scene in the floating house is a revelation of Huck's parricidal desires, then the subsequent scene at Judith Loftus's home justifies those desires through the mechanism of projection. Pap is changed from victim into villain, a conversion meant to vindicate a boy whose clever trick and ready cash led to his father's death. In a word: Pap got what was going to him. Parricide is justified as revenge for filicide.

This pattern of concealment is continued at the level of proxies. As Pap is eased out of the story, Jim is eased in as his double. This is made clear in striking similarities between scenes. In one, Pap comes back to the cabin with a jug of whiskey and a case of delirium tremens; he yells about snakes crawling up his legs and biting him, and he calls Huck the Angel of Death and suspects that the boy means to slay him. A few pages later, Jim meets Huck and also perceives the boy as a threat, a ghost who will harm him, and Jim falls down on his knees and prays, "Doan' hurt me" (51). Later, Jim gets bitten in the leg by one of the snakes Pap worried about, gets his own case of delirium, ends up drinking Pap's whiskey for the pain, and nearly dies.

Once Jim is established as a proxy for Pap, in other words, we should note that Huck is responsible for nearly killing this father figure; the boy killed a rattler and placed it on Jim's blanket as a joke, and the snake's mate came and bit Jim. Huck, notably, feels obliged to protest his innocence to the reader and explain how he forgot this habit of snakes to seek out their mates. And this may be the case. Still, this forgetfulness may give the reader cause to wonder if some truth lies behind those apprehensions shared by Pap and Jim, when they worry whether the boy means to do them harm. Equally notable is the fact that, unlike his prank on Jim in the fog, the snake episode doesn't conclude with an apology from Huck. Instead, Huck's actions reveal his desire to conceal his guilt: "I slid out real quiet and throwed the snakes clear amongst the bushes; for I warn't going to let Jim find out it was all my fault, not if I could help it" (65).

The march of events in the early chapters of the book, then, slowly makes clear the parricidal shape of *Huckleberry Finn.* From Huck's slaughter of a pig in one house, the story moves to another house, where swinish Pap lies murdered. Guilty, it seems, Huck is steadfastly unable (or unwilling) to identify the corpse and dumbly fixated by the question "Who killed the man?" An answer to this "Whodunit?" is given once Jim is established as a double for Pap; then Huck very nearly kills this proxy. That same answer is given again when the boy travels to the home of Mrs. Luftus; there it becomes clear how Huck's clever trick and his cash led to his father's murder. The answer is repeated once more on the steamboat *Walter Scott,* an episode that brings into even sharper focus the previous "floating house" scene: then, in a reenactment of the killing of Pap, Huck sympathizes with the murderers and says he can imagine himself like them.

Choosing Fathers

It is a matter of indifference who actually committed the crime; psychology is only concerned to know who desired it emotionally and who welcomed it when done.

Sigmund Freud, "Dostoevsky and Parricide"

The Adventures of Tom Sawyer is, undeniably, a maternal book, one that focuses on the relationship between Aunt Polly and her endearingly mischievous "bad boy." Still, to some degree, *Tom Sawyer* anticipated the paternal themes that loom so large in its sequel.

The role of father figures in this earlier book is a complex subject,[16] but what can be said simply is that fathers in *Tom Sawyer* (and in Twain's other novels) seem variations on two competing types: the High-born Good Father and the Low-born Bad Father,

Judge Thatcher and Injun Joe.[17] As Robert Regan has observed, though such a notion may appear too reductive and simplistic, it is in fact a recognizable kind of childlike logic often found in children's stories—in this case, the male equivalent of, say, the bifurcated mother figures in "Cinderella": the Fairy Godmother and the Wicked Stepmother.[18]

The conclusion of *Tom Sawyer* presents the results of a psychic competition between Judge Thatcher and Injun Joe within the heart of the fatherless boy. The savage dies, and Tom is indirectly responsible for the death because he did not tell anyone that Injun Joe was in the cave before Judge Thatcher had an iron door mounted at its entrance. The High-born Good Father is triumphant over the Other, and Tom makes his own preferences clear: he votes with his dollars and presents the money he has taken from Injun Joe to Judge Thatcher, the same man whose approval and attention Tom had sought earlier in the book. Finally, at the end of *Tom Sawyer,* just as Huck is adopted by the Widow Douglas, the fatherless Tom is virtually adopted by the Judge, who "conceived a great opinion of Tom," "hoped to see Tom a great lawyer or a great soldier some day," and said "he meant to look to it that Tom should be admitted to the National Military Academy and afterward trained in the best law school in the country."

This same Judge Thatcher crosses over into *Huckleberry Finn* and becomes, after a fashion, a father to Huck. Correspondingly, Injun Joe's role is taken over by Pap.[19]

There may be biographical sources for both these versions of the father. On various occasions, Clemens called his own father a "stern, unsmiling" parent and often described their relationship as strained: "My father and I were always on the most distant terms when I was a boy—a sort of armed neutrality."[20] Several critics have pointed out that Clemens's father was a small-town justice of the peace and have suggested that he reappears in both Judge Thatcher and the visiting judge who tries to convince Pap Finn to join the temperance movement—an attempt that resembles Judge Clemens's own unsuccessful attempt to do the same with the town drunkard, Jimmy Finn.[21] Other, psychological critics have suggested that Pap can be viewed as "a nightmare version of Twain's hardhearted father."[22]

Whatever the case, *Huckleberry Finn* essentially opens with a rivalry between these two kinds of father figures, now engaged in a custody fight over Huck. On the one hand, a surrogate family composed of Judge Thatcher and the Widow Douglas (whose late husband was also a judge) stands ready to adopt the boy. On the other hand, there is Pap and his undeniable biological claim. Like Tom Sawyer, Huck has already cast his vote with his dollars: he has kept Pap from his money and presented the entire $6,000 to the Judge. Nonetheless, the new circuit court magistrate, in his Solomonic wisdom, decides not to cut Huck in half and returns the boy to Pap.

This decision seems to go against Huck's own wishes, but, in truth, Huck is ambivalent: he both likes and doesn't like staying with the Widow Douglas; and he has similar feelings about the

HUCK AND HIS FATHER.

Edward Windsor Kemble for *Adventures of Huckleberry Finn*
(New York: C. L. Webster, 1885).

alternative of living with Pap. A few pages later, Jim emerges from this ambivalence, this competition between parents, as a compromise candidate. He is a paternal hybrid who is both Good Father and Lowly Father, both kindhearted and déclassé.

Jim is, of course, a complex character and not simply a father figure—or, rather, his complexity defines just the kind of father he is. He is also a double for Huck and a peer: both escape the same place at the same time; both are held captives in cabins; and when Huck learns that a search party is approaching the island to look for Jim, what the boy cries out is inclusive: "There ain't a minute to lose. They're after *us!*" (75). Ever afterward, their fates are linked.

Jim's plights can be said to parallel Huck's in the same way Miles Hendon's difficulties in the subplot of *The Prince and the Pauper* echo the problems of the prince. At the same time, however, Hendon and the prince are not exact reflections of each other: although a member of the nobility, Hendon still comes from a social stratum beneath that of the prince, and Hendon is an adult who cares for the boy. In the same way, Jim is socially subordinate, and he is an older man who cares for a youngster. Hendon and Jim, in other words, are only proximately fathers. They have a role somewhere between peer and older guardian. They seem elder brothers or Dutch uncles—the equivalents, perhaps, of Clemens's older brother Orion, who (when Sam was almost twelve and their father died) took the youngster under his wing; or the equivalent of Uncle Dan'l, an aged and beloved slave whom Clemens remembered as both a children's comrade and a sensible adviser.[23] In fact, Jim seems a version of the Fraternal Father—that enlightened creature imagined in nineteenth-century American works influenced by the child-raising practices of Locke and Rousseau, that kind of parent envisioned as an antidote to patriarchs (*vide* Pap) of the old school that held to "spare the rod and spoil the child."

With these qualifications in place, Jim's role as father to Huck can be acknowledged. Throughout the book, Jim is frequently seen as a concerned parent: in his plans to get his wife and children out of bondage, in the way he misses his family, in his remorse for having mistakenly struck his deaf daughter, in the irritation he feels about Solomon's nonchalance and readiness to cut a baby in half, and in the way he is shown lavishing care upon Huck once Jim (alone) knows that Pap is dead and the boy has been orphaned. To some extent, Jim's parental role is also suggested by his friendliness, which, like that of Judge Thatcher, provides an alternative to Pap's abuse; that they are opposites is also suggested by the fact that Pap goes out hunting for Jim when the black is suspected in the murder of Huck. So, too, the boy votes with his dollars; Huck gives or shares with Jim the money and loot that he has stolen from Pap or found in the wreck of the floating house, just as earlier the boy had made a similar votive offering to the Judge.

While Jim is connected to the Judge in a sketchy way, what is more striking are the resemblances we have already seen between Jim and Pap. There are the similarities between the scenes when they both see Huck as an avenging angel and when they resort to the same whiskey jug because snakes, real or hallucinated, are after them. The episode with Judith Loftus also links Jim and Pap when she says that the town considers both of them suspects in the supposed murder of Huckleberry Finn and that the search is on for them both. But perhaps the most direct suggestion that Jim is a father figure to Huck is, simply, that as Pap moves out of the story, Jim moves in; and after Pap's death, Jim's attention and concern for the boy increase.

This process of substitution reaches a kind of climax when Huck takes the canoe out to discourage the approach of two slave catchers. Huck claims that his family is on the raft, and he implies that they have smallpox. When asked if there is an escaped slave aboard, Huck replies that the man on the raft is white and his father: "It's pap that's there" (126).

This is an epiphanic moment. Huck himself has made an important link. Like the Wilks girls deciding between guardians, he has made a choice. As offbeat as it might at first sound, what Huck has said amounts to this: Jim is Pap with a skin problem. This is an intense moment of repudiation (exaggerated by the racial differences) and identification (a denial of those differences)—so intense a moment, in fact, that a few hundred words later Clemens came to an abrupt stop on his novel and couldn't start up again for two years.

Jay Martin suggests that Clemens stopped at this point because he had achieved a psychic satisfaction: he had replaced his own hardhearted father (symbolized by Pap) with an affectionate dream father (Jim). Clemens resumed the book, Martin argues, because his "emotional needs were omnivorous, and he could not long accept this solution of his imagination."[24]

It is important, however, to look at the entire episode. After identifying Jim as his "pap," Huck suffers a kind of vertigo: he is lost, unable to locate Cairo, and adrift in a fog. And then he is very nearly killed: a steamboat comes barging out of the night, crashes into the raft, and drives Jim and their floating home down into the watery depths. Steamboats serve three purposes in *Huckleberry Finn:* they search for missing children (all of St. Petersburg society is aboard one and looking for Huck); they kill fathers (as the scene on the *Walter Scott* suggests); and they kill "niggers" (as Huck explains when he arrives at the Phelpses' farm).

Such an event, then, does not appear to be the expression of psychic satisfaction, as Martin suggests. Instead, it smacks of punishment and reprisal, of guilt and repression. What we know from Clemens's letters is that he did not stop at this point in the novel because things were going well; like Huck, he was lost and adrift. Clemens was stymied. The tank had "run dry."

Having made that paternal repudiation and choice, Clemens's mind, like the raft, seems to have drifted into some taboo area for which he was unprepared, a foggy and volatile region in which he felt lost and endangered. Out of that darkness came a huge, dangerous, home-wrecking monster. Huck has made a paramount decision—one that he feels guilty about because of the "deep" ingratitude it implies, because it is a climactic expression of his parricidal passions. Huck has rejected Pap and *chosen* his own father, Jim.

The Missing Chapter

As a rule, [in legends of the hero's childhood] the child is surrendered to the water, in a box . . . [but eventually finds and] takes revenge on his father.

Otto Rank, "The Myth of the Birth of the Hero"

On the suggestion of his editor, Clemens threw one chapter out of his book at the last minute. Since then, others have recognized the importance of "The Raftsmen Chapter," and modern editors of *Huckleberry Finn* have generally restored it to its place in the novel.[25]

The centerpiece of the missing chapter is "The Mysterious Barrel," a tall tale told by one raftsman to his joshing companions and overheard by Huck, who has stolen onto their raft. It is a story about another group of raftsmen whose raft is eerily followed by a barrel that appears nightly and brings them bad luck. One of the raftsmen, Dick Allbright, reluctantly confesses that this barrel follows any raft he works on. Finally, dogged by trouble, the captain of the raft has the barrel hauled aboard and busts it open. Inside, they find the corpse of a naked baby. This discovery forces Dick to confess that the dead child is his, that he killed his son and sealed the body in the barrel. Chased down, the father now commits suicide by jumping overboard.

This ghostly yarn is extremely relevant to Huck and his narrative.[26] Huck himself makes this clear. Just after the tale is told, the raftsmen find Huck aboard, and when they ask his name, he responds by giving the name of the dead baby in the story, Charles William Allbright. Huck identifies with the dead child in other ways as well. He, too, is associated with barrels, since Huck regularly sleeps in hogsheads. He, too, is "dead," or presumed to be by those who searched for his body or later meet his ghost. At this moment Huck, too, is naked and a floater on the river. And finally, all along the river, Huck, too, brings bad luck to others—Pap, Jim, the robbers on the *Walter Scott,* the Grangerfords, the Duke and the King.

More important, however, is the connection between this episode and the scene in Judith Loftus's home. In both, filicide is a topic, since Pap is suspected of killing his own son, just as Dick Allbright has done. Both scenes present, as well, an extended exculpatory process. The scene in the Loftus home is meant to absolve Huck of responsibility in his father's death, even though the boy's clever trick in the cabin and his ready cash led to just that. This is accomplished by tarring Pap, by saying that most people suspect that Pap killed his own son, and by concluding that Pap got what he deserved. "The Mysterious Barrel" story does the same thing: a son brings about his father's death, but it is a well-deserved death since the man had killed his son. The operative excuse in both scenes is that parricide is justified as revenge for filicide.

But note the absence of logic. Huck *didn't* die in the cabin at Pap's hands. In fact, Huck is *not* dead—and that point is emphasized when Jim meets the boy's ghost on the island, and later when he finds the boy alive (again) after they have been separated in the fog. There is, in other words, a fatal flaw in this self-vindicating notion that parricide is justified as revenge for filicide—Huck is an only child! There is no way for such a murdered child to get revenge on its father—except in fantasy. The story of "The Mysterious Barrel" enters the novel at this point.

And Clemens emphasizes that "The Mysterious Barrel" is fantasy. The narrative frame of the tale is constantly made obvious by the storyteller, who keeps inserting his own editorial asides (for example, when he offers his own opinion in the middle of the story that Dick Allbright is a liar). Moreover, once the tale is told, the crew begins to provoke and josh the teller, to ask how much of this yarn he expects them to swallow, and then a fight breaks out between a listener and the teller, ostensibly over this issue of credibility. Clemens stresses, in other words, just how much this tale departs from the verisimilitude that is characteristic of the rest of the novel. Here is fantasy or wish rather than logic—or, rather, wishful logic.

Even so, "The Mysterious Barrel" is revealing fantasy. This upside-down version of the biblical tale of Moses in the bulrushes can be regarded as the novel *in brevis*. It encapsulates and encodes the scene that is repeated over and over again in *Huckleberry Finn:* a dead son traveling downriver in murderous pursuit of his father.

Discrediting Fathers

His mind centered itself upon a single problem—how to find his father, in case he was still alive—& upon a single purpose: to kill him when he should find him. He said he would make this the whole business of his life, & allow nothing to stay or divert him until it was accomplished.

Deleted passage from Mark Twain, *Pudd'nhead Wilson*

When Clemens reached a climactic moment in Huck's psychic biography, he sank the raft and Jim and set aside his novel for two years. When he resumed, he took up, once again, this unresolved issue of fathers. In a fashion, Jim had predicted this resurrection: after their visit to the floating house, Jim had advised Huck that the "unburied" man was likely to haunt them. And so he does. Throughout the journey downstream, Huck is forever quoting Pap (on the reasons for taking roosting chickens, for example, or the necessity for no miserableness on a raft) or re-creating hard-luck and drunken fathers in the lies he tells others to explain himself. This obsession is quite natural. After all, Huck does not know his father is dead until the end of the novel; he sees his entire trip downriver as an escape from Pap.

Yet at times, instead of fleeing his father, Huck seems to be pursuing him. Such paternal pursuit is, of course, the central point of "The Mysterious Barrel." But this stalking of the father is evident in a number of similar episodes. In the second part of the novel, Huck always seems to find himself in the company of fathers, both high and low, alive and dead: Colonel Grangerford, Boggs, the King, Peter Wilks, Silas Phelps. These various father figures seem lined up along the shore as if, in dreamlike fashion, they are something Huck seeks.

Huck's vacillation between escaping Pap and pursuing him is entirely consistent with the competing emotions in separation anxiety: the wish to be independent and the uneasiness that comes when the child is apart from the parents. It is akin to the ambivalence Huck feels about houses, viewing them alternately as prisons and as refuges. Separation anxiety may also explain what Keith Opdahl has identified as a pattern of ambivalence in Huck's encounters with adults: how the boy feels threatened when he first meets them (the Widow Douglas, Pap, Jim on the island, the Grangerfords, the Duke and the King, the Phelpses), then grows comfortable, then discovers that they represent a real threat to him.[27] Linked to all this, as well, is Clemens's tonal ambivalence: his admiration coupled with implicit condemnation of Colonel Grangerford and Colonel Sherburn, his amusement and disgust at the low tricks of the Duke and the King, his affection for and ridicule of the Phelpses.

This dreamlike irresolution marks (some would say mars) the second half of the novel, the events that follow the sinking of the raft. In this section, Huck encounters a series of father figures, and the novel vacillates wildly between triumphs and debunkings of both High-born and Low-born Fathers. It would be wonderful to be able to say that the plot moves in an orderly fashion to a recognizable resolution, but this is not the case. Clemens's novel is not a folk tale revised by countless storytellers until events march in economical fashion to a clear and satisfying conclusion. Instead, like a not-quite-satisfying dream or an improvisational novel, the narrative picks up a topic, experiments with it, reverts to it again in a transposed form, tries another gambit, and so forth. Here are improvisations still searching for a resolution. What ties these scenes together is their shared obsession and the parricidal nature of their various denouements. As Huck glides down the river, the novel moves from one episode to another in which father figures are discredited.

The first of these occurs when, with Jim apparently out of the novel forever, Colonel Grangerford is introduced: "He was a gentleman. . . . He was well born, as the saying is, and that's worth as much in a man as it is in a horse, so the Widow Douglas said, . . . and pap he always said it, too, though he warn't no more quality than a mud-cat, himself" (142). Huck's introduction is comparative and suggests that the colonel is that paradigmatic alternative to Pap, the High-born Father. Throughout this episode the colonel is also, like Judge Thatcher, a paternal guardian; in fact, Walter Blair and others have argued that Clemens had his own father in mind when he created the colonel, who, like John Clemens, "often wore a blue tail-coat with brass buttons."[28] Moreover, Huck's role is clearly that of a "son." Huck is taken in and adopted by the Grangerfords, and his place in the family is further indicated by the similarities (in names and ages and shared clothing) between him and their son Buck.

While these familial enactments are interesting, the thrust of the Grangerford episode is to discredit the High-born Father. As admirable as the colonel is, something is dangerously wrong with him: like Pap, he is a father who is a threat to his children; by perpetuating the feud, he makes sure that the sins of the father are visited upon his children and thereby brings danger to his family and to families in general. In fact, this episode ends with the killing of Buck and the colonel, a genteel replication of the son-and-father "murders" of Huck and Pap or Charles William Allbright and Dick Allbright.

Despite what is admirable about him, then, the High-born Father is discredited. Not surprisingly, Jim is now resurrected and brought back into the story. But his presence constitutes only a temporary solution, as the next episode makes clear.

In succeeding pages, the violent confrontation between Colonel Sherburn and the drunken Boggs recapitulates Clemens's perennial competition between the High-born and Low-born Fathers, between Judge Thatcher and the drunken Pap. In the previous episode, readers watched a colonel descend from the heights of admiration into a paternal disgrace that warrants the rebirth of the Lowly-born Father, Jim. This episode portrays its dreamlike opposite. It begins with the death of a Low-born Father (Boggs in the arms of his daughter)[29] and traces the ascension of another colonel from a disgraceful murder to an admirable height where he faces down a mob.

This vacillation is one of the most characteristic aspects of the novel. Reversing the trend of the Grangerford episode, the Boggs–Sherburn scenes come to an apparent resolution that marks, finally, the demise of the Low-born Father and the ascendancy of the High-born Father. Even this state of affairs doesn't last long, however. In the circus scene that follows, Boggs's double (the apparently drunken horseman) evades death and turns out to be a wonderfully competent trickster. The archetype with which Boggs is associated is, as it were, brought back to life—ultimately to be embodied in those lowlife tricksters, the Duke and the King. In a similar reversal a few pages later, the High-born Father is laid to rest when the image of Colonel Sherburn standing on his roof and facing down the mob of neighbors who mean to lynch him is replaced by the image of a crowd of neighbors attending a funeral and looking down on the corpse of Peter Wilks.

This image of the father in his coffin, surrounded by his children and Huck, is an important one. But an equally important part of the Wilks episode is Huck's placing a bag of gold on the chest of the corpse. What is striking is that it is exactly the same amount of money ($6,000) that Huck had kept from Pap and offered to Judge Thatcher. The dollars on the chest of the corpse seem, in other words, a guilt offering—and further, tacit acknowledgment of the parricidal nature of this narrative.

Still, this penance is done in secret; Huck hides the money when no one is looking and subsequently feigns ignorance when others are searching for the funds. He makes amends, in other words, but still conceals his guilt. This explains why the subsequent scene in the graveyard is so emotionally charged: like that atmospheric pyrotechnics last seen when Pap's corpse was discovered, this uncovering of another father's corpse occurs on a dark night with thunder booming and lightning crackling, with a gang of men holding prisoners and digging furiously to unearth a body and the truth. It is a scene of revelation. But what is revealed is not so much the corpse or a tattoo or even who are and are not the true brothers of Peter Wilks. What startles everyone is the discovery of the bag of gold that Huck has hidden there. In dream fashion, Huck is caught redhanded, as it were, and (equally important) at graveside.[30]

Later, explaining to the Duke and the King how he managed to escape, Huck coins a revealing lie: he claims that the man holding him saw a resemblance between Huck and his son, who had died the year before; sympathetic, this father forgives Huck and lets this "son" off the hook and urges him to flee. As in Huck's offering of gold, forgiveness between father and son is the issue here. This motif is continued when the Duke and the King confront each other after escaping the mob in the graveyard. In an interesting choice of similes, the Duke objects that the King has duped him: "I [was] a trusting you all the time, like you was my own father" (264). Angry, the Duke nearly strangles the older man until this "father" confesses to taking the gold. Later, this "son" forgives his "father," and they get drunk and make up.

The End of Pap: No More "Milk for Babes"

Some pages later, the Duke and the King are exposed and disappear from the story. But they have, in fact, been present in the story since the Grangerford episode. They are highly complex characters. In them, the microcosmic story of Huck and his father is translated into a simultaneous macrocosmic story of national politics, and the novel becomes a particularly American book.

We can begin to understand the Duke and the King by considering their fraudulence. The first book written for America's children was John Cotton's *Milk for Babes* (1641). One of its catechetical passages is worth considering in light of the parricidal motifs of *Huckleberry Finn*:

Q. *What is the fifth Commandment?*
A. Honour thy father, and thy mother, that thy dayes may be long in the land, which the Lord thy God giveth thee.
Q. *Who are here meant by Father and Mother?*
A. All our superiors, whether in Family, School, Church, or Commonwealth.
Q. *What is the honour due them?*
A. Reverence, obedience, and (when I am able) recompence.

The link here between the honor due parents and respect for institutional authority was entirely acceptable to the pre-Revolutionary America of 1641. But what was the case a hundred or so years later, when America was no longer John Cotton's nursing babe but a macrocosmic adolescent rebelling against its royal father in England? How was this understanding of the Fifth Commandment to be squared with the antiauthoritarian attitudes of the revolutionaries?

The answer is that American thinkers, in tour-de-force rhetoric, advanced the claim that King George III was not a "true" father, but a "bad" or "false" or "fraudulent" father. Patrick Henry, for example, argued that "from being a father of his people," the king "degenerated into a tyrant, and forfeit[ed] all rights to his subjects' obedience." Thomas Paine seconded this and insisted that the monarch only "pretended [to the] title of 'Father of his People.'"[31] This Revolutionary "mistrust of paternal pretenders" established an "American cultural pattern," Paul Rogin has argued, that continued through the Jacksonian era, manifesting itself in the way "American culture encouraged sons to suspect usurpers of the father's place."[32]

Clemens's portrait of the "Duke" and the "King," then, should be understood as an echo of this national rhetoric. They are villainous actors and royal pretenders. And when they falsely claim to be the rightful guardians of the Wilks girls, they are also usurpers of the father's place.

Huckleberry Finn, in other words, with its long parricidal dream pointing toward the end of a youth's reliance on Pap, rejects *Milk for Babes* (and its understanding of the Fifth Commandment). Instead of filial respect, it celebrates disrespect for patriarchs and institutional authority. In one of the novel's most memorable scenes, for example, Huck has to decide whether to continue to help Jim escape from slavery when this flies in the face of all he has been taught by institutions. He decides to continue. In an act of parricidal self-reliance, Huck throws over all the pap he has learned from school and church; he resolves, "All right, then, I'll *go* to hell" (271).

This universal disrespect seems, nonetheless, to have made Clemens uneasy. Whether guilty or cautious, he frequently disguises it with humor. However, as a careful reading indicates, beneath the amusing passages featuring the Duke and the King (and the later Phelps Farm episodes) lies a willful destruction of that honor John Cotton says is due "All our superiors, whether in Family, School, Church, or Commonwealth."

As their names suggest, the "Duke" and the "King" are burlesque versions of the High-born Father. The King, for example, is a caricature of Colonel Grangerford: while the colonel is noted for his "blue tail-coat with brass buttons" (142), the King sports a cheapjack version of the same, "an old long-tailed blue jeans coat with slick brass buttons" (160). As this dual description begins to intimate, the scenes involving the Duke and the King amount to comic assassination of the High-born Father; they are the farcical equivalent of Peter Wilks in his coffin. Moreover, between themselves (as the language following their escape from the graveyard suggests), the King and the Duke counterfeit the roles of father and son in a lampoon of family life.

Through them, all seriousness about parenthood is turned into theatrical travesty and sham Shakespeare. Huck's memories of his dead father (Pap's saying, for example, about no miserableness on a raft) are parodied in a minor key in the fractured soliloquy of Hamlet to his father's ghost. The tragedy of the Grangerfords becomes their drag and slapstick rendition of *Romeo and Juliet*. The scene of Boggs dying in his daughter's arms becomes, through their arrangement, Jim painted blue and dressed as King Lear in a horsehair wig and whiskers. Even Jim's touching story about mistakenly punishing his deaf-and-dumb child is deflated by the ludicrousness of the Duke's pretending to be deaf and dumb "whilst he made all sorts of signs and said 'Goo-goo—goo-goo-goo' all the time, like a baby that can't talk" (213).

But there is more than just high spirits and low comedy to the Duke and the King. These impostors are a genuine threat to families and children. They conspire to bilk the Wilkses; and, despite protests, they separate their servants, a family of slaves, and sell them down the river. Behind Huck's back, they also sell Jim and leave the boy destitute on the banks of the lower Mississippi. No Dutch uncles, they intend real harm to orphaned children.

Even more important, however, Clemens is able, by means of the Duke and the King, to move the novel's paternal themes into the larger arena of patriarchal politics and make his children's book distinctly American. Noting, for example, how the two abuse their roles as guardians to the Wilks girls, Huck is moved to a sweeping conclusion that "all kings is mostly rapscallions." He then expresses what amounts to an American desire: "I wish we could hear of a country that's out of kings" (201). The Duke and the King are actors and tricksters, but then the democrat Clemens often thought the same about actual royalty. The Duke and the King are, in other words, doubly pretenders. As Huck says about these miscreants, "You couldn't tell them from the real kind" (201).

About the same time he was writing *Huckleberry Finn,* Clemens was also composing *The Prince and the Pauper*—a novel that makes the point that when the two boys exchange clothes, people can't tell a prince from a pauper. What is revealed is something that might be called the Secret of Clothes—what, in another work, Clemens imagines the Czar discovers when he looks in a mirror: "Is it this that a hundred and forty million Russians kiss the dust before and worship? Manifestly not! . . . It is my clothes. There is no power without clothes. . . . Strip its chiefs to the skin, and no state could be governed; naked officials could exercise no authority; they would look and be like everybody else—commonplace, inconsequential."[33]

This is, of course, "The Emperor's New Clothes" redux. To the democrat, to Clemens, monarchy is pretense, a hoax. This is an emphatic theme in American children's books. It is not only the point of *The Prince and the Pauper,* for example, but the crux of the central scene in *The Wizard of Oz,* in which the ruler of the Emerald City is exposed as a humbug and shown to be just an ordinary man.

The naked truth about monarchs is also revealed in *Huckleberry Finn,* in the appropriately titled theatrical "The Royal Nonesuch": "At last when he'd got everybody's expectations up high enough, [the Duke] rolled up the curtain, and the next minute the king come a-prancing out on all fours, naked; and he was painted all over, ring-streaked-and-striped, all sorts of colors. . . . It was awful funny. The people most killed themselves laughing" (196). The Royal Nonesuch is a smoker, an all-male drag show, and something like a male initiation ceremony. But at a deep level, the ultimate point of this burlesque is to reveal the secret that the king is naked or, rather, that naked he is no longer a king but a man like any other. When one of the patrons realizes that that's all there is to a king's performance, he sings out what Dorothy and her companions might have said when they dicovered the truth about the Wizard: "We are sold—mighty badly sold" (197).

The laughter that accompanies this moment barely disguises the fact that this ludicrous exposure of the naked king is parricidal. It is the vaudeville echo of the discovery of Pap's nakedness in the floating house. It is a burlesque in which everyone in the audience is made an accomplice to Ham at the moment he comes upon the shameful scene of his naked father, Noah. This is comic assassination of the patriarch.

Such ridicule is continued in the Phelps family episodes. The ludicrous extravagance of these scenes and the scatterbrained nature of Aunt Sally and Uncle Silas—dumbly scratching their heads, for example, as they count the cutlery or stare at rat holes stuffed with wadding—make these pages seem a premonition of *I Love Lucy*. Ham-fisted farmers, pipe-smoking women inclined to low-country circumlocutions ("'s'I, Sister Darnell"), dizzy black slaves spooked by witches, seniors easily manipulated by their juniors—the point seems clear: adults are buffoons.

Even Jim becomes a victim of this parricidal lampooning, though Clemens, perhaps out of guilt, brings in someone so closely linked to Huck that their identities are merged—Tom Sawyer, who must be reckoned a double acting in Huck's stead. Whatever the case (no matter how innocent Huck may or may not be in the mischief that victimizes Jim), these late pages of Huck's own narrative are full of images of a ridiculed father figure. Jim is the butt of burlesque extravagances, an adult essentially told what to do by kids, a paternal guardian who appears in drag and hopping about in Aunt Sally's dress. He is the Parent now held captive in a snake-filled cabin by the Child—an image that is the dreamlike opposite and revenge for Huck's earlier captivity in Pap's snaky cabin.

It is not surprising, then, that the final appearance of the Duke and the King accompanies these episodes of parricidal ridicule.

This scene recalls another in Hawthorne's tale "My Kinsman, Major Molineux." There, Hawthorne tells the story of the American Revolution in miniature by speaking of a boy named Robin who, in the penultimate scene, watches his uncle (a royalist who has been appointed a colonial administrator) run out of town by the Sons of Liberty, who have tarred and feathered him. As critics have observed,[34] the reciprocity between Robin's need for filial independence and the colonists' drive toward political independence creates a vision of oedipal politics—uniquely American, we might add, in its duplex vision of America-as-Child.

The last appearance of the Duke and the King, then, can be read in this simultaneously political and psychological fashion. Like that famous nocturnal, dreamlike, and parricidal scene in Hawthorne's tale, the scene in Clemens's novel features a mob that seizes and tars and feathers the Duke and the King. Naked and shamed, these patriarchs, too, are run out of town on a rail. Like Robin, Huck watches all this from a place of concealment. While Robin laughs and joins in his countrymen's ridicule, however, Huck feels another emotion: "to blame somehow—though *I* hadn't done nothing" (290).

Huck feels this guilt throughout his long parricidal dream— "to blame somehow" when, for example, as an unintended result of his trick, Jim is bitten by the rattlesnake; "to blame somehow" when his very presence in a place seems to so consistently evoke visions of a dead father (whether that of Pap in the floating house or Colonel Grangerford or Boggs or Peter Wilks). To be sure, Huck "hadn't done nothing" directly to cause what happens to the Duke and the King—nothing except to express his desires a few pages earlier in this wish-fulfilling book: "I wish we could hear of a country that's out of kings" (201) and "I'd seen all I wanted of them, and wanted to get entirely shut of them" (275).

Variations on the Pattern

To the perceptive reader, then, the news that comes in the very last words of the novel that Pap is dead must seem the very essence of anticlimax. Huck, too, registers no surprise. And he expresses no sorrow.

At first glimpse, then, *Huckleberry Finn* would seem to describe the oedipal interlude or dream journey often seen in works for children—akin to the parabola found, say, in *The Wizard of Oz* when Dorothy whirls away from Kansas to kill witches and then returns to her family. Huck journeys from St. Petersburg to largely all-male worlds, and then returns to the domain of the family (marked by the presence now of maternal women and the reintroduction of people and news from St. Petersburg).[35] But there are differences. Uncle Silas and Aunt Sally certainly suffer a ridicule that is never directed at Dorothy's Uncle Henry and Aunt Em. And when Huck says he means to "light out" rather than return to St. Petersburg, his attitude is considerably different from Dorothy's "There's no place like home."

In truth, Huck's journey only counterfeits that parabola in which the child works through problems and, still a minor, eagerly rejoins the family. Instead, the pattern of the novel approximates, more or less, a straight line, downriver and aimed at an end—a maturity defined as filial independence. Robert Penn Warren puts it this way:

> Once [Jim] and Huck are ashore, [their] relationship ends; Huck loses his symbolic father. But—we must emphasize this fact— he also loses the literal father, for now Jim tells him that Old Pap is, literally, dead. So, to translate, Huck is "grown up." He has entered the world, he must face life without a father, symbolic or literal, the "good" father of the dream, or the "bad" father of the reality or shore.[36]

Other motifs also suggest this transformation and maturation. Since St. Petersburg, Huck has been "dead," but when he arrives at the Phelpses' farm he feels "reborn" (282). So, too, questions of identity are finally resolved; the boy who has impersonated so many others is finally identified as "Huckleberry Finn." But an even clearer signal of Huck's maturation and independence occurs when Jim tells Huck that, since Pap is dead, the boy can collect his $6,000. There is perhaps no stronger image of Huck's empowerment than his recovery of the very same amount of money that the boy had entrusted to Judge Thatcher, kept from Pap, and then guiltily placed on the chest of Peter Wilks when he came upon the scene of the father in his coffin. After that last funereal image, the money is his.

Nonetheless, consistent as this imagery seems, these observations might leave the wrong impression that Clemens's novel reaches a neat resolution or achieves some sort of climax in which Huck, having overcome his father, becomes an individual. An honest critic, however, must concede that loose ends remain.

The unfinished nature of the conclusion is suggested in at least one way by a strong father figure who appears in the wings, a self-possessed Adult who condescends to and patronizes the Boy: the doctor who ministers to the injured Tom Sawyer, a kindly and well-respected High-born Father who recalls other minor characters of his kind who have appeared earlier (the doctor and lawyer who look out for the Wilks girls' interests, the judge who organizes the audience into accomplices in the charade of "The Royal Nonesuch"). If positive images of male adults late in the novel can be construed as signs of irresolution (because of the book's view of maturity as a parricidal thrust to independence), then there is some backsliding as well when Jim (despite the ludicrous spectacle he makes in Aunt Sally's dress) recovers some of his dignity by jeopardizing his freedom in order to help the wounded Tom and aid the doctor.

A final sign of the conclusion's incompleteness may be the powerlessness that Huck suffers in the presence of motherly females. What should be remembered is that, in the case of a boy, the achievement of autonomy means working through *both* sides of the Oedipal Complex: the antagonism toward the father and affection for the mother. *Huckleberry Finn* is a "boys' book," however, in which the struggle with the father predominates. The novel does not take up, in any significant way, the boy's passing beyond the state of powerlessness that is inherent in the oedipal bond of affection with the mother.

At the beginning of the novel, Huck chafes under the ministering attentions of the Widow Douglas and Miss Watson. Maternal authority also appears when an otherwise compassionate Judith Loftus puts Huck in his place in a particular fashion. She indicates that she is not fooled by Huck's disguise as a girl and reminds him of his gender by throwing a lump of lead in his lap—"when a girl tries to catch anything in her lap, she throws her knees apart; she don't clamp them together, the way you did" (75). But this is the last scene of its kind before the river journey begins. Once it does, Huck travels into largely masculine worlds where most of the females are close to his own age. In other words, Huck's downriver trip provides him with numerous occasions where he can work through his oedipal problems with father figures, but the journey offers scant opportunities to pass beyond the juvenile impotence implied in the episode of Judith Loftus's maternal solicitude. While the novel, then, has all the earmarks of maturation, we might well suspect that it is not fully resolved.

That incompleteness is, in fact, suggested late in the book when Aunt Sally sits at Huck's bedside and wrings her hand in worry that the missing Tom (masquerading as "Sid") may be dead or drowned. This episode might be reckoned as regressive because it returns to that kind of scene of parental anxiety that is so common in *Tom Sawyer* and from which Tom derives so much juvenile pleasure: when, for example, Aunt Polly wrings her hands in the company of Sid and worries that the missing Tom may have drowned. Even more important, in this scene in the later novel, Huck is robbed of his maturity and made the child once again: he is immobilized. Tucked into bed by Aunt Sally and "mothered . . . so good I felt mean and couldn't look her in the face," the boy who has outwitted murderers and proved himself intrepid in thousands of ways is suddenly paralyzed by guilt and unable to slip out of his bedroom window for a night's escapade. His legs turn to water whenever he glimpses what Clemens had elsewhere lampooned as a cliché and a sentimental icon:[37] the scene of the "old grey head" of Aunt Sally watching the night for Tom, "setting there by her candle in the window with her eyes toward the road and tears in them" (349–50). In the same vein, shortly thereafter, Tom's Aunt Polly arrives from St. Petersburg, sorts things out, and puts both boys in their place.

In these ways, then, the conclusion of *Huckleberry Finn* is not fully resolved. It is like the end of a not-quite-satisfying dream. Still, these are the small imperfections born of improvisation. Clemens's children's book remains, to quote Jim, "de powerfullest dream" (104).

3

✤ ✤ ✤ ✤ ✤ ✤ ✤

Spinster Aunt, Sugar Daddy, and Child-Woman
Rebecca of Sunnybrook Farm

For all its improvisational complexity, *Adventures of Huckleberry Finn* intimates the oedipal pattern at work in the "boys' book." Kate Douglas Wiggin's *Rebecca of Sunnybrook Farm* (1903), in contrast, provides a clear example of the pattern's configuration in the "girls' book"—a formula already glimpsed in the oedipal geography of *The Wizard of Oz*, in which the land is divided into quadrants ruled over by bifurcated versions of the mother (the good witches and bad witches) and at the center of which resides the paternally benevolent Wizard.

At the same time, as we will see, discernment of the ur-story in *Rebecca of Sunnybrook Farm* goes a long way toward explaining the American conception of "the girl"—or, more accurately, "the Child-Woman." Rebecca is that hybrid. On the one hand, she is not simply a juvenile innocent; in that regard, the novel's unfortunate association with Shirley Temple and with "Pollyanna-ism" (with darling but empty-headed waifs) was something Wiggin had to combat among those who hadn't actually read the book, and she often did so by pointing to the novel's male fans (among them have been Mark Twain, Jack London, and Jack Kerouac). [1] On the other hand, Rebecca is not an ersatz adult, the worldly-wise trollop and Europeanized American girl of Vladmir Nabokov's *Lolita;* still, as we will observe, *Rebecca of Sunnybrook Farm* comes surprisingly close to Nabokov's novel.

Rebecca stands at a midpoint between these two extremes. She is between the two worlds of childhood and adulthood, poised on the threshold of maturity. But what is interesting is how she is frozen at that very point and effectively excluded from maturity. Rebecca, and her sisters in the other girls' books, remain (to use Louisa May Alcott's words) both "little" and "women." They are mature minors or underage women, incarnations of the American icon of the Child-Woman played in contemporary films by such actresses (until they grew older) as Jodie Foster and Brooke Shields.

The Spinster Aunt

Rebecca is a hybrid, both a Sawyer and a Randall. She is the offspring of Aurelia Sawyer, a Yankee from an established family in Maine, and Lorenzo de Medici Randall, a generous but improvident Italian who roamed New England giving dancing lessons and from whom Rebecca inherited her dark complexion and "gypsy" spiritedness.

Like many another youth in American childhood classics, Rebecca was the issue of a marriage that others disapproved of. Her mother's family objected to the union with the extravagant Italian, who, they worried, might fritter away her modest inheritance. And events seemed to have proved them right when, after siring his children and making unsound investments, the father died and left his family penniless. For this reason, Rebecca's mother decides to send the child to live with her aunts, who have the wherewithal to see to the girl's education. So, like other American literary children, Rebecca is separated from her one remaining parent (made a "virtual orphan") and embarks on a journey. As the stagecoach departs from Sunnybrook Farm to Riverboro, Maine, her mother says that the stay with the aunts will be "the making of Rebecca."[2] And, in fact, the *Bildungsroman* begins.

In the second of "The Three Lives of the Child-Hero," at the end of the journey, the literary child typically arrives at the Big House, where he or she is adopted into a second family of parental surrogates of a different social rank, and encounters both a same-sex antagonist and helpers. Rebecca arrives at the Brick House, where she is taken in by her two spinster aunts, Miranda and Jane, whose modest means compare favorably with the penury she has left behind at Sunnybrook Farm. Her Aunt Miranda is a "stiff, grim, martial" woman (33), constantly irritated by Rebecca, and the child's antagonist. Aunt Jane, the Good Mother half of the bifurcated mother figure, is the quieter of the two and the child's sympathetic supporter.

Aunt Miranda recalls Aunt Em of *The Wizard of Oz*, Dorothy's grave aunt who "never smiled" and who "had been so startled by the child's laughter [when Dorothy first came to live with her] that she would scream and press her hand upon her heart whenever Dorothy's merry voice reached her ears." Rebecca's lively and spontaneous ways have a similar effect on the sclerotic Miranda:

> Rebecca irritated her aunt with every breath she drew. She continually forgot and started up the front stairs because it was the shortest route to her bedroom; she left the dipper on the kitchen shelf instead of hanging it up over the pail; she sat in the chair the cat liked best; she was willing to go on errands, but often forgot what she was sent for; she left the screen door ajar, so that flies came in; her tongue was ever in motion; she sang or whistled when picking up chips; she was always messing with flowers, putting them in vases, pinning them on her dress, and sticking them in her hat; finally she was an everlasting reminder of her foolish, worthless father. (59)

This last objection is the crux of the oedipal antagonism between Rebecca and Aunt Miranda, and it is over this subject alone that the child stands up to her critic. When Miranda levels yet another slur against her "vain, foolish, and shiftless" father, Rebecca answers in a flash: "Look here, aunt Mirandy, I'll be as good as I know how to be. I'll mind when I'm spoken to . . . , but I won't have my father called names. He was a perfectly lovely father" (79–80).

So the stage is set for the contest. At first, the irritable Miranda seems the more powerful, insisting that Rebecca is all Randall and not a Sawyer, that she is her father's child and does not share in the maternal bloodline of her aunts. But Rebecca is, in the words of another character, the "winning-est child ever." Typical of the child-hero in the second of its three lives, Rebecca does eventually triumph over her antagonist, not in the parricidal manner of Huck Finn, but by humbling her aunt and melting the curmudgeon's heart.

To be sure, it is a long campaign. Rebecca's first victory comes when both of her aunts are sick and she is sent as their representative to the Missionary Society meeting. Afterward, the visiting missionary asks if there is a place where his family might spend the night, and Rebecca grows embarrassed that none of the townspeople offer their hospitality. Goaded by a neighbor who reminds the girl that her late grandfather, Israel Sawyer, always had a place for traveling missionaries, Rebecca stands up and offers to take them in at the Brick House. Her aunt is livid when first told of the invitation. But during the course of the pleasant evening, Miranda changes when she hears Rebecca included in the missionaries' praise of the Sawyer family and listens to neighbors' memories of old days when Miranda's father was alive:

> A certain gateway in Miranda Sawyer's soul had been closed for years; not all at once had it been done, but gradually, and without her full knowledge. If Rebecca had plotted for days, and with the utmost cunning, she could not have effected an entrance into that forbidden country, and now, unknown to both of them, the gate swung on its stiff and rusty hinges, and the favoring wind of opportunity opened it wider and wider as time went on. All things had worked together amazingly for the good. The memory of old days had been evoked, and the daily life of a pious and venerated father called to mind; the Sawyer name had been publicly dignified and praised; Rebecca had comported herself as the granddaughter of Deacon Israel should, and showed conclusively that she was not "all Randall," as had been supposed. (156)

Having cleared up this issue of her identity, Rebecca solidifies her triumph in succeeding pages. She wins over her aunt and, as much as it is possible, thaws the old woman's hard heart. Not surprisingly, the child's further successes come at the expense of her aunt. It is not simply that, in sending Rebecca for further schooling at Wareham Academy, Miranda has to scrimp and save and do without. It is rather that the trajectory of Rebecca's successes seem inversely proportional to Miranda's own fate.

Rebecca piles up accomplishment after accomplishment at

Wareham Academy—winning the essay contest, becoming the first girl editor of the student newspaper and the foremost figure at the school. All of this reaches an apex on Graduation Day, when Rebecca is the class president, leads her group in a floral procession to the stage, delivers the first interesting commencement speech in the school's history, and is informed that she has two offers of teaching positions waiting for her. If this is an oedipal success, it is not surprising that the girl's triumph is matched simultaneously with her aunt's demise; at this very moment, in the midst of her crowning glory, Rebecca receives word that Aunt Miranda has suffered a debilitating stroke.

As if this image of a girl's coming into her own and replacing a mother was not sufficient, the motif is echoed a few pages later. While attending to her ailing aunt, Rebecca is told that her own mother has been injured in an accident at Sunnybrook Farm, and the daughter returns there and takes charge. Ministering to her injured mother and running the household herself, Rebecca then receives a telegram and learns that her Aunt Miranda has died.

In the third of "The Three Lives of the Child-Hero," after the triumph over the oedipal antagonist (by death or humbling or both), the child typically comes into its own, an event usually symbolized by the resolution of questions of identity and recognition ceremonies. At the same time, the child has to strike some accommodation between its first two lives: the First Life with the biological parents and the Second Life where, in some distant place, oedipal problems are worked through with parental surrogates.

The last chapter of Wiggin's novel is titled "Aunt Miranda's Apology." When Rebecca returns for the funeral, her Aunt Jane says about Miranda, "I'm sure she was sorry for every hard word she spoke to you; she didn't take them back in life, but she acted so't you'd know her feeling when she was gone, . . . Rebecca. Your aunt Mirandy's willed all this to you,—the brick house and buildings and furniture, and the land all round the house, as far's you can see" (253–54). Miranda's "apology" is a touching one and an acknowledgment, finally, that Rebecca is a Sawyer and Miranda's heir. It is also a financial bequest that provides Rebecca with a way to yoke her two lives; in the concluding paragraphs, Rebecca decides to rescue her mother, brothers, and sisters from poverty and bring the inhabitants of Sunnybrook Farm to the Brick House, where they will all live together. While not as dramatic as Dorothy's house falling on a witch or Huck's discovery of Pap's naked body in the floating house, the death and post-mortem concession of the girl's same-sex antagonist provides its own conclusion to this story of "the making of Rebecca."

The Sugar Daddy

By focusing on Rebecca's relations with her aunts, we have been paying attention to one side of the oedipal triangle. We now need to consider another corner of that triangle: Rebecca's relations with another character, her neighbor Adam Ladd. He is an adult and bachelor who develops a keen interest in the child and eventually becomes the opposite-sex helper so frequently seen in American children's books.

They first meet when Rebecca is selling cakes of soap door to door in order to buy a banquet lamp for an impoverished family that lives in her neighborhood. The philanthropic Mr. Ladd listens sympathetically to the child's pitch and shocks her by taking 300 cakes of soap. He has been charmed by Rebecca, and that fascination deepens in succeeding pages as the gentleman becomes both her friend and her patron—regularly sending her gifts, visiting her at home and school, offering to pay for her education, and secretly arranging the essay contest she will win. What are we to make of this?

There are many clues in the novel that the relationship between Mr. Ladd and Rebecca will end in marriage. Rebecca is often mentioned when Ladd's marital future is discussed by gossips:

> "It is strange he hasn't married . . . and him so fond of children. . . ."
>
> "There's hope for him still, though," said Miss Jane smilingly; "for I don't s'pose he's more than thirty."
>
> "He could get a wife in Riverboro if he was a hundred and thirty," remarked Miss Miranda.
>
> "Adam's aunt says he was so taken with the little girl that sold the soap . . . that he declared he was going to bring her a Christmas present," continued Miss Ellen. (124–25)

Mr. Ladd does bring Rebecca a Christmas gift and, in the years that follow, showers her with gifts. On each occasion, he also provides a gift for Emma Jane (the girlfriend who accompanied Rebecca on her soap-selling expedition), though in succeeding years he acknowledges how difficult it is to keep up appearances and remember Emma Jane "at all the proper times" (211).

This, too, leads to a discussion of Rebecca when the gossips discuss the marriageable Mr. Ladd:

> "He's given Emma Jane about the same present as Rebecca every Christmas for five years; that's the way he does. . . ."
>
> "Like as not," assented Mrs. Peter Meserve, "though it's easy to see he ain't the marryin' kind. . . ."
>
> "'Tain't likely he could be ketched by any North Riverboro girl," demurred Mrs. Robinson; "not when he prob'bly has had the pick o' Boston. I guess Marthy hit it when she said there's men that ain't the marryin' kind."
>
> "I wouldn't trust any of 'em when Miss Right comes along!" laughed Mrs. Cobb genially. "You never can tell what 'n' who's going to please him. You know Jeremiah's contrairy horse, Buster? He won't let anybody put the bit in his mouth if he can help it. . . . Rebecca didn't know nothin' about his tricks, and the other day went int' the barn to hitch him up, . . . and when she put her little fingers into his mouth he opened it so fur I thought he'd swaller her for sure. He jest smacked his lips over the bit as if 'twas a lump o' sugar. 'Land, Rebecca,' I says, 'how'd you get him to take the bit?' 'I didn't,' she says, 'he seemed to want it.'" (220–21)

It seems no coincidence that the question of whether Adam Ladd will ever put on the traces of marriage is so closely accompanied by the story of Rebecca's ease at getting the bit in the horse's mouth.

All this subconscious matchmaking, then, seems to be moving the book to a concluding scene in which Mr. Ladd and Rebecca marry, but this is not the case. What prevents it?

First of all, there is a difference in their ages. Rebecca is ten when she meets a twenty-eight-year-old Mr. Ladd, "a good-looking young man, or was he middle-aged?" (116). Because he buys the soap that permits her to get the lamp, Rebecca nicknames him "Mr. Aladdin," a familiarity that shocks her peer and companion Emma Jane almost as much as his familiarity with them:

"Oh, Rebecca!" said Emma Jane in an awestruck whisper.
"He raised his hat to us, and we not thirteen! It'll be five years
before we're ladies."

"Never mind," answered Rebecca; "we are the *beginnings* of
ladies, even now." (121)

Later, age does not seem such an obstacle to a courtship between Mr. Ladd and Rebecca,[3] but a second explanation is offered.
In her adolescence, Rebecca remains uninterested in the opposite
sex: "boys were good comrades, but no more. . . . From the
vulgar and precocious flirtations she was preserved by her ideals.
There was little in the lads she had met thus far to awaken her
fancy" (192–73). Even Wiggin seems surprised by this: "It was a
fact that Rebecca's attitude toward the opposite sex was still somewhat indifferent and oblivious, even for fifteen and a half!" (191).

But later, this obstacle, too, is removed. When Rebecca passes
on to finishing school at Wareham Academy, she takes pride in not
being a boy-crazy flirt like fellow student Huldah Meserve. But
when she sees Mr. Ladd walking with Huldah—"Huldah, so saucy
and pretty, so gay and so ready" (186)—she seethes with jealousy
and recognizes her own romantic and possessive interest in the
gentleman.

There is, finally, one thing that prevents a courtship, and it is
hinted at in the gossip's observation about Mr. Ladd: "It's strange
he hasn't married yet . . . and him so fond of children." Mr.
Ladd is a devotee of children; in fact, he prefers the "beginnings" of
ladies to the full-grown kind. On a visit to Wareham Academy, he
suddenly takes Rebecca's hands in his and comments on how she
has grown up:

"This will never do in the world! How will Mr. Aladdin get
on without his comforting little friend! He doesn't like grown-
up young ladies in long trains and wonderful fine clothes; they
frighten and bore him!"

"Oh, Mr. Aladdin!" cried Rebecca eagerly, taking his jest
quite seriously; "I'm not yet fifteen, and it will be three years
before I'm a young lady; please don't give me up until you have
to!" (189)

On an occasion like this, *Rebecca of Sunnybrook Farm* seems to
dimly resemble Vladmir Nabokov's *Lolita*. Adam Ladd (who is

thirty-two at this moment) has a special interest in the unripe Rebecca, an interest similar to that of Nabokov's Humbert Humbert, who is fascinated by "nymphets"—girls "between the age limits of nine and fourteen." In his description of this type of fascination, Humbert adds, "There must be a gap of several years, never less than ten . . . between maiden and man to enable the latter to come under a nymphet's spell."[4] In a way, then, *Rebecca of Sunnybrook Farm* reads like *Lolita* without sex. Unlike Humbert, Mr. Ladd is asexual in his fascination with Rebecca. And unlike Lolita, Rebecca is sexually innocent.

Mr. Ladd wouldn't have it any other way. When he spies Rebecca walking with a sixteen-year-old boy at Wareham Academy, he explodes at Miss Maxwell, "I am a trustee of this institution, but upon my word I don't believe in coeducation!" (203). He is relieved to learn that what he saw was only an innocent meeting of the editors of the school newspaper.

The trouble is (and Rebecca seems subconsciously aware of this), Mr. Ladd prefers the young and sexually innocent. But Rebecca is growing older and developing a womanly interest in men—two things likely to make her unattractive to Mr. Ladd, the one man she desires. Although he says to her, I'm "glad I met the child, proud I know the girl, longing to know the woman" (229), Rebecca knows that Adam Ladd prefers lassies to ladies. She says to him shortly before her graduation:

> "I know what you are thinking, Mr. Aladdin,—that my dress is an inch longer than last year, and my hair different; but I'm not nearly a young lady yet; truly I'm not. Sixteen is a month off still, and you promised not to give me up till my dress trails. If you don't like me to grow old, why don't you grow young? Then we can meet in the halfway house and have nice times. Now that I think about it," she continued, "that's just what you've been doing all along. When you bought the soap, I thought you were grandfather Sawyer's age; when you danced with me at the flag-raising, you seemed like my father; but when you showed me your mother's picture, I felt as if you were my [brother] John." (200)

This link between Adam Ladd and Rebecca's John seems all the more significant a few pages later, when Rebecca learns that her Aunt Miranda has had a stroke and she must return to the Brick

'DON'T BE KIND, MR. ALADDIN'

Helen Mason Grose for *Rebecca of Sunnybrook Farm*
(Boston: Houghton Mifflin, 1925).

House and give up her debutante future. This hard news quickly makes her older, and in her sorrow "she longed to steal away into the woods with dear John, grown so manly and handsome, and get some comfort from him" (231).

Surely, this is a Freudian slip, and one that Adam Ladd would find unacceptable. He prefers his vision of Rebecca as a little slip of a thing, and he needs constant reassurance about her sexual immaturity. Most revealing are the last pages of the book, when he encounters Rebecca at a train station just after Aunt Miranda's death. Although she strikes him as "all-womanly," he is relieved when "he had looked into her eyes and they were still those of a child; there was no knowledge of the world in their shining depths, no experience of men and women, no passion, nor comprehension of it" (250).

After that meeting, Adam Ladd wanders away and throws himself under a tree. He reads the book he meant to give Rebecca, *The Arabian Nights,* and the story of Aladdin's enchantment with the beautiful Princess Badroulboudour. It is a moment not unlike that in *Lolita* when Humbert Humbert finds himself near a playground full of children and thinks, "Ah, leave me alone in my pubescent park, my mossy garden. Never grow up."[5]

The Child-Woman

In Twain's personal activities during his last decade . . . [what] was especially evident [was] the enormous energy and attention he devoted to creating and augmenting his collection of what he called "Angel Fish" for his "Aquarium." His "Angel Fish" were young, preadolescent, presexual girls whom he induced to gather round him; from them, as Hamlin Hill says, "he demanded unquestioning devotion and frequent companionship," and he "lavished affection" on them in return. . . . "Don't get any older," he wrote to one in 1906; "I can't have it." When this same girl became sixteen, he demanded she regress to fourteen for his sake.

Jay Martin, "The Genie in the Bottle: Huckleberry Finn in Mark Twain's Life"

We are left with Adam Ladd's final glimpse of Rebecca, situated in a kind of fairyland of girhood, frozen on the threshold of maturity

where she seems "all-womanly" but with eyes that reveal she is still
a child. Wiggin, too, never let Rebecca grow up. Despite repeated
requests, she refused to write a sequel to *Rebecca of Sunnybrook
Farm*. In fact, the letters pouring in from readers requesting one
were so numerous that Wiggin had to compose a form letter to be
sent out in reply. Eventually she did write another book, *New
Chronicles of Rebecca* (1907), but it was full of stories meant to be
added between the chapters of the original book. Wiggin steadfastly refused to take Rebecca beyond her maiden years.

One ten-year-old Pennsylvania girl was so disappointed by this
that she composed her own sequel and sent it to Wiggin. As
Wiggin's sister observed, the child's conclusion "wastes no words
on . . . psychological hair-splitting. It goes straight to the point
and settles things to the satisfaction of everybody": Mr. Ladd presents Rebecca with a ring on Christmas Day, and the next day they
are married.[6] Wiggin's inability to be so straightforward bears
examination.

Rebecca is frozen out of maturity. On the one hand, Wiggin's
novel is progressive, a *Bildungsroman,* a story about "the making of
Rebecca." On the other hand, she can only grow to a certain point
and then she is locked into the ever-youthful world of Peter Pan's
Never-Never Land. What should be noted is that Rebecca is
stopped at the threshold of sexual maturity. While the trajectory of
Rebecca's growth would seem to lead quite naturally to her becoming a marriageable woman, throughout the novel Wiggin is busy
in the background arresting her character's growth.

Notice should also be taken, in this regard, of Rebecca's name.
When they first meet, Mr. Ladd asks the child her name and she
replies:

> "Rebecca Rowena Randall, sir."
> "What?" with an amused smile. *"Both?* Your mother was
> generous."
> "She couldn't bear to give up either of the names, she says."
> (120)

In this manner, Wiggin signaled that her novel joined a long list of
American adaptations of Sir Walter Scott's *Ivanhoe*. There are two
heroines in Scott's novel—the Anglo-Saxon and fair Lady Rowena,
and the Jewish and dark-complexioned Rebecca—and the combi-

nation of both names in Wiggin's character may mean to suggest Rebecca's twin bloodlines (her inheritance of Anglo-Saxon virtues from her Yankee mother, and her dark complexion and gypsy ways from her Italian father). Since Wiggin never mentions the child's middle name again, we need to pay attention to the Rebecca with whom she is conspicuously associated: Scott's Rebecca is the Dark Maiden, a figure of musky eroticism, a saucy *femme fatale* who is conspicuously sexual; the villain, Sir Brian de Bois-Gilbert, is taken with Rebecca and tries forcibly to steal her virtue.

What seems odd is that, having made this association with Scott's erotic character, Wiggin is strenuously engaged elsewhere in subtracting sexuality from her namesake. For example, Wiggin stresses Rebecca's prolonged uninterest in the opposite sex, something even the author concedes is remarkable for a fifteen-and-a-half-year-old. Sexual subtractions are also emphasized (in negative constructions and in Adam Ladd's sigh of relief) when Rebecca appears at the end of the novel: though she appears "womanly," "there was *no* knowledge of the world in [the] shining depths [of Rebecca's eyes], *no* experience of men and women, *no* passion, *nor* comprehension of it" (250).

Why did Wiggin feel such an imperative to desexualize her character? Certainly some of these subtractions can be explained by the fact that Wiggin was writing a children's book and not a romance novel like *Ivanhoe*. But that answer still leaves questions. Why did Wiggin take Scott's romantic story as her inspiration and then fill it with erasures? Why did Wiggin put herself in jeopardy to begin with by associating Rebecca with Scott's erotic character so that she was subsequently obliged to backpedal furiously and desexualize *her* Rebecca? To restate this question once more, what explains Wiggin's emphatic wish to freeze Rebecca in a state of emphatic girlhood innocence?

Adam Ladd can't be blamed. His wish to preserve the immature Rebecca, his idealized pedophilia, is only an intermediate explanation of the girl's arrested growth. His wish coincides with Wiggin's. He is, after all, her creation. It is, in fact, by paying attention to his characterization that we can discover the reason behind Rebecca's arrested maturity.

Adam Ladd is young but old, a paternal patron but still full of romantic possibilities, fatherly yet a marriageable bachelor—in short, a wistful oedipal dream.[7] Here is why Rebecca is never permitted to grow up, why she is so strenuously desexualized, why she is kept a "Child-Woman." As Wiggin's readers recognized, the whole trend of the novel seems to be moving to a moment where Adam Ladd and Rebecca marry. By freezing Rebecca on this side of the threshold of sexual maturity, Wiggin prevents her character from crossing over into oedipal taboo.

If we understand *Rebecca of Sunnybrook Farm* in this fashion, as a novel that walks a tightrope between oedipal romance and taboo, then many of its complications can be understood. Specifically, this interpretation explains:

- Why, despite the strong undercurrents in the novel that move it toward a marriage between Rebecca and Adam Ladd, Wiggin's psyche would not allow it and bristled with inventions to prevent it.

- Why, despite her readers' repeated requests for a sequel, Wiggin steadfastly refused to take Rebecca beyond her maiden years.

- Why, despite having given Rebecca a name associated with the sexuality of the Dark Maiden of the *Ivanhoe* tradition, Wiggin bowdlerized and subtracted sexuality from the story with such ferocity that she finally arrested her character's development.

- Why, despite the novel's constant discussion of the marital prospects of Mr. Ladd, Wiggin desexualized *him* in the same manner she desexualized Rebecca, by making this middle-aged man into an innocent and arrested adult—as his name implies, an Adamic lad—who "doesn't like grown-up young ladies in long trains and wonderful fine clothes; they frighten and bore him!" (189).

- Why, despite the hint that Aunt Miranda shared a romantic interest in the man who would become Rebecca's father (59), Miranda, too, is desexualized and rendered a spinster whose views on marriage are unflattering.

- And why, despite the fact that this is *Bildungsroman* about the maturation of Rebecca, at the end of the novel she only *appears* to be a woman, since her eyes reveal that she is still a child with "no knowledge of the world" and "no experience of men and women, no passion, nor comprehension of it."

The Pattern of the Girls' Book

The Spinster Aunt, the Sugar Daddy, the Child-Woman—these are stock characters in American girls' books. They constitute a kind of desexualized oedipal triangle. In this surrogate family, the literary girl can work through oedipal problems with a hardhearted maternal substitute and an affectionate paternal substitute.

This pattern can be found in other American girls' books. Later in this study, we will discuss *Little Women* and *Pollyanna* in greater detail, pursuing other facets of their stories. But if we take a glimpse at them now, we can note the remarkable similarity among these three girls' books and the particular nature of their similarities.

Like *The Wizard of Oz,* much of *Little Women* can be understood by its geography. At the center is the home of the daughter, the household of the March sisters—which consists entirely of children, once their father has departed for the war and been injured and their mother has left for a Washington hospital to nurse him. In a sense, however, these parents never depart, since surrogates for them appear in the form of guardians who watch over the girls during this absence. Across town from the daughterly house is the all-female household of their termagant Aunt March. Next door live the philanthropic bachelors of the all-male Laurence household.

Aunt March is Rebecca's Aunt Miranda reborn: a spinster residing in a wealthy but cheerless home, someone who disapproved of the marriage that brought the girls into the world, and a fixed and sclerotic antagonist who is put off by the lively and spontaneous ways of Jo. The Laurence household, in contrast, consists of three males: the fatherly and philanthropic Mr. Laurence, the eligible bachelor Mr. Brooke, and the youthful friend Laurie. We can indicate something of their nature by saying that, in *Rebecca of Sunnybrook Farm,* Adam Ladd is, at once, all three of these men.

In *Little Women,* in other words, we see again the oedipal configuration of Spinster Aunt and Sugar Daddy (albeit divided into three characters). And, as Alcott's title suggests, we see as well the Child-Woman (again divided, into the four March sisters). This is perhaps easiest to observe by looking at one character, America's most famous literary child heroine, Jo March.

Like Rebecca's, Jo's maturation (at least in the novel in which she is introduced) is arrested. At the beginning of the book, when her elder sister Meg tells Jo she is "old enough to leave off boyish tricks" and advises her to put up her hair and "remember that you are a young lady," Jo's response is determined: "If turning up my hair makes me one, I'll wear it in two tails till I'm twenty. . . . I hate to think I have to grow up, and be Miss March, and wear long gowns."[8] Several hundred pages of maturation ensue, and the March sisters eventually earn their father's acknowledgment that they have become "little women," but Jo's wish remains unchanged. Near the conclusion, she tells her mother, "I wish wearing flat-irons on our heads would keep us from growing up."[9]

Given a choice, Jo would rather be "little" than a "woman." Her resistance to sexual identity is conspicuous. Throughout, Jo is determined to be a tomboy, and others often remark on her "boyish" haircut and "boyish" behavior (whistling, running, using slang). At the same time, Jo often identifies with males: wishing she could go off to war, playing the male roles in home theatricals, assuming her father's place in her parents' absence (while sister Meg assumes her mother's), wishing she were a man so she could marry Meg and keep her from leaving the bosom of the family.

Moreover, Jo is made anxious by the prospect of romance. Her great disappointment is her older sister's "horrid" interest in John Brooke, and she does what she can to undermine this courtship. When Laurie takes a chance and kisses Jo, she pushes him away and says, "Don't!"

How are we to understand all this resistance? The presence of the Spinster Aunt and the Sugar Daddy offers a clue. Like Rebecca, Jo remains a Child-Woman, frozen on the threshold of sexual maturity. If we take *Rebecca of Sunnybrook Farm* as a model for our understanding, we can see that behind Jo's vehement desire to remain "little" are oedipal issues.

Those familiar with what biographers have had to say about Louisa May Alcott's relationship with her father, Bronson, will not be surprised by this suggestion.[10] Nor will readers of Alcott's other works. As Madelon Bedell observes, "Alcott's writing repeatedly portrays a romance between a child-woman and an older man; the latter often a guardian, an uncle, or an older male friend; in short, a displaced father. The theme is constant."[11]

Bedell's comment offers an intimation. Here, as with *Rebecca of Sunnybrook Farm,* we have an explanation of why Jo doesn't wish to grow up and cross the threshold of sexual maturity: on the other side of that threshold lies oedipal taboo. Here, too, is an explanation of something not present in *Rebecca*—Jo's wish to be and remain a tomboy and her consistent identification with males. Karen Horney's observation in *Feminine Psychology* seems applicable: "The desire to be a man is . . . clung to tenaciously, the reason being the desire to avoid the realization of libidinal wishes and fantasies in connection with the father."[12] And here, too, is the explanation of Jo's considerable consternation whenever one of the inhabitants of the fatherly house next door (be it John Brooke or Laurie) becomes a romantic suitor.

If we turn now to Eleanor Porter's *Pollyanna,* we can see another example of these fundamental similarities among American girls' books. When she is orphaned, Pollyanna travels to the New England home of her well-to-do Aunt Polly, who becomes the child's guardian. Aunt Polly is a spinster, and, like Rebecca's Aunt Miranda or Jo's Aunt March, she is fixed in her ways and put off by the lively manner of the girl. Like these others, Aunt Polly disapproved of the marriage that brought the child into the world, and the aunt expressly forbids the child to speak of her late father. Like Rebecca, Pollyanna is a junior philanthropist and works with the Church Aid Society. Likewise, she eventually melts the curmudgeon's hard heart, overcomes her aunt-antagonist, and humbles the woman. In the denouement of Porter's novel, as in that of *Rebecca of Sunnybrook Farm,* the aunt apologizes to the girl.

Sugar Daddies also appear in *Pollyanna* in the two fatherly bachelors who take a special interest in the girl. The most conspicuous of these is the wealthy Mr. Pendleton, who, readers subsequently learn, was in love with Pollyanna's late mother. When he breaks his leg, Pollyanna nurses him, and he is taken by her charm. When Mr. Pendleton finally articulates his heart's desire and asks the girl to take her mother's place by coming to live with him, the oedipal nature of their relationship becomes surprisingly manifest. Appropriately, Pollyanna declines the offer because it would mean leaving Aunt Polly, her maternal guardian.

The other fatherly bachelor who takes a keen interest in Pollyanna is Dr. Chilton. Here the novel falls into murky confusion and revealing reduplication. Dr. Chilton was Aunt Polly's lover, but (given license by the similarity of their names) the girl and her aunt are confused when others in the novel try to sort out hearsay.

It is only many pages later that we discover that Dr. Chilton's protracted interest in Pollyanna is, sub rosa, a continuation of his courtship of her Aunt Polly.

In addition to the Spinster Aunt and the Sugar Daddies, *Pollyanna* features the Child-Woman. Pollyanna's precocious maturity is evident throughout, in the sage advice she is always giving to adults and in the fact that she is nurse to all the bedridden and heartbroken grownups in her town. Yet her youthfulness is clear in the prolonged naiveté and juvenile optimism with which her name has become synonymous. Like Rebecca and Jo March, Pollyanna matures in a story of thickening oedipal complications until she reaches the threshold. At that point in *Rebecca of Sunnybrook Farm*, the author stops short and refuses to go any further, freezing her character *in media res*. At that point in *Little Women*, matters are unresolved and left in limbo as Jo March digs in her heels, resists growing up, objects to Meg's betrothal, and zealously remains the tomboy. At that point in *Pollyanna*, the girl suffers a "fortunate fall." Late in the book, Pollyanna is struck by a car. Her injury, in a sense, gets her out of the way and provides an opportunity during her convalescence for Aunt Polly and Dr. Chilton, the Spinster Aunt and the Sugar Daddy, to get to know each other better. They decide to marry and adopt Pollyanna. This is Porter's method of resolution: at the threshold, the roles of father, mother, and daughter are restored.

Here, then, in all their manifold similarities, are America's girls' books. But here, too, are America's boys' books. Change the gender of the child-hero, and a summary of *Little Lord Fauntleroy*, for example, sounds like a plot recapitulation of these girls' books: the story of a boy who travels to the wealthy mansion of a disagreeable male relative who becomes his guardian, a same-sex antagonist who disapproved of the marriage that brought the child into the world and who forbids the child to talk of its affectionate opposite-sex parent, but who is eventually won over by the philanthropic, adultlike child and humbly apologizes.

In *Rebecca of Sunnybrook Farm*, then, as in *The Wizard of Oz*, *Huckleberry Finn*, *Little Women*, *Pollyanna*, and *Little Lord Fauntleroy*, we glimpse variations of the ur-story behind American childhood classics. Having done so, we can now consider more precisely how this oedipal pattern was put to specifically American uses.

TWO

✦ ✦ ✦ ✦ ✦ ✦ ✦

Manuals of
Republicanism

4

✣ ✣ ✣ ✣ ✣ ✣ ✣

Motherland, Fatherland, or Oedipal Politics

Little Lord Fauntleroy

Samuel Clemens's *Adventures of Huckleberry Finn* and Frances Hodgson Burnett's *Little Lord Fauntleroy* are often compared because both works appeared in 1885. Literary historians have seized on this coincidence to point out the two books' different portraits of the American boy: one vernacular, the other genteel; one the barefoot rascal in tatters, the other well behaved and well dressed in the famous Fauntleroy suit. At the same time, these differences have been used to explain how Burnett's novel came to acquire the unfortunate reputation of being a book about a sissy.[1] But what is perhaps more remarkable is the similarity between Clemens's and Burnett's novels: in them, the microcosmic world of the family and the macrocosmic world of politics are mingled and interchangeable.

As we observed in Chapter 2, Clemens, with the Duke and the King, extends the parricidal thrust of *Adventures of Huckleberry Finn* to include a critique of patriarchal politics. Although this conjunction of the small realm of the family with the grand world of politics might now seem quite an imaginative leap, this linking was in fact a familiar one during the Golden Age and frequently appears elsewhere in Clemens's novel. When Jim, for example, learns of Solomon's decision regarding the disputed baby, he concludes that all kings are irresponsible fathers (94–96). On another occasion, when he hears about the atrocities of "Henry the Eight," Jim's next thoughts are about the time he, too, was guilty of parental injustice—when he whipped his daughter for not obeying him, only to discover later that she was deaf (199–202).

The linking of parents and kings, the antipatriarchal motifs of *Huckleberry Finn,* reflect earlier myths of national identity. As George Forgie and others have shown, from the Revolution through the mid-nineteenth century, America's political writers and thinkers consistently understood their country's history in terms of the story of a child engaged in oedipal rebellion against the tyranny and despotism of its macrocosmic father, the king. [2] Indeed, this vision of America-as-Child engaged in oedipal rebellion is, Christopher Looby has observed, the "quintessential motif" of American political thought before the Civil War. [3]

Both Forgie and Looby suggest that the Civil War might be generally reckoned the terminus of this motif because that calamitous event revealed the shortcomings of a myth of national identity framed in oedipal terms of ceaseless rebellion and antipatriarchal attitudes. After the war a revised myth was needed, one that pictured America as having achieved a more advanced state of childhood. Instead of constant "filial" rebellion and secession, politicians spoke of the need for the restoration of "domestic harmony." Absent, too, was the antipatriarchal rhetoric; instead, the preeminence of a national government seemed to go hand in hand with Reconstruction. At the same time, America's position in the world had changed. By the time *Fauntleroy* was published, nearly ten years after the United States had celebrated its centennial, the country had become a considerable presence in the international community. This development called for a revised myth that defined America not in terms of its youthful antagonism toward Europe, but as a mature nation-state taking its place among the "family of nations." What was needed was a new national myth of post-oedipal identity. [4]

This was true in political circles, but (given the metaphoric reciprocity between the microcosm of the family and the macrocosm of politics) it is interesting to observe that the very same topic was also being discussed in pediatric circles. In the Introduction we noted, as an example of this reciprocity, Samuel Osgood's remarks in his essay "Books for Our Children" in the December 1865 issue of the *Atlantic Monthly*. Now, in light of these historical circumstances, they are worth considering again:

> The war is over, yet our fight is not through. . . . We shall settle the Reconstruction problem, the Negro, the Debt, John Bull, and Louis Napoleon, all in due time. . . . But there is a question to be settled which comes nearer home to each family . . . —What shall we do with our children? . . . The Slaveholder's Rebellion is put down; but how shall we deal with the never-ceasing revolt of the new generation against the old? and how keep our Young America under the thumb of his father and mother without breaking his spirit? . . . and how does our legion of juvenile infantry compare with the young legions of England, France, Germany, Russia, or Italy?[5]

After the Civil War, American parents *and* American political thinkers were asking the same question: What follows oedipal rebellion? If parents were seeking a conception of post-oedipal identity, politicians were also seeking a new vision of America-as-Child who had made its Declaration of Independence and achieved autonomy; who no longer fomented domestic squabbles, but could see to it that family harmony was restored; who no longer needed to struggle against the father, but could make peace with him.

Given this reciprocity between these familial and political tropes, between the micro and the macro, what better place might there be than the domestic novel to signal this new vision of national identity? Remarkable as it seems, *Little Lord Fauntleroy* did just that.

The Oedipal Pattern of the Domestic Story

In the autumn of 1884, Frances Hodgson Burnett wrote to Mary Mapes Dodge, who (after the success of her novel *Hans Brinker*) had become the editor of America's foremost juvenile periodical, *St. Nicholas*. Burnett asked if Dodge would be interested in serializing a story about a likeable American boy of English descent:

> It is called "Little Lord Fauntleroy"—His father (the hero's) was a younger son of a noble house—he came to America and mar-

ried a pretty American girl to the fierce indignation of his fiery
old father—(this part of the story is merely sketched in a few
sentences)—He is cast off by his family, lives in a simple middle
class way in America a few years & then dies leaving the little
boy and his pretty young mother—

This is where the story begins—the two older brothers die
suddenly—the only heir to the family splendors and titles—after
his grandfather's death—will be the little Anglo-American boy.

The fierce old grandfather sends for him—still hating his
mother . . . [and] Little Lord Fauntleroy is taken from his
shabby little home in New York where he has made friends with
the milkman & hobnobbed sweetly with the grocery store
keeper . . . —and is borne off to the magnificence of his ancestors.[6]

Dodge immediately wanted *Fauntleroy* for her magazine. The
plot Burnett had proposed was sure-fire—the Cinderella story, a
little New York street urchin who suddenly finds himself an English lord, the reversal-of-fortunes theme already popular in
Twain's *The Prince and the Pauper* (1882) and the rags-to-riches
novels of Horatio Alger. Moreover, Burnett's proposal must have
sounded attractive because of its suggestion of a highly dramatic
and emotional clash of personalities: the "fierce" and "fiery" grandfather who, still bearing a grudge, sends for "the little boy and his
pretty young mother."

The domestic story of *Little Lord Fauntleroy* is easily told, and
its fidelity to the pattern of "The Three Lives of the Child-Hero"
easily recognized. "Dispossessed royalty," "the violation of a marriage prohibition," "poverty"—these motifs of the child-hero's
First Life are evident in the opening of Burnett's book. Then,
predictably, the child-hero embarks on "the journey," and Cedric
Errol (Little Lord Fauntleroy) takes a steamship to England and
comes to the "Big House," the castle of his grandfather.

In this way, Cedric becomes a "virtual orphan"; his father is
dead, and his grandfather, the Earl of Dorincourt (still bearing a
grudge against the boy's mother), insists that Cedric live in the
castle and apart from his mother, though he concedes that the boy
can visit her for a few hours every day in her distant residence.
Cedric, in other words, is "adopted into a second family" headed by
his grandfather, a "surrogate parent of a different social rank."
While Cedric can depend on the affection of his mother (an

opposite-sex helper), his relations with his grandfather (a same-sex antagonist) are strained. But over the course of the novel, like Rebecca with her Aunt Miranda, Cedric melts the curmudgeon's heart and wins his affection. As a result, the earl apologizes to the boy's mother and the previously estranged members of the family are reconciled.

This rapprochement is solidified according to the pattern of the Third Life of the child-hero. "Issues of identity are resolved" when impostors advance false claims to the title of Lord Fauntleroy and the truth has to be sorted out. "Recognition ceremonies" appear near the end of the novel, when the boy's birthday is celebrated and the earl, in front of all his retainers and tenants, acknowledges the boy as his heir. And "an accommodation between the hero's two lives" is struck when Cedric, of both America and England, brings his American friends to England to live with him.

Oedipal Politics: Motherland, Fatherland

If the domestic story of *Little Lord Fauntleroy* is easily told, what is remarkable is the way this variation on "The Three Lives of the Child-Hero" is yoked to nationalistic issues. One of the oddest things about Burnett's novel is its highly exaggerated antagonism between England and America. The Earl of Dorincourt, for example, disowns his favorite son simply because the young man married an American. At the same time, Mr. Hobbs, a Yankee grocer, spends many pages lecturing the young Cedric Errol about the glories of the American Revolution and the vices of the British— their grasping tyrants, their corrupt nobility.

Needless to say, these Anglo-American antagonisms seem odd and contrived. They can't be explained in terms of circumstances. By the late nineteenth century (the time of the novel), relations between the two countries were largely cordial, and ocean liners regularly moved citizens of both nations back and forth across the Atlantic like caravans of visiting relatives.

Nor did Burnett have any axe to grind. The facts of her life suggest that Burnett was completely comfortable with her own Anglo-American identity. She was born in England, but at the age of twelve moved to the United States and became an American citizen. In her later life, she spent an equal amount of time in both countries, traveling back and forth across the Atlantic thirty-three times. She told an interviewer:

> I hold that no one today, in our complex civilization, can be thoroughly and symmetrically developed unless he knows and lives in both countries, England and America. We are nowadays too complicated and many-sided to be satisfied by what either one of those countries alone can offer us; we need them both. I have a home in England and one in America, and I live in them by turns.[7]

In truth the novel's flamboyant and anachronistic antipathy between Americans and British serves a conscious, literary purpose: *Fauntleroy* is a remarkable novel in which the domestic story (the troubled relations between the earl and his family) is simultaneously a political allegory of Anglo-American relations. Burnett's readers seem to have recognized this story behind the story. William Gladstone, then prime minister of England, told Burnett he believed the novel "would have a great effect in bringing about added good feeling between the two nations and making them understand each other"[8]—certainly unusual praise for a children's book!

Early in the novel, America seems to be the Land of Rebellious Sons. The earl has "a very violent dislike of America and Americans,"[9] which would seem an inexplicable and irrational prejudice except that it is linked with his animosity toward his son for marrying an American woman. Moreover, when the earl reveals what he dislikes about the country, he sounds like an irritated father talking about an errant child: "American impudence! . . . I've heard it before. They call it precocity and freedom. Beastly, impudent bad manners; that's what it is!" (65).

In a similar fashion, England seems to be the Land of Tyrannical Fathers. When the reader is told about the earl's unfair treatment of his loving son, which resulted in the break between them, it hardly seems coincidental that this account of a father's despotism is immediately followed by a discussion in which Mr. Hobbs tells Cedric "the whole story of the Revolution, relating very wonderful and patriotic stories about the villainy of the enemy, . . . being especially indignant against earls and marquises" (13). *Fauntleroy* begins, then, in the throes of the oedipal situation.

Cedric and his widowed mother are especially close, and Burnett goes to great lengths to indicate the extraordinary affection these "best friends" feel for each other. This alliance is attacked by the grandfather, the father surrogate. The oedipal nature of these hostilities is made even clearer by the fact that readers are to understand the grandfather's antagonism toward Cedric and his mother as a continuation of the hard feelings the old man harbored against his late son for marrying an American woman against his wishes—an act that caused the earl to disown his child and led to the son's exile in America.

This is the situation Cedric inherits. In the early stages of the novel, the earl often tries to push his grandson into identifying with him and deserting the mother. This, too, has innuendoes of national and domestic politics—a choice between the motherland and the fatherland. At one point, Cedric is talking with his grandfather about the Fourth of July and the Revolution, but suddenly stops:

> Little Lord Fauntleroy was embarrassed by the thought that just occurred to him. "I forgot you were an Englishman. . . ."
>
> "You forgot you were an Englishman too."
>
> "Oh, no," said Cedric quickly. "I'm an American!"
>
> "You are an Englishman," said the Earl grimly. "Your father was an Englishman. . . ."
>
> "I was born in America," he protested. "You have to be an American if you are born in America." (78)

Which is to say, his mother and motherland gave birth to this native son.

This is the status quo. It falls to Cedric to end this stalemate, and the larger part of the novel concerns his efforts to do so. Cedric must move things to a stage beyond childhood rebellion, a postoedipal phase in which hostilities between father and son come to an end and family harmony can be restored. Or, to say this differently, Cedric must end the warfare between England and America and avoid the situation that requires him to choose between the fatherland and the motherland. Before he leaves for England, he promises: "If there is ever to be another war with America, I shall try to stop it" (23).

Over the course of the novel, Cedric's peacemaking mission succeeds. He wins his grandfather's affection and love, and through him, hostility within the family is brought to an end. This rapprochement is made all the easier by an opportunity that is provided for the earl to discharge his hostility upon the false claimants. The American woman and her son who dishonestly claim to be the earl's heirs are just the kind of ill-bred and avaricious Americans the earl first expected to meet in Cedric and his mother, and their false claim allows the earl an opportunity to vent his paternal anger outside the family, upon these doubles, in a safe and justifiable way. At the same time, just as Lear recognizes his mistreatment of Cordelia, [10] the earl recognizes how badly he has treated Cedric's mother, a woman whom others have praised for her virtue and kindness.

Family harmony is restored, then, when the earl is humbled, comes and meets the boy's mother, acknowledges her, and invites her to join him and her son in the castle. An end to the oedipal period is symbolized when the boy no longer has to choose between parents, between fatherland and motherland. Cedric's identity is established as Anglo-American.

Natural Nobility and the Need for Ancestors

When Prime Minister Gladstone told Burnett that he believed *Little Lord Fauntleroy* "would have a great effect in bringing about added good feeling between the two nations and making them understand each other," he was probably acknowledging what other readers may have recognized. The Anglo-American solution Burnett proposes in her novel suggests that there is something each country can learn from the other. The English can learn from Americans the notion of "natural" nobility; Americans can learn from England a respect for ancestry.

Fauntleroy's message to the English concerns the advantages of egalitarianism. As Burnett observed, what is unique about Cedric is his ability to say, "'My friend, the Duke of Blankshire,' as affectionately as he had said, 'My friend, the milkman.'"[11] In a class society like that of England, there is the danger that differences between high and low may be arbitrary and unjust, rather than differences in rank that accord with inner worth. America's democratic elections and republican form of government, in contrast, are more likely to permit the rise of a "natural nobility." Cedric's American childhood among common folks, his natural nobility already evident when he was playing in the streets of New York, will make him the best kind of ruler. As an Anglo-American heir, he is the ideal hybrid: someone whose virtues happily accord with his high station.

And what can America learn from England? The answer is the value of tradition. America's notion of itself prior to the Civil War had its shortcomings: antipatriarchal rhetoric argued for ceaseless rebellion, and, in always making itself anew, the nation had no enduring sense of continuity between the generations. As Norman O. Brown has observed, there is an inner contradiction in a republican government like America's, in a country formed by sons rebelling against the father: "Sonship and brotherhood are espoused against fatherhood: but without a father there can be no sons or brothers."[12]

Before the Civil War, American writers would celebrate America as the fatherless child: *sui generis,* entirely new, "emancipated from history, happily bereft of ancestry," at the beginning of time, separated from the past and connected only with the future. R. W. B. Lewis has described this vision of America, this myth of national identity, as the "American Adam," and this figure appears in the literature of the time in the celebration of the Indian, the innocent, the frontiersman, and the child.[13]

By mid-century, America needed to revise this view of itself. The growing power of the federal government, the urbanization of the populace, the linking of the country into a grid of railroads and telegraph lines—all these and other forces called for a new conception of America as a unified nation-state, rather than a loose confederation of Adamic individuals. At the same time, 100 years after its birth, this relatively young country had become a considerable presence in the world community. Instead of a negative identity defined by its denial of Europe, America required a positive myth of itself as a legitimate nation-state taking its place among others.

This wish for legitimacy meant abandoning the idea that America was parentless, ahistorical, emancipated from the past, and connected only to the future. Instead, the new myth needed to stress America's legitimacy in terms of genealogy and ancestry. This concern was reflected in the great historical works of Francis Parkman and George Bancroft, in the introduction of information

"My grandfather says these are my ancestors"

Reginald Birch for *Little Lord Fauntleroy*, new ed.
(New York: Scribner, 1911).

into schoolbooks about such founding fathers as George Washington, in the retrospective nature of such celebrations as the Centennial, and in similar enterprises. This wish for historicity would also appear in the late nineteenth century's enthusiasm for historical novels like Clemens's *The Prince and the Pauper*, in which the most pressing issues concern legitimacy and succession. Finally, although America had originally defined itself as a society based on a radical discontinuity with the past, the new myth of national identity had to be based on the conviction that if the nation was to endure, it was necessary to reassert order and continuity rather than flounder in a state of perpetual revolution. The calamities of the Civil War were, as we have noted, a great argument for just that.

This need for generational continuity is finally acknowledged in *Little Lord Fauntleroy* by the novel's greatest critic of England, Mr. Hobbs. When the cranky grocer goes to England, he grows to like it, opens a store there, and "would often walk from the village . . . [to] spend half an hour or so wandering about the gallery" at the earl's castle, where hang the portraits of Cedric's "aunt-sisters"—as Mr. Hobbs pronounces the word "ancestors." Mr. Hobbs, too, becomes an Anglo-American. When he is asked why he doesn't return to America, Mr. Hobbs identifies (in the very last words of the novel) the shortcoming of a country that defines itself solely in terms of oedipal rebellion: "It's a good enough country for them that's young and stirrin'—but there's faults in it. There's not an aunt-sister among 'em" (190).

Little Lord Fauntleroy sounded themes that would echo throughout American children's books of the Golden Age. In *Tarzan of the Apes*, Edgar Rice Burroughs would take to their imaginative extreme these apparently competing notions of natural nobility and the need for ancestors, and he would resolve them by creating a character who is at once Adamic and ancestral. If we understand that another meaning for Mr. Hobbs's "aunt-sister" is "mother," then Tarzan's final statement in the novel is the Darwinian last word on the subject of ancestors: "My mother was an Ape."

5

❖ ❖ ❖ ❖ ❖ ❖ ❖

Ur of the Ur-Stories
Tarzan of the Apes

Despite its stylistic drawbacks—passages of wooden and purple prose, occasional episodes of stagey melodrama, and some characters who seem straight from central casting (including an absent-minded professor who wears top hat and tails in the jungle and a pickaninny servant who rolls her eyes)—Edgar Rice Burroughs's *Tarzan of the Apes* remains a remarkable, exciting, compelling book. Testaments to its power have come from many—including Ronald Reagan, Leslie Fiedler, Ray Bradbury, and Gore Vidal.[1] Arthur C. Clarke put it this way: "Whatever the literary establishment may say, . . . [Burroughs's] influence has been enormous—and is, even now, underrated. A writer who can create the best-known character in the whole of fiction is not to be ignored, whatever the deficiencies of his prose style."[2]

Whatever his fortunes among critics, Burroughs's Tarzan has never been ignored by readers. First appearing in *All Story Magazine* in 1912 and then published as a book in 1914, *Tarzan of the Apes* immediately jumped onto the best-seller lists. In the years that followed, readers would demand some twenty-five sequels from Burroughs. The statistics are staggering: by 1970, according to one estimate, there were more than 36 million Tarzan books in print in thirty-one languages. Others put these numbers three times higher.[3]

Somehow, Burroughs's private dream spoke to millions of readers and became a shared dream, a public dream, a myth. The proof, Leslie Fiedler suggests, is in the way the story and its hero leaped out of the pages of a book and, like a myth, became embodied in countless other commercial (i.e., popular and vulgar) forms.[4] There have been more than fifty Tarzan films, from the countless Saturday matinees in which Johnny Weissmuller let out his famous Tarzan yell to the most recent version, *Greystoke: The Legend of Tarzan.* There have also been a television series, a radio program, a comic strip, countless Tarzan objects (from wristwatches to swimsuits), Tarzan Gasoline, and Tarzan Bread (of which 3 million loaves were baked). Surveying all of American culture, scholar Russel Nye finally concluded, "Tarzan remains the greatest popular creation of all time."[5]

Why?

The answer is unwittingly revealed in the novel itself, when (in a wonderful specimen of his prose) Burroughs explains a moment that would become familiar in the B movies based on his work, when someone hears the ominous sound of distant jungle drums:

> Many travelers have seen the drums of the great apes, and some will have heard the sounds of their beating and the noise of the wild, weird revelry of these first lords of the jungle, but Tarzan, Lord Greystoke, is, doubtless, the only human being who ever joined in the fierce, mad, intoxicating revel of the Dum-Dum.
>
> From this primitive function has arisen, unquestionably, all the form and ceremonials of modern church and state, for through the countless ages, back beyond the uttermost ramparts of a dawning humanity our fierce, hairy forebears danced out the rites of the Dum-Dum to the sound of the earthen drums, beneath the light of a tropical moon in the depth of a mighty jungle which stands unchanged today as it stood on that long forgotten night in the dim, unthinkable vistas of the long dead past when our first shaggy ancestor swung from a swaying bough and dropped lightly upon the soft turf of the first meeting place.[6]

This, then, is what Edgar Rice Burroughs offers in *Tarzan of the Apes:* to take us Back, to the Darwinian Dream, the fierce

Origin, the Dionysian Beginning. For Burroughs, there is none of the timidity of George Santayana, who wondered whether it is ever possible to find the very Beginning of things and speculated that life may be composed only of small episodes of sequence rather than some simpler Alpha from which everything else evolved.[7] There is none of that uncertainty in Burroughs's "doubtless" and "unquestionably." What he offers is nothing less than a return to the Ancestral, the Source, the Adamic, the "wild" and "hairy" *Fons et Origo*.

And that means loincloth nakedness! Strip away the gradual accretions of civilization, the Emperor's New Clothes.

And that means apocalyptic truth! Frank admission that, at bottom, we are basically animals—fiercely competitive, concerned with only our own survival. That beneath politics and good manners lie sex and the wish for dominance. That rationality is only a fragile lid covering a potent and fundamental stew of drives, impulses, and passions.

And that means freedom! From restrictions, rules, and concern for others, from the pettiness of office politics and civilized bureaucracies. Here is unchecked and untrammeled egotism. Here, it is only man to man, *mano a mano*. Here, only the fittest survive.

What Burroughs offers is the Fierce Dream of the Primordial: this is the forest primeval. . . .

Permutations of the Child

Orphaned in Africa by the death of his parents, and raised by great apes in the jungle, Tarzan is one of the many incarnations of that timeless figure known as the Wild Child—Romulus and Remus, Mowgli, Pecos Bill, Kaspar Hauser, the Wild Boy of Aveyron, and others. The Wild Child is cousin to that hairy man Robinson Crusoe and all other shipwrecked or orphaned solitaires bristling with self-sufficiency and rampant egotism: the boys in *Lord of the Flies*, for example. The Wild Child is related, as well, to half-animal creatures, especially those that smoulder with eroticism and hint at beastly amours: satyrs and mermaids, nightmare yeti and King Kong, werewolves and others of Dracula's tribe, Beauty and her Beast.

Fundamentally, basically, primarily, the timeless fascination with the figure of the Wild Child is an attempt to answer one question: What are we at bottom? It is a Rousseauistic exercise: strip away civilization, and then what are we, or what were we? Under the tyranny of necessity—*in extremis*, in variously imagined situations, after the Bomb has fallen, after we have been stranded on an island or in the jungle, after any such truth-evoking apocalypse—what would we *really* be like?

The answers have varied. At bottom in *Robinson Crusoe* is the rugged individual. In *Lord of the Flies*, what is discovered is the savage heart of darkness. What is unique about Burroughs is that he hunts for his answer-at-the-bottom in the realms of Darwin and Freud.

As much as Burroughs borrowed from legends about the Wild Child and from Kipling's Mowgli stories, he made an important departure from tradition when he had Tarzan raised by apes instead of wolves. Seeking his own set of origins, Burroughs followed Darwin's lead in *The Origin of Species*.

Burroughs's Darwinism is hardly sophisticated. Instead, he seems to have gotten many of his ideas from the loose talk about and popularizations of the naturalist's ideas that appeared in newspapers and magazines (which bandied such terms as "survival of the fittest" and "evolution" and "lower orders"), from the propositions advocated by Social Darwinians and others keen on eugenics, and from discussions evoked by the Scopes Monkey Trial, on which Burroughs himself commented.[8]

But Darwin's ideas must also have seemed personally relevant to Burroughs, and thereby true. *Tarzan of the Apes* was started in the midst of one of the country's great economic depressions, by a failed businessman who was writing in a rented office in Chicago and who had seen that it was a dog-eat-dog world out there, a "jungle" where only the fittest survived. So in December 1911, Burroughs started a story to experiment, as he said, with the ideas of heredity and environment:

> For this purpose I selected an infant child . . . at an age at which he could not have been influenced by association with creatures of his own kind, and I threw him into an environment as diametrically opposite than that to which he had been born as I might well conceive. As I got into the story I realized

that . . . for fictional purposes I must give heredity some
breaks that my judgement assured me the facts would not have
warranted.[9]

This book would be, in other words, no strict accounting of the
naturalist's ideas but, rather, Darwinian Dream.

What goes without notice, even by Burroughs himself, is the
fact that he intended the Child to bear the freight of this dream.
Conducting his fantasy experiment, following his Darwinian trail
back to the progenitor, Burroughs encounters aboriginal man and,
notably, finds that Adam is a minor. On another occasion years
later, Burroughs would say offhandedly, "Really Tarzan was but a
child, or a primeval man, which is the same thing anyway."[10] This
casual, post-Darwinian equation implies so strikingly new a figure
of the juvenile that it bears noticing—this vision of *the child as
primeval man*.

Darwin's ideas, in a sense, loosely permitted this claim. Of all
the naturalist's notions, Burroughs seems to have been most impressed by the theory that ontogeny recapitulates phylogeny; Tarzan's own evolution from ape to man, after all, is meant to echo the
ascendancy of the human species. What biologists have in mind, of
course, is something cellular: the growth of a human fetus is said to
mirror, by analogy, the process of evolution from single-celled
ameba, through amphibians, to the most complex forms of life. By
extrapolation, then, Burroughs is correct. The missing link is not
missing. Positioned at a midpoint in the process of evolution,
where animal becomes human, in an embryonic way, it is possible
to see *the child as missing link*.

For this reason, too, Tarzan in the jungle is (in two senses of
the word) "close" to animals. This, apparently, inspired Burroughs's own son Jack when he read the books. One of the frequently repeated stories in their household was the day Burroughs
found the boy following him around the yard on all fours with his
nose to the ground:

> "What in the world are you doing, Jack?" Mr. Burroughs
> questioned.
> "Why, father," replied the boy, "I am following your scent
> spoor."[11]

In his romance upon facts, Burroughs created an orphaned infant who was to be raised by his next of kin, the great apes. Like other versions of the Wild Child raised, say, by coyotes (Pecos Bill) or wolves (Mowgli, Romulus and Remus), this Darwinian permutation shares the motif of *the child as animal*.

Another motif, especially relevant to Burroughs, is *the child as frontier*. The most significant period in Burroughs's life began in 1889 when, at the age of fourteen, he left his parents behind in Chicago and joined his older brothers on their cattle ranch in Idaho, then one of the last outposts of the Wild West. Unfortunately, two years later, friends of his parents visited and mailed back word that an unsupervised life among cowboys was no place for an adolescent. He was sent home and ever afterward hankered for the unbridled freedom he had experienced in the West.

Back home, the young Burroughs reluctantly accepted a summer job at the Chicago World's Fair so that he could visit his favorite exhibit, Hagenbeck's Wild Animal Show, where he would moon around the cages of those powerful beasts, trapped like so many adolescents in the Chicago of his parents. After graduation, the teenager once more lit out for the territories to recapture what he remembered of the West. He joined the cavalry only to discover, after months of digging ditches in the baked earth of Arizona, that the heyday of the Seventh Regiment had been some twenty years earlier, before Custer and the regiment tooted their last at Little Big Horn.

Chagrined, Burroughs went back to Chicago, married, and took a job at Sears, Roebuck. In 1903, however, when Jack London published *The Call of the Wild,* Burroughs heard his own call and returned to Idaho to try silver dredging with his brothers. When things didn't pan out, he returned once more to Chicago and eventually took up writing about a character born in the wilderness and first introduced by his tiny wail in the African jungle. In Burroughs's stories, the voice crying in the wilderness is a child's.

Writing about this connection between the Mowgli stories and the frontier, Marcus Cunliffe said something equally applicable to Burroughs's Tarzan books:

> It is an odd feature of [the work of British writers like Kipling, R. M. Ballantyne, and Rider Haggard], as of American writers

like James Fenimore Cooper, Mark Twain, and Jack London, that in [writing about the frontier] they tended to produce stories either about children or (not always intentionally) for children. Among other things, they provided the myth of escape for a society whose edges seemed to be closing in. Mowgli . . . has affinities with Huckleberry Finn. . . . Both are orphans, boy-heroes of the last frontier, given their fling before it is too late. [12]

Just as Huck wished to light out to the territories to escape the civilizin' of the Widow Douglas, the appeal of the Tarzan stories (and the Wild Child stories in general) is the wish "to get away" from it all—where "it" means Chicago and parents, civilization and its discontents as Rousseau and Freud defined them. Burroughs once tried to puzzle out the popularity of his Tarzan:

His appeal to an audience is so tremendous that it never ceases to be a source of amazement to me. This appeal, I believe, is based upon . . . the constant urge to escape that is becoming stronger in all of us prisoners of civilization as civilization becomes more complex. We wish to escape not alone the narrow confines of the city streets for the freedom of the wilderness, but the restrictions of man-made laws, and the inhibitions that society has placed upon us. . . . We would each like to be Tarzan. At least I would; I admit it. [13]

And so, in the *Tarzan* books, the child is a symbol of something more than freedom of a territorial kind. The child becomes the locus of the unrestricted, the uninhibited, the unrepressed. Although Burroughs might never have used the term, in his books we see the motif of *the child as id*.

Burroughs saw himself as an "unconscious"—or, as he put it, "subconscious"—writer. After a certain point in the Tarzan series, in fact, he gave up writing and simply dictated his fictional dreams to his secretary. In another of his novels, he offers what might be taken as a description of his process of composition: "The impulse that moves me and the doing of the thing seem simultaneous; for if my mind goes through the tedious formality of reasoning, it must be a subconscious of which I am not objectively aware. Psychologists tell me that, as the subconscious does not reason, too close a scrutiny might prove anything but flattering." [14]

Indeed, when Burroughs opens his Pandora's box, what spills out in his books is a number of sordid things that are hardly flattering: hostility to anything "other," manifested in blatant racism and sexism; voyeuristic and sadmasochistic erotica, in which white women often seem to be in danger of "the fate worse than death" at the hands of hairy brutes while the hero looks on from concealment with his knife or sword in hand; and, most conspicuously, the wish for dominance, evident in the antisocial behavior of this solitary and self-made man who is pictured in retrograde fantasies of self-importance that sometimes make Tarzan seem kin to comic-book characters like Superman and the Hulk. Here, then, is no repression or embarrassment. Here come spilling out all the violent and erotic fantasies of the white male. Here, unchecked, is naked id.

Following Rider Haggard, Burroughs made Africa the locale for this kind of physical and psychological nakedness. It is, of course, an "Africa" that has no objective correlative. At one point, for example, Tarzan pelts a tiger (an animal found only on the Indian subcontinent) with a pineapple (a fruit found in the Caribbean and now grown in Hawaii). Still, it is worth noting that, though the movies based on the books took even greater liberties with facts, Emperor Haile Selassie of Ethiopia made one request of America when he ascended the throne: that Hollywood send him all the Tarzan films. Burroughs's books, to state the point differently, while not true to facts, are true to the Dream of Africa. This is the Africa of Freud, the Absolute Elsewhere, a psychological zone of untrammeled freedom, the Dark Continent.

In Burroughs's Wild Child, then, Darwin meets Freud. The primeval becomes equated with primal urges, and the feral child becomes the aborigine of the unconscious.

Ur of the Ur-Stories

The hero is the child of most distinguished parents, usually the son of a king. His origin is preceded by difficulties. . . . He is then saved by animals, or by lowly people (shepherds), and is suckled by a female animal or by a humble woman. After he has grown up, he finds his distinguished parents, in a highly versatile fashion. He takes revenge

*upon his father, on the one hand, and is acknowledged, on the other.
Finally he achieves rank and honors.*

Otto Rank, "The Myth of the Birth of the Hero"

Tarzan of the Apes is first about descents and descendants, and then about the Ascent of Man. The first descent occurs when Tarzan's parents are marooned on the African coast by mutineers. Plucky English nobility, they take courage from history: "Hundreds of years ago our ancestors of the dim and distant past faced the same problems which we must face, possibly in the same primeval forests. That we are here evidences their victory" (16). They soon build a snug cabin and hunt for game and fruit. In this, *Tarzan of the Apes* descends no further than *Robinson Crusoe*.

But Burroughs's novel descends a second time. The idyll ends when John and Alice Clayton, Lord and Lady Greystoke, are attacked by gangs of apes. Clayton is forced to kill one of these "great man-like figures" (21) and "to drag the ape from his wife's prostrate form" (23). Not surprisingly, a child is born to them shortly thereafter. Alice Clayton then dies, and, once again, the great apes attack and this time kill John Clayton. Hearing a wail from the crib, the male apes are inclined to kill the human orphan; but a female of the tribe, Kala, mourning the loss of her own infant, does something else:

> As she took up the live baby of Alice Clayton she dropped the dead body of her own into the empty cradle; for the wail of the living had answered the call of universal motherhood within her wild breast which the dead could not still.
>
> High up among the branches of a mighty tree she hugged the shrieking infant to her bosom, and soon the instinct that was dominant in that fierce female as it had been in the breast of his tender and beautiful mother—the instinct of mother love— reached out to the tiny man-child's half-formed understanding, and he became quiet.
>
> Then hunger closed the gap between them, and the son of an English lord and an English lady nursed at the breast of Kala, the great ape. (30)

Here is where *Tarzan of the Apes* touches bottom.

At bottom in Burroughs's novel is the hairy family, the primal family ruled by primal impulses. Mother is Kala, the great ape who

Burne Hogarth for *Tarzan of the Apes* (New York: Watson-Guptill, 1972).
Copyright Edgar Rice Burroughs, Inc. All Rights Reserved.

suckles and loves her "white ape"—pronounced "Tarzan" in her language. Father is the ape Tublat, who dislikes his "son" because Kala pays too much attention to the child. Tarzan returns this antagonism and sees his "father" as a rival. After much harassment, an adolescent Tarzan finally seizes his "father" by the throat and plunges a hunting knife into the ape's breast a dozen times: "As the body rolled to the ground Tarzan of the Apes placed his foot upon the neck of his lifelong enemy and, raising his eyes to the full moon, threw back his fierce young head and voiced the wild terrible cry of his people" (56).

Here, remarkably, without blinking or disguise, is the Oedipal Complex and its primal solution. And Tarzan's ascent begins from this moment. To be sure, he subsequently has to dispose of other father figures (e.g., Kerchak, the leader of the tribe and "King of the Apes") and deal with sibling rivalry (his English cousin Cecil Clayton and his ape stepbrother Terkoz share his interest in Jane), but his ascent begins when Tarzan kills his ape "father" with his own (what else?) knife. This is an old story, some would say the oldest, and it is just one more facet of Burroughs's endeavor to discover and reveal the Basic, the Elemental, the Prototype.

Burroughs recasts this oedipal drama within the pattern of "The Three Lives of the Child-Hero" evident in other American children's books: the story of an orphan (of Lord and Lady Greystoke) who travels (from the cabin into the heart of the jungle) and is adopted into a surrogate family of a different social order (apes) where the child encounters a helper in an opposite-sex parent figure (Kala) and a same-sex parental antagonist (Tublat) who is eventually overcome. But at this point *Tarzan* differs from the pattern. This deviation bears examination.

Typically, in the Third Life of the child-hero, issues of identity are resolved; at the end of *Huckleberry Finn,* for example, Aunt Polly unmasks the grand impersonator and identifies him as Huck Finn. More common, however, are resolutions of controversies surrounding parenthood: Miranda acknowledges that Rebecca of Sunnybrook Farm is not "all Randall" and only her father's child, but is a Sawyer as well and shares in her maternal bloodline; Aunt Polly, who has forbidden Pollyanna to speak of her late father, finally admits that she has been wrong and lifts that taboo in the book's conclusion; and the Earl of Dorincourt, whose paternal claim on

Little Lord Fauntleroy leads to a similar exclusion of the boy's mother, finally admits his error and acknowledges that the child is also his mother's offspring. This admission of the true nature of the child-hero's parentage is also often accompanied in the Third Life by the bestowal of inheritances: indirectly suggested in *Huckleberry Finn* when the boy regains access to his $6,000, but more obviously, for example, when Rebecca inherits the Brick House or Lord Fauntleroy is acknowledged in a public ceremony as the earl's heir.

Tarzan of the Apes presents only a simulacrum of this pattern. Much is made in the conclusion of the convincing proofs that Tarzan is, in fact, the son of John and Alice Clayton. Fingerprint tests, the diary of his father, and forensic comments on the skeleton found in the crib—all these offer clear evidence of Tarzan's true parentage. Moreover, given that, Tarzan is Lord Greystoke. *He* is the rightful heir to his father's title and holdings, not his rival and cousin Cecil Clayton, who became Lord Greystoke when no other successor was presumed to be alive.

Nonetheless, despite these similarities, Burroughs's novel deviates from the pattern. Tarzan's true identity is never revealed, and his claim to his father's title is never acknowledged. Instead, Tarzan denies what he has learned about his parentage. In the last lines of the novel, he maintains, "My mother was an Ape, and of course she couldn't tell me much about it. I never knew who my father was" (245).

It is a strange moment in the novel—akin to, say, an adult insisting on the legendary stork as the explanation of his or her nativity—and one that needs to be understood. Read in a psychological fashion, the fantasy of the animal mother (like any of the surrogate parents who appear in the middle of "The Three Lives of the Child-Hero") are a fiction that permits the child to grow up and (guiltlessly) separate from its parents to achieve autonomy. As Otto Rank explains, "The lowering of the mother into an animal is meant to vindicate the ingratitude of the son who [eventually] denies her."[15] Tarzan, however, never denies her.

Instead, the novel ends with Tarzan's willful embrace of what he knows to be a lie. But it is a lie that is also the truth, a truth of a different kind, the ur-truth-at-the-bottom that Burroughs has been seeking. In Tarzan's insistence on his ape parentage, Darwin would agree. Freud would also agree when Tarzan insists that the animal who nursed him is his true mother; as Rank, Freud's student, observes, when the disguise is stripped away, "when all is said and done, . . . an animal or strange nurse—does not express anything beyond the fact: The woman who suckled me is my mother."[16]

Natural Nobility Meets Natural Selection

From the gradual evolution of Tarzan, Burroughs turns in the second half of the novel to the civilizing of Tarzan. It begins when Tarzan develops an interest in Jane Porter, an American woman who is stranded in the jungle. Tarzan rescues her from Terkoz, his ape stepbrother, who abducted her and planned to rape her. When Tarzan carries Jane off, his motives are no different. He takes the woman to his bower to have his way with her. Then, suddenly and unbelievably, something else happens. Tarzan's English DNA begins to crackle with communiqués about good manners and "acting like a gentleman":

> Now, in every fiber of his being, heredity spoke louder than training.
>
> He had not in one swift transition become a polished gentleman from a savage ape-man, but at last the instincts of the former predominated, and over all was the desire to please the woman he loved, and to appear well in her eyes.
>
> So Tarzan of the Apes did the only thing he knew to assure Jane of her safety. He removed his hunting knife from its sheath and handed it to her hilt first, again motioning her into the bower. (168–69)

As Freud observes, the cornerstone of civilization is the repression of aggressive instincts,[17] and this act by Tarzan (the surrender of the phallic knife he had used to slay his ape stepfather) is the beginning of his own process of becoming civilized. This repression of instinct is followed by many others. Later, for example, Tarzan emerges from the jungle for the first time and enters a settlement, and his companion, the French lieutenant D'Arnot, successfully persuades him to restrain his first impulse—to kill every black person he meets.

Out of his love for Jane and under the tutelage of D'Arnot,

Tarzan leaves the forest primeval behind and becomes civilized. It is a process that continues through the novel's conclusion when Tarzan comes to America, to "prosaic Wisconsin," and presents himself to Jane, not only as someone who now knows how to use silverware and can read, but as an impeccable gentleman speaking French, wearing white clothes, and driving a Citroën. He asks for her hand. In a conclusion that has surprised and disappointed generations of readers, Jane chooses, instead, Tarzan's cousin Clayton.

What is significant in this final scene is that Tarzan possesses the power to undermine his cousin's suit. Clayton had become Lord Greystoke when it was believed that Tarzan's parents had left no heir. Nonetheless, in this *Casablanca*-like conclusion, Tarzan does not reveal that he is the rightful Lord Greystoke because that revelation would jeopardize Jane's future. Although he is aggrieved, in other words, Tarzan once more represses his aggressive instincts in a final act of renunciation that offers convincing proof that he has, in fact, become a gentleman. It is proof, too, of the accuracy of Freud's title—*Civilization and Its Discontents.*

But what shouldn't escape notice is that Burroughs runs into difficulty in the second half of the book, once Jane is introduced. There, essentially, Burroughs offers his own version of Nietzsche's *The Genealogy of Morals.* Still, his logic is flawed in one major way: by the notion that Tarzan's evolution continues more or less seamlessly into his becoming civilized. This notion implies that the rise of morality is coextensive with natural selection; that the ultimate victor in "the survival of the fittest" would be not only the strongest, but the most ethical; and that hereditary progress might inevitably lead to a situation in which, say, every professional football player would perforce be a paragon of deportment. To say this differently, when Burroughs suddenly has Tarzan's DNA send him messages about ethics and fair play—and hastily explains Tarzan's innate knowledge of the Ten Commandments and Emily Post's *Book of Etiquette* as a genetic bequest from generations of fine breeding among English aristocracy—Darwin meets Rousseau, and natural selection suddenly becomes equated with natural nobility.

This imaginative equation is Burroughs's own contribution, and with it *Tarzan of the Apes* drifts most decidedly in the direction of fantasy. Nonetheless, this equivalency (or equivocation) deserves attention because in it is found a solution to the dilemma presented in *Little Lord Fauntleroy,* in which an American advocacy of a kind of ahistorical natural nobility clashed with a perceived need at the time to emphasize the ancestral.

Two of Burroughs's favorite books during his childhood were *The Prince and the Pauper* and *Little Lord Fauntleroy* (which he reported having read more than six times), and the evidence is everywhere in *Tarzan.* [18] These three books share a concern with the perennial American theme of natural nobility. In each, a child of aristocrats is stripped of his perquisites, survives and prospers and demonstrates his superiority (or natural nobility) while among the *sans-culottes,* and then achieves a high social rank.

These fundamental similarities point to an American dissatisfaction with European monarchal government evident in so many American childhood classics, from the tar and feathering of the Duke and the King in *Huckleberry Finn* to the exposure of the ruler of the Emerald City. More specifically, the New World's democratic complaint against the Old World—so ably stated in *Little Lord Fauntleroy,* so cleverly shown in *The Prince and the Pauper*—is that a hereditary aristocracy creates situations in which social rank does not necessarily correspond to inner worth.

We might add that this was a general American obsession, not only evident in literature. During the same period, Andrew Carnegie, for example, repeatedly advocated the transformation of European government by abolishing inherited wealth; in this form of survival of the fittest, he argued, every man might start off on an equal footing—ahistorically, as it were. This is, of course, once more, the idea of the American Adam, that self-conception and myth of national identity that posited America and Americans as unprecedented, freed from history, beginning anew.

While, as we have pointed out, this notion was entirely satisfactory through the early nineteenth century, it was at odds with another emphasis in the latter part of the century, when social change and the Civil War seemed to argue for the replacement of antipatriarchal and ahistorical rhetoric with motifs of continuity and succession. As Mr. Hobbs says in the last lines of *Little Lord Fauntleroy,* an America of constant fresh beginnings is "a good enough country for them that's young and stirrin'—but there's faults in it. There's not an [ancestor] among 'em."

What should be noted, consequently, is that Burroughs found in Darwin an answer to this dilemma. By yoking natural nobility with natural selection, he offered in *Tarzan* a vision that was at once Adamic *and* ancestral.

The American Omega

In the beginning all the world was America.

John Locke, *Of Civil Government*

Locke had it wrong, according to Burroughs. In the beginning all the world was Africa. America is to be found at the Darwinian end.

One of the books in Burroughs's library was Darwin's *The Descent of Man,* purchased when he was twenty-three and on the flyleaf of which he doodled a picture of an ape and captioned it "Grandpa." In that work Burroughs would have read Darwin saying, "The wonderful progress of the United States and the character of its people are the results of natural selection; for the more energetic, restless and courageous men from all parts of Europe have emigrated during the last ten or twelve generations to that great country and have succeeded there best."[19]

Perhaps this explains why Burroughs's book begins among apes in Africa and ends in twentieth-century America. This is a novel about evolutionary progress. Tarzan's ontogeny, we are to understand, recapitulates the phylogeny of the human race. Where Burroughs's hero reaches the culmination of his development, where the novel ends, we would expect to find, consequently, the acme of human evolution—at least as far as progress has taken the species by the early twentieth century. *Tarzan* ends in the United States.

Whatever one might think about this quasi-scientific jingoism, it is important to note its implications. America's legitimacy is established not just by natural nobility, but by natural selection. Its superiority is the result not just of genealogy, but of evolution.

Few European cultures have employed the figure of the Wild Child in this way. France's Wild Boy of Aveyron and Germany's Kaspar Hauser are not viewed as myths of the race; instead, they seem test cases in a Rousseauistic debate between heredity and environment. Even Mowgli, despite his association with the British Empire, does not seem a figure for the race but, rather, an occasion for Kipling to debate the competing appeals (and discontents) of wildness and civilization.

To understand the use of the Wild Child as a myth of national identity, one would have to turn to the ancient legend of Romulus and Remus. Only in this story, of orphans who are raised by wolves and who go on to found the Roman Empire, is there something like the subtext offered Americans in Burroughs's book—in which the word "natural" (natural nobility, natural selection) seems about to be slurred to sound like the word "national."

6

❖ ❖ ❖ ❖ ❖ ❖ ❖

Imposters, Succession, and Faux Histories
The Prince and the Pauper

There is something mythic about Samuel Langhorne Clemens's *The Prince and the Pauper* (1881). As Peter Brunette has observed, the novel has "managed over the years to worm its way into the American collective unconscious, so thoroughly in fact that many seem to have absorbed the tale without ever having read the book."[1]

What accounts for this enduring, mythic appeal? Victor Fischer has suggested that an answer is to be found in the way the book addresses "universal childhood fears": "death of a parent, cruel substitute parents, abandonment, lost identity, kidnap, unjust punishment and imprisonment."[2] Certainly part of its appeal, too, is its working out of the conviction of those of us on the pavement when Richard Cory or some other wealthy merchant prince goes by: "There but for the grace of God go I." And certainly part of the pleasure is its shadowed opposite, since what Clemens's prince wants is a chance to play in the mud, an excremental enthusiasm not denied his lookalike, who lives in a squalid room in the pointedly named Offal Court just off Pudding Lane.

When Clemens began his story about the exchange of places between the pauper Tom Canty and the prince Edward Tudor, he apparently meant to undermine the Victorian enthusiasm for Olde Englande that was sweeping America and manifesting itself in everything from historical novels to crossbeam architecture in the "Tudor" homes of Hartford. His intention, he explained to William Dean Howells, was to show that the England of the sixteenth century had, in truth, been a cruel place—a fact that would become obvious once the boys exchanged positions and the prince became subject to his country's unusually harsh and unenlightened laws.[3]

Then, too, Clemens was enjoying himself. As Albert Paine said, "Of all Mark Twain's stories none brought him greater joy in the writing than *The Prince and the Pauper*."[4] The book was "affectionately inscribed" to his daughters, Susie and Clara Clemens, who waited daily for the next installment and who enacted scenes from the novel in theatricals they arranged for their Hartford neighbors.

There was still one other motivation behind the writing of the book. *The Prince and the Pauper* was to be Clemens's bid for respectability. "Mark Twain" had a reputation as a western humorist who dealt with low material: jumping frogs and claim jumpers. Now living in genteel Hartford, married to a woman who believed his real genius was yet unrecognized, Clemens felt a need to be regarded seriously. Choosing the acceptable genre of historical fiction and writing about regal England instead of lowlife Mississippi, Clemens meant to show everyone that he could do what other, more respectable writers did.[5] The result was a novel for the Gilded Age: embossed, heavily illustrated, with sixteen footnotes, maps, and the like. To save the book from the taint of "Twain," Clemens even thought about publishing the book anonymously.

Perhaps he should have, but for the opposite reason. Many American critics have dismissed *The Prince and the Pauper* not because there is too much "Twain" in it, but because there is not enough. In their eyes, in this "English" novel, Clemens "sold out" in his bid for propriety. Although he was composing *Huckleberry Finn* and *The Prince and the Pauper* at virtually the same time, nativist critics have invented the notion that they are the work of two separate authors, the genius and the hack—and never the twain did meet.[6]

In truth, *The Prince and the Pauper* is as much a work of genius as its companion book; at one time, Twain thought of binding the two together in a single volume, Siamese-twin fashion.[7] Although the novel is at times "longwinded," as Howells observed when he read his friend's manuscript,[8] Twain's ability to coordinate the dual and synchronous stories of his twins (while echoing them once again in the Miles Hendon subplot) is nothing short of dazzling. At the same time, perhaps no other work by Clemens reveals so much about its author.

Juxtaposing the Romance and the Myth

The symmetrical genius in *The Prince and the Pauper* amounts to a juxtaposition of what psychologists call "The Family Romance" and what Otto Rank calls "The Myth of the Birth of the Hero." They are shadowed opposites, two sides of the same coin; and Clemens makes this clear in his parallel stories of Tom Canty and Edward Tudor.

The Family Romance, first of all, is a familiar childhood fantasy that most adults can still remember entertaining during their youth. It is the dreamy conviction that "I was adopted. The people that I live with are not my real parents, but my foster parents. My real parents are more important, royal perhaps, better looking, wealthier, and someday they will come and get me."

Tom Canty's story is essentially the Family Romance come true: a boy pauper who, through happenstance, exchanges places and comes to be regarded as the real prince; who becomes a member of the royal family and the son of a king; and who would just as soon forget the poor folks and impoverished family that he lived with originally. This transition is prepared for by those circumstances which Rank identifies as the usual ones that give rise to the Family Romance.[9]

Feelings of being a neglected or unwanted child. Clemens's novel begins with an account of Tom's birth, and it is compared with that of Prince Edward in such a way that his unwelcome status is exaggerated:

> In the ancient city of London, on a certain autumn day . . . a boy was born to a poor family named Canty, who did not want him. On the same day another English child was born to a rich

family of the name of Tudor, who did want him. All England wanted him, too. England had so longed for him, and hoped for him, and prayed for him, that now that he was really come, the people nearly went mad with joy. (1)

An active imagination regarding royalty. Tom's manner of play when he is still at home is notable:

> [He] organized a royal court! He was the prince; his special comrades were guards, chamberlains, equerries, lords and ladies in waiting, and the royal family. Daily the mock prince was received with elaborate ceremonials borrowed by Tom from his romantic readings; daily the great affairs of the mimic kingdom were discussed in royal council, and daily his mimic highness issued decrees to his imaginary armies, navies, and viceroyalties. (8–9)

A conviction that "a prophet is not without honor, save in his own country and in his father's house." Tom does not just feel like an unrecognized genius, but is one, according to Clemens. Although the boy only plays in the streets at being a prince, he miraculously begins to seem like one:

> Tom's influence among young people began to grow, now, day by day; and in time he came to be looked up to, by them, with a wondering awe, as a superior being. He seemed to know so much! and he could do and say such marvelous things! and withal, he was so deep and wise! . . . [Even elders began] to regard him as a most gifted and extraordinary creature. Full grown people brought their perplexities to Tom for solution, and were often astonished at the wit and wisdom of his decisions. In fact, he has become a hero to all who knew him except in his own family—these, only, saw nothing in him. (8)

"[Chance] meetings with the lord of the manor or the proprietor of the estate, in the country; with the reigning prince, in the city; in the United States, with some great statesman or millionaire." And so, Tom's chance moment near the gates of the castle, when he spies the prince and is invited in, begins the story.

If Tom Canty's story is the Family Romance, then to understand the story of the prince, Edward Tudor, we have to turn our discussion upside down. If the Family Romance is not regarded as a childhood fantasy, but is taken as fact, then we have Rank's "Myth of the Birth of the Hero." In this case, the childhood dream—of being a high-born child temporarily being raised by lowly foster parents, of being a child who will eventually be recognized and achieve its royal birthright—is a true description of actual circumstances. As Rank observes, this is the typical history presented in the legends of Oedipus, Cyrus, Romulus, and dozens of other heroes. It is also, we should add, the story found in *Little Lord Fauntleroy, Tarzan,* and in those parts of Clemens's novel that deal with Edward Tudor—a prince who finds himself a temporary member of a pauper's family, but who is eventually recognized and achieves his birthright.

Twain's twinning genius in the novel, then, lies in his symmetrical and synchronous presentation of the Romance and the Myth. They are mirrored opposites, in that the relation between the two is the relationship between fantasy and fact. So, for example:

- While Tom has fantasies about being a member of the nobility, Edward really is of noble blood.

- While Tom feels as though he is "a prophet without honor in his own country," Edward really is.

- While Tom is paranoid (believing that servants and nobles alike are sneering at him and plotting), Edward really is pursued by people who are out to get him (John Canty, the Hermit, the vagabonds).

- While Tom has delusions of grandeur, Edward is well acquainted with actual grandeur.

Such juxtapositions do more than intimate Clemens's symmetrical genius in organizing his parallel plots. They also suggest how much of *The Prince and the Pauper* turns on a careful separation of fact from fantasy. As Tom's story, especially, makes clear, the ability to make such a separation is an important part of growing up if a youth is ever to pass beyond the childhood fantasy of the Family Romance.

The Fear of Impostors

The endurance past puberty . . . [and] the compulsive pressure to
live out the Family Romance [is most] characteristic of the impostor.

Phyllis Greenacre, "The Impostor"

Over the years, psychologists have studied the personality of the impostor—those individuals whose stories occasionally appear in the newspapers after they have masqueraded as, for example, policemen or doctors. In recent years, however, psychologists have recognized another, related malady that they have named "the impostor phenomenon." This is a debilitating anxiety of individuals who feel *as if* they are impostors: the successful trial lawyer who worries that he will be exposed as a phony on some elementary point of law; the computer programmer who is fearful of the mistake that will show others that he has just been faking it; the middle-aged person who believes that she is still a child and only pretending to be an adult; the student who gets good grades but is still troubled about the exam that will reveal she is actually a dunce. [10]

Visions of both the genuine impostor (if that is the right term) and the impostor phenomenon are present throughout *The Prince and the Pauper*. In the first case, Edward Tudor is thought to be an impostor when he claims to be the prince; Miles Hendon is wrongly accused of being an impostor when he claims to be himself; John Canty (a master at disguises) often pretends to be someone other than he is; and eventually Tom Canty has to be an impostor and play at being the monarch until the real one is found. But it is really in terms of the impostor phenomenon that much of *The Prince and the Pauper* can be understood. What baffles many of the characters in the book is Tom Canty's continual insistence that he is not the prince; as one of the royal ministers observes, "Now were he impostor and called himself prince, look you that would be natural; that would be reasonable. But lived ever an impostor yet, who, being called prince by the king, . . . denied all his dignity and pleaded against his exaltation!" (50).

Generally speaking, victims of the impostor phenomenon are frequently individuals who find themselves in new circumstances, often through sudden and unanticipated success: the executive, for example, who is suddenly promoted to the top echelons and thinks,

"I'm really just a kid from the streets who used to play stickball, so I'll have to fake it." The malady that results may be said to have four pronounced characteristics: first, a conviction of a split between a "true" self and a "false" self; second, guilt about this discrepancy, about being a "hypocrite"; third, a terrible need to hide a "secret" identity; and, finally, an acute fear of exposure—real insecurity and genuine worry about unpredictable situations that might result in humiliation, particularly social situations in which some accident might occur that would bring the hoax down like a house of cards.

To readers familiar with *The Prince and the Pauper,* the applicability of these concepts to Tom Canty's situation may already be apparent. He constantly feels a discrepancy between his "true" and "false" identities; for example, he "tried hard to acquit himself satisfactorily, but he was too new to such things, and too ill at ease to accomplish more than a tolerable success. He looked sufficiently like a king, but he was ill able to feel like one" (123). And Tom has the impostor's anxiety about being exposed and worries that some sudden event will topple the edifice of his charade. This only makes him feel more acutely that he is a fake and a hypocrite. In a moment when he is enjoying his royal perquisites, for example, Tom thinks about his mother and sisters and grows worried "of their coming some day in their rags and dirt, and betraying him with their kisses and pulling him down from his lofty place and dragging him back to penury and degradation and the slums. . . . Whenever their mournful and accusing faces did rise before him now, they made him feel more despicable than the worms that crawl" (252).

But more than anything else, what signals the presence of the impostor's anxieties is the fact that throughout the book the most acute pain comes from humiliation or the fear of it. This is a novel in which hurt is inflicted publicly through jeering, shaming, and ridicule. Poor Tom is jeered by crowds when he comes in his rags to see the castle. After the exchange of clothes, a mob hoots at Prince Edward, and later he is ragged by charity children. While in regal habiliment, Tom worries that the servants are sneering at him behind his back. Recalling the mockery Christ suffered, Edward suffers his own mock coronation and public ridicule at the hands of taunting vagabonds unable to stomach his claims to the throne. And when Miles offers to take Edward's place to save him from a public flogging, the boy monarch is grateful for something other

"THRONE HIM."

John J. Hartley for *The Prince and the Pauper*
(New York: Harper and Brothers, 1881).

than being spared physical injury; such injury, he says, is "less than nothing!—when 'tis weighed against the act of him who saves his prince from SHAME!" (241). In the conclusion, as well, Tom has to confess in front of all the assembled gentry of England that he used the King's Great Seal as a nutcracker and then hear the guffaws that follow. Even when shaming and public humiliation do not occur, characters are anxious that they are just about to; when Tom is posing as royalty, his most excruciating moments occur at state dinners, where he worries that hundreds are watching him eat and monitoring his proper or improper use of utensils.

Clemens's own sudden ascendancy—from poor white folks eating cornpone in frontier Missouri to the well-to-do sitting down to china place settings in the gilded parlors of Hartford—provided, no doubt, fertile ground for the particular kinds of fantasies and anxieties that appear in *The Prince and the Pauper*. His own childhood, Clemens explained, was marked by financial reversals. His father was one of the most "honored and opulent citizens of Fentress County" until the crash of 1834 reduced him to a pauper, and he was forced to relocate to Hannibal.[11] There his father slowly rebuilt his fortunes until they were lost once again when he was obliged to honor a loan made by another man who declared bankruptcy. They were paupers, Clemens confessed, living in a muddy little river town. And it was a town infected with "gold fever," since Hannibal was one of the last jumping-off points for get-rich-quick folks headed overland to make their fortunes in the Gold Rush. Mining a similar vein in the evenings, the family enjoyed talking about their vanished grandeur and speculating about their noble ancestors— their kinship with one of the judges of King Charles I, a claim they had on the earlship of Durham.[12]

Clemens's own Cinderella-like ascendancy from barefoot Missouri boy to newspaper royalty was certain to seem a dislocation. Clemens himself not only acknowledged this, but emphasized it: he was a Southerner living in the North, a frontiersman in genteel company, an American in Europe. As others have observed, this sense of "twin" identity is suggested in everything Twain/Clemens did, from the day he coined his doubled moniker to his last words on his deathbed, when he mumbled incoherently about Dr. Jekyll and Mr. Hyde.[13]

These obsessions are reflected in his work: in the fascination with Siamese twins, the exchanged identities of Tom and Huck in the conclusion of *Huckleberry Finn,* the changelings of *Pudd'nhead Wilson,* the transpositions of *The Prince and the Pauper,* and elsewhere. The episode in *Huckleberry Finn* in which two sets of brothers both claim to be related to Peter Wilks is repeated over and over again in Clemens's work: the question is always who is the true and genuine and who is the fraud and impostor.

There may be no other author in the world who can match Clemens in his bona fide obsession with genuineness. His work reveals a consuming preoccupation with frauds, pretenders, con men, hoaxes, dupes, shams, and deceptions. His greatest characters ply this trade: the Duke and the King, Colonel Sellers, and several boys who move in and out of ruses with incredible alacrity. At the beginning of his career, as a journalist in Nevada, Clemens made a name for himself as a perpetrator of hoaxes. At other times, especially late in his life, he seemed to be a Catcher in the Rye eager to preserve others from various fads that he perceived as frauds—be it the Christian Science movement or Sir Walter Scott's novels.

It may not be surprising, then, that one of the most memorable moments in Clemens's early life occurred in 1877 when he was asked (as a writer of the young, upcoming generation) to speak at a dinner to celebrate John Greenleaf Whittier (an *éminence grise* of the previous generation). Clemens told a yarn about a miner who is taken advantage of by three impostors who claim to be Ralph Waldo Emerson, Henry Wadsworth Longfellow, and Oliver Wendell Holmes. The conclusion of the story amounts to an inadvertent revelation: when "Mark Twain" shows up, the miner asks whether he is an impostor, too.

In her extensive study of fraudulent personalities, psychiatrist Phyllis Greenacre has noted a special affinity between impostors and writers. Examining Thomas Mann, Ossian, and others, she observes: "Many artists feel as though they were impostors, especially at the beginning of their careers. The possession of an extraordinary gift is, apparently, not easily taken for granted."[14]

The Cause: Problems of Succession

In psychiatric studies, Greenacre and others have been surprised to discover so much consistency in the backgrounds of impostors that they have been able to draw up a profile.[15] The typical impostor is a male who has had a doting mother and an "absent" father (whether absent by death, departure, or ineffectuality). The lack of a father creates postpubertal problems, since the son has no one to rebel against and so directs oedipal aggression toward others to "get the better of them" through imposture. At the same time, the son gains the early sense of having replaced his absent father in some undeserved way and feels guilty about this unwarranted ascendancy. In a word, the problem of the impostor is the problem of succession.

Those familiar with Clemens's life will notice the congruence with this profile. His mother lavished attention on him, especially when he was young and sickly and thought to have little chance of surviving. His father, the son always said, was "distant" and "stern" and died before Sam's twelfth birthday.

Clemens's books tell a similar story. He is often concerned with succession: from the comic complaints of the King and the Duke about their lost birthrights in *Huckleberry Finn,* through the central question of *The Prince and the Pauper* about who is the true heir to the throne, to the muddle over inheritances that motivates *Pudd'nhead Wilson.* Moreover, and again with surprising frequency, Clemens seems drawn to boys at a pubertal age. It is not only that he chooses to make youths like Tom Sawyer and Huckleberry Finn his principal characters; even in a historical novel like *The Prince and the Pauper* (in which the author trumpets his historical accuracy and the facts dictate that Edward and Tom should be about nine years old), Clemens instructed the illustrators to picture the boys as he saw them: "as lads of 13 or 14 years old."[16]

This issue of a boy's succession conspicuously appears in the novel's opening words: "I will set down a tale as it was told to me by one who had it of his father, which latter had it of *his* father, this last having in like manner had it of *his* father—and so on, back and still back, three hundred years and more, the fathers transmitting it to the sons and so preserving it." But there is something absent here that begs to be noticed. Despite the prologue's emphasis on narrative inheritances, the passage does not begin as might have been expected: the passage does not begin "I had this tale from my father."

To understand *The Prince and the Pauper,* it is only necessary to allegorize this prologue in a psychological fashion. What happens in other kinds of situations, when the father is absent and does not "transmit" to his son? What happens when the boy becomes an heir without having earned the right? Will the boy feel as if he has prematurely stolen from the father something that should have been "transmitted"? In that case, shouldn't the usurper, this impostor, be punished?

These conflicted issues of succession are the major themes of *The Prince and the Pauper,* and they are visible *in brevis* in "The Whipping Boy Episode," a section of the novel that Clemens left out at the suggestion of William Dean Howells.[17] It is the story of a thirteen-year-old boy who does what is forbidden. While his father is absent, he steals into the wardrobe and puts on the man's favorite possession, a special multicolored cloak—so special that "even the king their father" had praised the garment on those few occasions when it was taken out of storage. When the boy transgresses and dresses himself in his father's raiment, there is hell to pay: a wild bull ride, bee stings, and eventually a whipping.[18]

Here is the opposite of the novel's prologue, with its cameo of uninterrupted transmission of the story from father to son. Here, instead, are the problems of succession that mark the impostor phenomenon—where what is conspicuous, Greenacre observes in a singularly appropriate passage, is the impostor's desire to over-throw "the king-father [revealed in] an assumption of his mantle in a real or illusory assumption of power."[19] Such an episode may intimate the "guilt" Clemens felt about his own premature succession upon his father's early death. Be that as it may, for the Whipping Boy, at least, the day he put on the robe stolen from his father changed his life: "It was there my sorrow and my shame began. Naught fitted—all was a world too large."[20]

The Solution: Memory

Someone in Missouri has sent me a picture of the house I was born in. Heretofore I have always stated that it was a palace but I shall be more guarded now.

Samuel Clemens, *The Autobiography of Mark Twain*

The problems of the impostor, then, arise when life is not succes-sive. As we noted earlier, the person suffering from the impostor phenomenon often feels some pronounced discontinuity with the past. Genuine impostors, too, psychiatrists have pointed out, char-acteristically have problems with succession: their premature re-placement of the father is often seen as usurpation.

If interrupted succession is the cause behind the rise of fraudu-lent personalities, the effect is often seen in one particular kind of personality disorder. As Greenacre has observed, "The endurance past puberty . . . [and] the compulsive pressure to live out the Family Romance [is most] characteristic of the impostor."[21] As Rank also observes, the prolongation of the Family Romance into adulthood is evident in the delusions of the psychotic who finally issues his apodictic statement, "I am the emperor."[22]

Here is Tom Canty's problem. Impostors—who, even into adulthood, persist in the childhood fantasy that they were born of royal parents and who demand their birthright—turn their backs on the facts. In their denial of their actual or genuine past lies a discontinuity of identity. Memory is rejected.

Memory is what makes life successive. And given that the principal concern of *The Prince and the Pauper* is usurpation and the dangers of interrupted succession, it is not surprising that memory plays so large a role in the novel.

The danger Tom Canty faces is that he will forget who he is in his intoxication with his impostrous identity. The satisfactions are considerable. While masquerading as the prince, Tom witnesses how his every wish is a command and how he is universally honored, the Child Regent. In this heady and egocentric atmosphere, as his coronation approaches, he seems ready to unthinkingly embrace the fantasy and forget the facts—but in that way lies madness.

Sanity is finally restored, however, during "The Recognition Procession" that precedes the coronation in the book's conclusion. In the parade to Westminster Abbey, "Tom found himself once more the chief figure in a wonderful floating pageant" (253). With cannons booming, surrounded by the King's guard and all the guilds of London, with the people of the city turned out to shout "God save the king," the pauper's egocentric wishes seem to have been finally answered: "All these wonders and these marvels are to welcome me—me!" (257). But at the very moment when he seems most willing to embrace his impostrous identity,

he caught sight of a pale, astounded face which was strained forward in the crowd, its intense eyes riveted upon him; a sickening consternation struck through him—he recognized his mother! . . . In an instant more she had torn her way out of the press and past the guards, and was at his side. She embraced his leg, she covered it with kisses, she cried, "O, my child, my darling!" lifting toward him a face that was transfigured with joy and love. The same instant an officer of the King's guard snatched her away, with a curse, and sent her reeling back from whence she came, with a vigorous impulse from his strong arm. The words "I do not know you, woman!" were falling from Tom Canty's lips when this piteous thing occurred; but it smote him to the heart. . . . In his own breast, in his accusing conscience—a voice kept repeating those shameful words, "I do not know you, woman!" . . .

The Lord Protector was quick to notice these things [and said,] . . . "O, dread sovereign, shake off these fatal humors —the eyes of the world are upon thee!" Then he added in sharp annoyance, "Perdition catch that crazy pauper!—'twas she that hath disturbed your highness."

[Tom] turned a lustreless eye upon the duke, and said in a dead voice—"She was my mother!"

"My God!" groaned the Protector, . . . "He is gone mad again!" (258–61)

Actually, he has grown sane. Just as Tom is about to erase the last traces of his ascent, he begins to feel guilty and reverses his course. Through this acknowledgment of his mother, he is finally able to sort out fact from the fantasy that threatens to suck him away. Memory, not denial, is the answer.[23] This is, of course, the basis of most psychiatric practice. It is, as well, the remedy for those problems of the impostor that arise from discontinuities in identity.

Throughout *The Prince and the Pauper*, wherever memory is absent there is the suspicion of madness. Memory and madness are opposite poles. When rumors begin to circulate around the castle that "the prince hath gone mad, the prince hath gone mad!" (30), Tom Canty is brought before the king, who tests his powers of recognition: "Am I not thy loving father?" (37). When Edward Tudor finds his way to the hovel of the Canty family and is regarded as crazed because he claims to be the prince, Tom's mother pleads to him, "Call back thy poor wandering memory. Look upon me. Am I not the mother that bore thee and loveth thee?" (67).

Disappointed by the responses of the boys they presume to be their sons, both parents make further tests of their memory. Henry VIII makes trial of the youth's familiarity with Latin and French, and is disappointed by Tom's replies. Dame Canty—remembering that her son, ever since an explosion of gunpowder, has had a curious habit of holding up his hands palms outward when he is startled, rather than palms inward as most people would—wakes the boy three times during the night while she holds a candle. She, too, is disappointed by the results. Each time Edward holds up his hands in the wrong fashion, and she wonders if it is possible that he could so quickly forget the gesture that had been engraved on his memory.

For Henry VIII, these are worrisome circumstances, since the mental state of his heir puts the kingdom in jeopardy. This situation prompts him to issue a command: no one shall speak of the boy's mental condition or take notice of his lapses, while the prince "shall strive with diligence to bring unto his memory again" all he has forgotten (40). Tom is a dutiful subject and takes his king's orders to heart, but for him it means engaging in an elaborate charade. He must pretend to be the prince. And so, when he is caught short and ignorant of one thing or another, the little actor exclaims, "How I am forgetting! . . . 'Tis strange how my memory doth wanton with me these days" (117). At other times, he expresses gratitude to others for "reminding" him of something, or, when assisted, he feigns to dimly recall what he never really knew. For Tom, his whole period of imposture requires the construction of a huge edifice of counterfeit memories.[24]

Unlike Tom, Edward has the memory of the proverbial elephant. He never forgets who he is. Edward's persistence in this is nothing short of incredible, since it brings him only pain and ridicule from those (like John Canty and the vagabonds) who cannot stomach his assertions that he is actually the prince, or patronizing kindness from those who simply think the boy is crazed. In his insistence, they think him mad, unable to remember who he really is. Even Miles Hendon is surprised by "the grip his memory doth take upon his quaint and crazy fancies" (201).

But it is Edward's strength of memory that brings about his salvation and leads to the improvement of life in England. During his period among his people, Edward constantly exercises his memory, and not just in remembrance of who he really is or in the affairs of court. When he is rudely treated by a group of orphans, he decides that they need learning as well as food and shelter, and he resolves: "I will keep this diligently in my remembrance, that this day's lesson be not lost upon me, and my people suffer thereby" (24). When he is forced to witness Baptist women being burned at the stake, he determines to change the laws when given the chance: "That which I have seen, in that one little moment, will never go out of my memory" (237). And when Miles takes a public flogging originally intended for him, Edward promises to reward his honored subject: "this loyal deed shall never perish out of my memory. I will not forget it!" (241).

Edward's memory receives its most important test, of course, in the resolution of the novel. In front of all the assembled nobles, with the crown of England hanging in the balance, Edward must remember where he hid the Great Seal on the day he and Tom exchanged clothes. Tom encourages him, "Bethink thee, my king—spur thy memory. . . . Recall everything!" (272–73). And he finally does.

Memory puts all things right. The boy who never forgot who he was now ascends the throne. And in the denouement, Edward, recalling the good the pauper has done during the time he was thought to be the prince, rewards Tom with a position and a special set of clothes, a "dress of state, [by which] he shall be known, and . . . wheresoever he shall come, it shall remind the people that he hath been royal" (286). So, too, Edward remembers the promises he made to the man who was his protector when others thought him a mad pauper, remembers even his promise that his friend could sit in the king's presence, and makes Miles Hendon the Earl of Kent.

But even more that this, it is Edward's memory that explains why his reign is remembered, in Clemens's words, as "a singularly merciful one for those harsh times":

> As long as the king lived he was fond of telling the story of his adventures. . . . He said the frequent rehearsing of the precious lesson kept him strong in his purpose to make its teachings yield benefits to his people; and so, whilst his life was spared he should continue to tell the story, and thus keep its sorrowful spectacle fresh in his memory. (288–89)

Counterfeit Memory: The Faux Histories of Democracies

Impostors, problems of succession, the Family Romance (both as fantasy and as fact), the salvific power of memory—what has all this to do with America, and how does it explain the unusual popularity of Clemens's book? Until now, we have, for the most part, been examining Clemens's novel at close range and in a psychological and biographical manner. If we widen our discussion now in a psychohistorical fashion, we can begin to see how Clemens's private concerns echoed larger, cultural concerns. William Dean Howells intimated this when he reviewed *The Prince and the Pauper* for the *New York Tribune* and called the novel "a manual of republicanism."[25] Although modern readers may find it surprising to be advised that a children's book ought to be read in a political fashion, we have already seen how this is true of other juvenile classics published during the Golden Age.

In these works we have noted a consistent critique of European monarchism and an advocacy of the American alternative of natural nobility. This theme is especially conspicuous in *The Prince and the Pauper*. The pauper is a kind and wise ruler for a time because, when he assumes his royal office, he brings with him a heart that has been educated among the people. So, too, the prince becomes a better ruler because of his moral reeducation among hoi polloi. In the same way, Cedric Errol makes a benevolent Lord Fauntleroy because he has first been an ordinary kid on the streets of New York. And Tarzan, the offspring of Lord and Lady Greystoke, is all the better because, instead of depending on his nobility, he has had the occasion to descend to the bottom of the evolutionary ladder and (in free competition) prove his mettle in nature and rise to the top.

But we should note a contradiction. In these three American books what is offered is a compromised version of "natural nobility." Except for Tom Canty's brief interlude in *The Prince and the Pauper*, none of these novels tells the democratic story of a prole who rises to a position of power. Instead, in each, the hero is nobly born but finds himself in reduced circumstances. In each, the noble child goes through a process of reeducation among the people and then (following the pattern of the Family Romance) resumes his rank in a manner that suggests a reification and renewal of the notion of nobility.

In these three novels, in other words, the major emphasis does not fall on the democratic and antipatriarchal rhetoric that marks, say, the exposure of the Wizard as a humbug in *The Wizard of Oz* or the King as naked in *Huckleberry Finn*. To be sure, this is a minor motif in all three.[26] Still, instead of a *break* with the father, *Fauntleroy* and *Tarzan* and *The Prince and the Pauper* are post-oedipal and concerned with continuity: with succession, ancestry, and lineage.

This concern is also suggested by the differences between Clemens's companion books, the two he once thought of binding together. With the characters of the Duke and the King, for example, *Adventures of Huckleberry Finn* rejects *paternal* impostors, who are both royal pretenders and usurpers of the father's place (when, for example, they falsely claim to be the rightful guardians of the Wilks girls). *The Prince and the Pauper,* in contrast, presents this theme's counterpart, its twain: a concern with *filial* impostors, usurpers of the son's place and rightful birthright. In the second work, in other words, parricidal impulses are largely absent;[27] they are replaced by the worries of a son—of being bereft, orphaned, disowned. *The Prince and the Pauper,* we might say, addresses post-Revolutionary concerns, ones that arose after America had so forcefully separated from its European parents. While *Huckleberry Finn* celebrates the break with the father, *The Prince and the Pauper* addresses the anxiety that arose after that break had occurred.

If *The Prince and the Pauper* is understood in this psychohistorical manner, then it is easier to see why this novel found its place on the best-seller lists of the period and to understand how private dream became public myth. First of all, Clemens's preoccupation with frauds in his writings (as well as his own personal anxieties about being an impostor and usurper) matched the times. His age, after all, was also the age of P. T. Barnum and aptly named (by Clemens himself) the Gilded Age. During the 1870s, the most celebrated news story concerned the Tichborne Claimant, a butcher from Australia who claimed to be the missing son and heir of Lady Tichborne and who was shown in court to be an impostor. The notoriety of the Tichborne case spawned a generation of music-hall plays about missing heirs, may have inspired *Little Lord Fauntleroy,* and captured the attention of Clemens.[28] He paid a researcher to collect twelve scrapbooks full of newspaper clippings on the story. Clemens and his times had a ravenous appetite for such incidents.

Moreover, in writing this genteel novel, Mark Twain's personal bid for respectability echoed similar national wishes of a mature and post-oedipal America. This America wished to emphasize the ancestral. It had seen in the Civil War the dangers of ceaseless oedipal rebellion and wished to emphasize continuity. It was preoccupied (via Bancroft and Parkman) with solidifying the country's historicity. It had grown up and settled its antagonism with the fatherland.

This milieu may also explain why Clemens chose the *historical* novel as his genre and why he went to such great and tedious lengths to point repeatedly to his book's fidelity to the facts. The novel begins with an epigraph about the faithful transmission of this story from father to son. As the story proceeds, faithful memory becomes the primary tool for undoing confusion, for separating fantasy from fact. And all along the way, Clemens feels a need to assert the book's historical accuracy. This is a novel with footnotes! It is also full of bibliographical references to the histories Clemens consulted, frequent editorial intrusions meant to indicate to the reader the unusual care he took in the accurate presentation of costumes and customs, and an incredibly conscientious use of "Olde Englishe" language.

Clemens doth protest too much. Despite all the appurtenances of the historical novel and Clemens's strenuous assertions of historicity, what has to be remembered is that *The Prince and the Pauper* is not folklore but—to use the most accurate term—fakelore. Like *Tarzan of the Apes*, Clemens's novel offers an Invented Past, Faux History.

The Prince and the Pauper, *Tarzan*, and *Fauntleroy*, then, may be regarded as "manuals of republicanism" because of their political critique and American advocacy of natural nobility. But in their compromised version of natural nobility and in their anxieties about succession, they reveal another side to this American sense of self-identity: a country that has made its forceful break with European parents now worries about being bereft, disowned, disinherited. The need to make ancestral assertions, in other words, the need to create Impostrous Pasts, reflects the subsequent anxieties of a country self-defined, parentless, Adamic, and ahistorical. Clemens's own response to his boyish fear of becoming an orphan took shape in a "historical" novel that likewise answered a national need for fictions of legitimacy.

THREE

✦ ✦ ✦ ✦ ✦ ✦ ✦

The Theater
of Feelings

7

✣ ✣ ✣ ✣ ✣ ✣
Remorse and Regrets
The Adventures of
Tom Sawyer

Having identified the basic plot that lies behind American classics of the Golden Age of Children's Literature, and having discussed the way authors addressed American issues in the variations they played on this plot, we can turn now to consider them *sui generis* and identify their native themes. Humphrey Carpenter has argued that British children's books of the same era move outward to create imaginary paradises—treasure islands, never-never lands, pastoral paradises.[1] For the most part, American children's books head in the opposite direction.

The land of Oz would seem to be an exception. However, as we have seen, the movie develops what is nascent in Baum's book and makes clear that its oedipal geography is a psychological landscape that finally retreats into Dorothy's head as she wakes up. In the same way, in the internal monologue and first-person narrative of *Huckleberry Finn,* the river world (with its father figures lined up along the shore) is a dreamlike extension of Huck, whose adventures end with word that Pap is dead. So, too, the elaborate sociology of *Rebecca of Sunnybrook Farm* and other girls' books, with their populations of sclerotic spinster aunts and benevolent Sugar Daddies, is the Child-Woman's oedipal feelings writ large. In American children's books of the Golden Age, in other words, landscape leads inward: the England and America of *Little Lord Fauntleroy* are the boy's fatherland and motherland; the Africa of Tarzan, the aboriginal homeland of id; and the Olde Englande of *The Prince and the Pauper,* an imagined ancestral locale where the impostor's anxieties are played out.

These American childhood classics take place in an internal world we might call the Theater of Feelings. Here we encounter Tom Sawyer contriving melodramatic tableaus in which he fancies himself the martyred child, and what is important is that others feel remorse and regret when they think of his passing. Here we encounter the March sisters of *Little Women* engaged in an internal struggle with their negative emotions, their "bosom enemies." And here we encounter Toby Tyler tossed this way and that by a single feeling, hunger.

In a curious way, *The Adventures of Tom Sawyer* presents the best example for delineating this phenomenon because it is an antitype. Samuel Langhorne Clemens's novel is a comprehensive parody of American Children's Literature, but we can glimpse, in what it pokes fun at and subverts, the shapes of what others took more seriously.

Generally speaking, there were two kinds of American Children's Literature before the publication of *Tom Sawyer* in 1876: Aesopian tales of Good and Bad children (which finally became codified in the Sunday school story) and spiritual biographies of woebegone but saintly waifs (a genre that eventually became the stories of the child-victim in sentimental fiction). In his early attempts at parody, Clemens took on the first kind of story, turned it on its head, and celebrated the Bad Boy. But, as we will see, when Clemens delved deeper into his novel, he widened his critique to include this second kind of story in his comic vision of Tom as the pale martyr. For this reason, *Tom Sawyer* should be seen historically, within the context of the earlier American Children's Literature that it so wonderfully lampoons.

The Bad Boy

By the middle of the eighteenth century, many of America's progressive parents had come to adopt John Locke as their Dr. Spock and made the bachelor philosopher's *Thoughts Concerning Education* (1693) their bible of child raising.[2] Among his other recommendations (cold showers, a stiff upper lip, and the great outdoors), Locke championed Aesop's fables. That advocacy would shape the nature of America's literary offerings to juveniles.

In *A New Gift for Children* (ca. 1750)—perhaps America's first secular storybook—the author, "Mary Homebred," tacitly acknowledges Locke's ideas in her Introduction and goes on to tell such tales as:

- "The Good Boy," in which the virtuous Billy Manley pleads for mercy for a bad boy who tried to harass him, and so impresses the bad boy that the latter reforms.

- "A Good Girl," about Miss Polly, who gives money to a stranger who, fortunately, saves her from a mad dog later in the day.

- "The Undutiful Child," who falls through the ice and drowns because he made a habit of ignoring his father's warnings.

- "The Lost Child," who parades through the town to show off his new clothes and is kidnapped by villains and brought home naked.[3]

Like Aesop's tales, these secular stories are forcefully didactic. But what is also striking is the shortening of the span of justice to Aesopian dimensions. In the absence of heaven and hell, America's literary children reap what they have sown only a few hours later. When George snubs a poor boy in the morning in *The Grateful Return* (1796), for example, he cannot share in the gift the boy brings that afternoon. "You should have recollected," his brother tells him, "the Fable you read this morning of the Mouse that released the Lion from the net."[4]

American Children's Literature in the first half of the nineteenth century continued in this didactic fashion in Parson Weems's *The Life of Washington the Great* (1806), Samuel Griswold Goodrich's "Peter Parley" books (1828–1856), Lydia Maria Child's *The Girl's Own Book* (1831), and Jacob Abbott's "Rollo" series (1835–1840). The genre reached its acme by mid-century in the Sunday school books (cheap volumes offered by such organizations as the American Sunday School Union and the American Tract

Society) by means of which countless Americans learned to both read and be good. As Anne Scott MacLeod has observed, these books consisted of "innumerable small tales of temptation resisted, anger restrained, disobedience punished, and forbearance learned."[5] In these, too, justice is swift and does not wait for the afterlife: boys who fail to go to church on Sunday morning are struck by lightning in the afternoon; and those who climb trees to steal apples inevitably fall and break their arms.

It was not long before the simple-mindedness of this quid pro quo morality was recognized. Experience as old as Job's indicated that, often enough, the wicked *do* prosper and the good *do* go unrewarded. But there was something else wrong with these tales. In the mid-1850s, Oliver Wendell Holmes would complain that even their language seemed unreal: "James was called *Jem*, not *Jim*, as we heard it; . . . naughty schoolboys [stole] 'Farmer Gile's red-streaks,' instead of apples."[6]

Apparently having read his Holmes, Clemens, just a few years later in 1865, wrote a magazine article meant to parody the Sunday school tale. He called it "The Story of the Bad Little Boy":

> Once there was a bad little boy whose name was Jim—though, if you will notice, bad little boys are always called James in your Sunday-school books. . . . Everything about this boy was curious—everything turned out differently with him from the way it does to the bad Jameses in the books. [He stole apples from a farmer but did not fall from the tree and break his arm. He did not confess to his crime when the teacher punished the wrong boy, and he did not feel guilty. He went boating on Sunday but was not struck by lightning.] He ran off and went to sea at last, and didn't come back and find himself sad and alone in the world, his loved ones sleeping in the quiet churchyard, and the vine-embowered home of his boyhood tumbled down and gone to decay. Ah! no; he came home as drunk as a piper . . . got wealthy by all manner of cheating and rascality . . . and is universally respected, and belongs to the Legislature. So you see there never was a bad James in the Sunday-school books that had such a streak of luck as this sinful Jim with the charmed life.[7]

In a companion piece, Clemens wrote "The Story of a Good Little Boy," in which a dutiful child has a hard time of it, and again nothing comes out the way it does in Sunday school books.

Both essays were sent to the *Atlantic Monthly,* but William Dean Howells returned them, saying it would cost the magazine too many subscriptions among God-fearing folk if he were to publish them. But Howells may have had another reason for rejecting them. This time Mark Twain had misfired. As a parody of the Sunday school story, the essays were unsophisticated, too simple and obvious. But Clemens like the idea and kept it in mind until, five years later, he apparently found a clue in another author's book that suggested how the parody might be handled better.

In 1870 Clemens's Hartford neighbor Thomas Bailey Aldrich published *The Story of a Bad Boy.* Aldrich gave his book that title, he explained in its opening pages, so that it wouldn't be confused with that kind of account of boyhood with which most of his readers would be familiar, the Sunday school tale of the Good Boy:

> I call my story the story of a bad boy, partly to distinguish myself from those faultless young gentlemen who generally figure in narratives of this kind, and partly because I was really *not* a cherub. I may truthfully say I was an amiable, impulsive lad, blessed with fine digestive powers, and no hypocrite. I did not want to be an angel and with the angels stand; I did not think the missionary tracts presented to me by the Rev. Wibird Hawkins were half so nice as Robinson Crusoe; and I failed to send my little pocket money to the natives of the Feejee Islands, but spent it royally in peppermint-drops and taffy candy. In short, I was a real human boy.

From Aldrich's book Clemens seems to have taken away the idea that his own parody of the Sunday school story would have been all the better if he had presented a Bad Boy who was not so much a nascent criminal as (to use Aldrich's synonym) "a real human boy"—that is, a rascal, a mischief maker, a red-blooded kid with a little spunk, the kind given to tipping over outhouses. The result was the publication of *The Adventures of Tom Sawyer.*

Clemens makes clear that Tom is not a Good Boy like his tattling half-brother Sid, the mama's boy Willie Mufferson, or the German youth who memorized the entire Bible and became brain-damaged. Instead, *Tom Sawyer* celebrates the Bad Boy and turns the Sunday school book on its head. It is an admiring portrait of a boy who plays hooky, upsets church services, plagues adults with pranks, and engages in other forms of misbehavior. And unlike the conclusion of the Sunday school book, by the end of the novel this miscreant is universally admired and wealthy to boot.[8]

But Clemens's lampoon of earlier American Children's Literature does not stop with this simple parody of the Good Child–Bad Child stories. Its ridicule is far more comprehensive.

The Pale Martyr

Besides the Aesopian tale with its story of the Good and the Bad, the other major and longer-lived tradition in American children's books before the publication of *Tom Sawyer* might be described—to use the title of a work often reprinted in *The New England Primer*—as "Martyrology." This genre's origins are to be found in Protestant works for children in the eighteenth century, with their familiar deathbed scenes of juvenile saints taken too soon from this world.[9]

The pattern was established in the first work published in America directly intended for the young: Cotton Mather's *A Token for the Children of New England; or some Examples of Children in whom the Fear of God was remarkably budding before they dyed: in several parts of New England* (1700). Whether the subject is five-year-old Ann Greenough or two-and-a-half-year-old Elizabeth Butcher, Mather's ten biographies tell virtually the same story, a recurring scene that might be described as the "Protestant Pietà": In the sickroom, a child is dying. After godly instruction, the child recognizes its sinful condition and, with much wailing and tears, secret fasting and hours of prayer, finally expresses the wish to leave carnal life behind. After issuing advice to the adults and children huddled around the bed, this commendable child dies. Those who have witnessed the child's passing are smitten with admiration and filled with remorse that their own lives do not compare favorably with that of their puerile exemplar.

Mather's book was like countless others printed in America or imported from England and used by Puritan parents to educate their children. The Quakers of Philadelphia, perhaps to prove that New England and the Puritans had no monopoly on youthful sanctity, published in 1717 another book that may be said to be representative: *A Legacy for Children; Last Words and Dyeing Expressions of Hannah Hill, aged 11 years and near three months*. Hannah's story is a familiar one: her illness, her contrition, her "grave and pithy counsel" to the living, and her ability to inspire regrets and remorse in all those around her deathbed who have not been as zealous as this child in securing their salvation. Hannah was also blessed with the dubious talent of never being able to say something simply when a poetic or quasi-scriptural phrase would serve; in her sickbed, for example, she does not simply wish to die but proclaims, "Oh! that the Messenger would come! That my glass was run!" In retrospect, Hannah's stylistic gifts recall those of a character who would appear some years later in *Huckleberry Finn*—Emmeline Grangerford, the fifteen-year-old who wrote poems with such titles as "Shall I Never See Thee More Alas" and "Art Thou Gone Yes Thou Art Gone Alas." Indeed, by the end of *A Legacy*, a modern-day reader may come to the same conclusion about the young Quaker that Huck comes to about Emmeline Grangerford: "Everybody was sorry she died, . . . but I reckon with her disposition, she was having a better time in the graveyard."

By 1860, Oliver Wendell Holmes had had enough of these kinds of stories and their offspring. In *The Professor at the Breakfast-Table*, he looked back at American Children's Literature and observed:

> There have been many interesting children . . . who have shown a wonderful indifference to the things of earth and an extraordinary development of the spiritual nature. There is a perfect literature of their biographies, all alike in their essentials: the same "disinclination to the usual amusements of childhood," the same conscientiousness, in short, an almost uniform character, marked by beautiful traits, which we look at with pained admiration. It will be found that most of the children are the subjects of some constitutional unfitness for living. . . . I am convinced that many healthy children are injured morally by being forced to read too much about these little meek sufferers and their spiritual exercises. Here is a boy that loves to run, swim, kick football, turn somersets, make faces, whittle, fish, tear his clothes, coast, skate, fire crackers, . . . cut his name in fences, read about Robinson Crusoe and Sinbad the Sailor, . . . "stick" knives, call names, throw stones, knock off hats, set mousetraps, chalk doorsteps . . . —isn't that a pretty nice sort of boy? . . . Now, when you put into such a hot-blooded, hard-fisted, round-cheeked little rogue's hand a sad-looking volume or pamphlet, with the portrait of a thin, white-faced child,

whose life is really as much a training for death as the last month
of a condemned criminal's existence, what does he find in common between his own overflowing and exulting sense of vitality
and the experiences of the doomed offspring of invalid parents?
The time comes when we have learned to understand the music
of sorrow, the beauty of resigned suffering, the holy light that
plays over the pillow of those who die before their time, in
humble hope and trust. But it is not until he has worked his way
through the period of honest, hearty animal existence, which
every robust child should make the most of, not until he has
learned the use of his various faculties, which is his first duty,
that a boy of courage and animal vigor is in a proper state to read
these tearful accounts of premature decay. I have no doubt that
disgust is implanted in the minds of many healthy children by
early surfeits of pathological piety. I do verily believe that He
who took children into His arms and blessed them loved the
healthiest and most playful of them as well as those who were
richest in the tuberculous virtues. [10]

Implicit in Holmes's comments are two views of the American child. One—the "thin, white-faced" sufferer, unfit for living,
conscientious, an example of "premature decay"—is the older figure, with a history that runs from its origin in Puritan juvenile literature to its apotheosis in frail Beth March of *Little
Women*. The other—ordinary, healthy, "hot-blooded [and] round-
cheeked," full of robust vitality and "hearty animal existence,"
inclined to knock off hats and chalk doorways and shoot
firecrackers—represents a countertradition best exemplified by
Tom Sawyer.

Something else should be said about these two figures. While
Tom is the hearty and robust child whom Holmes describes, the
humor of Clemens's novel rests in Tom's attempts to appear to be
the other kind, the white-faced sufferer. Or, to say this differently,
Tom Sawyer wishes to be Beth March.

Tom often tries to re-create the Protestant Pietà. He likes to
imagine himself the pale martyr, to arrange deathbed scenes, to see
others filled with regrets and remorse when they think of his passing. Clemens means for us to chuckle about all this. And it *is*
amusing to watch Tom arrange to be both "dead" and yet alive
enough to see how badly he is missed, to watch his strenuous

activities to enlist all of St. Petersburg in his Quixote-like attempt to replicate the familiar and funereal scenes of earlier Children's Literature.

Tom Sawyer should be seen, then, as elaboration on Holmes's denunciation of earlier children's stories. It is an effort to carry to comic excesses Holmes's criticism of the figure of the literary child as pallid sufferer.

An Atmosphere Thick with Remorse and Regret

The brave though trembling chin, the artfully timed tear trickling down the pale cheek—I loved [stories] about woebegone waifs. I yearned to be poor. Poor, and an orphan. Mistreated, misunderstood; an innocent . . . victim, set upon by fate and misfortune, . . . immobile in a bed of pain, commanding the undivided attention of friends and family, who would gather around, sobbing, I expected, and beg my forgiveness for the slights and wrongs they had inflicted on me in the past.

Lois Lowry, Afterword to *Pollyanna*

Tom Sawyer amusingly treats a familiar childhood sentiment: that kind of exaggerated self-pity which leads children to imagine themselves as aggrieved victims; that kind of melodramatic self-indulgence which results in daydreams of "What if I died? How would they feel *then?*" This is self-righteousness. This is the stuff of tear-jerking Pietàs.

Consider, for example, the occasion when Tom's half-brother Sid has broken a sugar bowl and Aunt Polly, presuming she knows the culprit, mistakenly gives Tom a rap with her knuckles. When Aunt Polly learns of her error, she is filled with regret: "Then her conscience reproached her, and she yearned to say something kind and loving; but she judged that this would be construed into a confession that she had been in the wrong, and discipline forbade that. So she kept silence, and went about her affairs with a troubled heart."[11]

Tom, for his part, wallows in self-pity. He enjoys the theatrical gorgeousness of being a martyr:

> Tom sulked in a corner and exalted his woes. He knew that in her heart his aunt was on her knees to him, and he was morosely gratified by the consciousness of it. He would hang out no signals, he would take notice of none. He knew that a yearning glance fell upon him, now and then, through a film of tears, but he refused recognition of it. He pictured himself lying sick unto death and his aunt bending over him beseeching one little forgiving word, but he would turn his face to the wall, and die with that word unsaid. Ah, how would she feel then? (22)

Clemens himself finds this romantic posturing—Tom's righteously imagined Pietà—quite amusing. This becomes clear as he continues with his description of Tom's aggrieved state:

> [Tom] pictured himself brought home from the river, dead, with his curls all wet, and his sore heart at rest. How [Aunt Polly] would throw herself upon him, and how her tears would fall like rain, and her lips pray God to give her back her boy and she would never, never abuse him any more! But he would lie there cold and white and make no sign—a poor little sufferer, whose griefs were at an end. He so worked upon his feelings with the pathos of those dreams, that he had to keep swallowing, he was so like to choke; and his eyes swam in a blur of water, which overflowed when he winked, and ran down and trickled from the end of his nose. And such a luxury to him was this petting of his sorrows, that he could not bear to have any worldly cheeriness or any grating delight intrude upon it; it was too sacred for such contact; and so, presently, when his cousin Mary danced in, all alive with the joy of seeing home again after an agelong visit of one week to the country, he got up and moved in clouds and darkness out at one door as she brought song and sunshine in at the other. (22–23)

There are other moments in the novel when Tom luxuriates in this kind of self-pity. When Becky Thatcher finds out about Tom's former girlfriend, she jilts him. Tom feels this is an injustice. Again, he is the stylish martyr. Choosing the graveyard as the ideal locale, he broods about his mistreatment:

> The boy's soul was steeped in melancholy. . . . It seemed to him that life was but a trouble, at best, and he more than half

envied Jimmy Hodges, so lately released [into death]. . . .
Now as to this girl. What had he done? Nothing. He had meant
the best in the world, and been treated like a dog—like a very
dog. She would be sorry some day—maybe when it was too late.
Ah, if he could only die *temporarily!* . . . What if he turned
his back, now, and disappeared mysteriously? What if he went
away—ever so far away, into unknown countries beyond the
seas—and never came back any more! How would she feel then!
(63–64)

Clemens means for us to be amused by this, too. Having
dismissed death as regrettably impractical, Tom opts for this other
gambit, the equivalent of the French Foreign Legion. Then, in an
extravagantly romantic departure—after "'looking his last' upon
the scene of his former joys and his later sufferings, and wishing
'she' could see him now . . . going to his doom with a grim
smile on his lips" (102)—Tom runs away. He becomes a pirate
and, with Joe Harper and Huck Finn, travels "ever so far away, into
unknown countries beyond the seas." This is, of course, contrived
melodrama: Tom takes a raft out into the Mississippi to Jackson's
Island, a few miles from home.

But then, in a wonderful turn of events, Tom *does* get his wish
"to die temporarily." After he and his companions journey to the
island and are missing for a few days, the townspeople conclude the
boys have drowned. From their hideout, Tom and his friends curiously watch a steamboat searching the river for corpses. Then it
occurs to Tom: "Boys, I know who's drownded—it's us!" This
delights Tom: "Here was a gorgeous triumph; they were missed;
they were mourned; hearts were breaking on their account; tears
were being shed; accusing memories of unkindnesses to these poor
lost lads were rising up, and unavailing regrets and remorse were
being indulged. . . . This was fine" (111).

This passage is a revelation of Tom's hopes throughout the
novel. Here, too, is the desired answer to the righteous question
put twice in the book: "How would she feel then?" To Tom Sawyer, a "gorgeous triumph" occurs when others think about him and
are smitten by "accusing memories" and filled with "unavailing
regrets and remorse."

Milking his "death" for all it is worth, Tom, once he realizes
that he is presumed drowned, swims ashore, returns home, con-

ceals himself, and listens to find out how badly he is missed. He is pleased to learn that Aunt Polly is heartsick, can only remember the times she mistakenly disciplined him, and rues all her missed opportunities to have done otherwise.[12] Tom's "death" has a similar effect on Becky Thatcher. She berates herself for having jilted him: "Oh, if it was to do over again. . . . But he's gone now; I'll never never never see him any more" (129). Even more important, when he returns, Becky comes to him and "with shame and repentance" admits her mistreatment of him (152). Tom basks in such occasions.

When the town arranges a funeral for the "drowned" boys, Tom is provided with another opportunity to see "how they would feel then." With his friends, he sneaks back into town and hides in the choir loft to hear the eulogies. He is pleased. The minister so works upon the feelings of the congregation with memories of the lost children that their acts of mischief, which had annoyed so many, are now put in a new light and come to be regarded as episodes of nobility. Whitewashed in this fashion, the boys are now seen as departed angels who were not valued enough during their lifetimes, and the congregation is filled with "unavailing regrets

"The Mourner." True W. Williams for *The Adventures of Tom Sawyer* (Hartford: American Publishing, 1876).

and remorse." This is Tom's very definition of a "gorgeous triumph."

This constant evocation of tableaus of belated contrition is the emotional center of Clemens's novel. For the most part, these episodes are amusing.[13] Clemens means for us to chuckle at Tom's cleverness in imagining or contriving scenes in which he is the martyred innocent and others are guilt-stricken. For example, when Aunt Polly is concerned about Tom's listlessness, she regularly gives him a patent medicine called Painkiller, described as "simply fire in a liquid form." One day, she finds the boy giving a dose of the medicine to the family cat, which tears around the house, somersaults, and jumps out the open window. Aunt Polly asks Tom, "Now, sir, what did you want to treat that poor dumb beast so, for?" He cleverly gets off the hook by explaining:

> "I done it out of pity for him—because he hadn't any aunt."
>
> "Hadn't any aunt!—you numbskull. What has that got to do with it?"
>
> "Heaps. Because if he'd a had one she'd a burnt him out herself! She'd roasted his bowels out of him 'thout any more feeling than if he was a human!"
>
> Aunt Polly felt a sudden pang of remorse. This was putting things in a new light; what was cruelty to a cat *might* be cruelty to a boy, too. She began to soften; she felt sorry. Her eyes watered a little, and she put her hand on Tom's head and said gently:
>
> "I was meaning for the best, Tom." (94–96)

And there he has her! She is put in the wrong, and the air grows thick with her self-reproach.

These emotions and sentiments, then, are the subjects of Clemens's novel. In *Tom Sawyer* we enter the Theater of Feelings and see, for the most part, a comedy that (like Oliver Wendell Holmes) pokes fun at the pallid sufferers of earlier American Children's Literature, the aggrieved child who is the center of attention in an atmosphere thick with remorse and regret. This same world—of the pathetic child and the Pietà, of the wronged and the guilt-stricken—appears in *Little Women,* but there it is taken seriously.

8

✤ ✤ ✤ ✤ ✤ ✤ ✤
Bosom Enemies
Little Women

Louisa May Alcott's life was irrevocably changed when she assented to publisher Thomas Niles's request that she write a book for girls. As Madeline Stern has observed, the publication of the book in 1868 was the pinnacle of the author's life, dividing it in two parts, before and after *Little Women*.[1] As Alcott said, her story of the March sisters was her "truest" work and its success was due to the "use of real life & one own's experience": "Many of the things in my story truly happened, and much of *Little Women* is a reflection of the life led by us sisters. I am 'Jo.'"[2]

In this sense, her subsequent work was less "true," a concatenation of fiction and compromises required by her publisher. This is the case with *Good Wives* (also known as *Little Women* Part II), a sequel unanticipated in the writing of the first part, in which literary spinster Louisa May Alcott sold out and had Jo marry because "publishers won't let authors finish up as they like but insist on having people married off in a wholesale manner which much afflicts me [because] 'Jo' should have remained a literary spinster."[3] Even the recent discovery of many of the gothic thrillers and melodramatic potboilers that Alcott wrote under a pseudonym, despite the subsequent critical hoopla over the fact that the "hidden" Alcott had been found,[4] does not make her masterpiece *Little Women* (Part I) less true.

Besides being faithful to real-life events and circumstances, *Little Women* is psychologically true, an accurate reflection of its author. Alcott's sister Anna once confided to her journal what she felt was the touchstone of Louisa's personality: she "always seems to feel the moment she is having a good time that she is doing wrong and that her duty in life consists in doing exactly what she doesn't wish to do."[5] This sense of wrongness is everywhere in this remorseful book, and is most often associated with feelings.

In her story of the March sisters, Alcott takes as her subject the control of "wrong" feelings or negative emotions—anger, envy, shyness, and the like. This theme is established in the novel's opening words, which contrast the wrong attitudes of three of the March sisters with the right attitude of Beth:

> "Christmas won't be Christmas without any presents," *grumbled* Jo. . . .
> "It's so dreadful to be poor!" *sighed* Meg. . . .
> "I don't think it's fair for some girls to have plenty of pretty things, and other girls have nothing at all," added little Amy, with an *injured* sniff.
> "We've got a father and mother and each other," said Beth *contentedly*.[6]

The other sisters know that Beth's disposition is the correct one. They often know what they *should* feel, yet they confess that they feel otherwise. As the story continues, for example, Meg notes, "We can make our little sacrifices, and ought to do it gladly. But I'm afraid I don't" (11). Jo says, "It's naughty to fret; but I do think washing dishes and keeping things tidy is the worst work in the world" (12). And although Jo knows she should act in a more proper fashion now that she is becoming a young lady, she insists that she won't and adds, "I hate to think I have to grow up" (13). Even though they consider these attitudes wrong, the March sisters admit they are their own.

There is another impulse in *Little Women* that runs opposite these moments of guilty self-assertion: an impulse toward self-denial. It is introduced in the first chapter when the girls receive a letter from their father, who is away with the troops in the Civil War. He urges self-abnegation, encouraging them in another form of internecine warfare by asking them to master their personality faults: to "do their duty faithfully, fight their bosom enemies bravely, and conquer themselves so beautifully that when I come back to them I may be fonder and prouder than ever of my little women" (20). In this way, then, the stage is set in the Theater of Feelings: pitting guilty individuality against the ideal of self-denial.

Their father's letter prompts a bout of public confession. Like a cell meeting in Red China, each girl admits to her own "bosom enemy" and makes resolutions. Amy says, "I *am* a selfish girl! but I'll truly try to be better, so he mayn't be disappointed in me." Meg admits, "I think too much of my looks and hate to work, but won't anymore, if I can help it." Thinking about her tomboy nature, Jo resolves, "I'll try and be what he loves to call me, 'a little woman,' and not be rough and wild." And even Beth, who seems without a fault, determines to mend her own shortcomings, which lie "in envying girls with nice pianos, and being afraid of people" (21–23). In this condition of contrition, in this atmosphere of self-reproach, the melodrama of *Little Women* unfolds.

Why Jo Has Her Hair Cut

If the most famous scene in *Hans Brinker* is the one in which the little Dutch boy sticks his finger in the leaking dike, if the most famous scene in *Tom Sawyer* is the whitewashing of the fence, the most famous scene in *Little Women* (readers seem to agree) is the one in which Jo has her hair cut.[7] Once we understand this emblematic episode, we can understand much about Alcott's novel.

A telegram arrives from a Washington hospital: "Mrs. March:. Your husband is very ill. Come at once." While others fall into a frenzy of activity to ready Marmee for her departure, Jo goes to a shop that buys hair. She offers her "mane," her "one beauty," and brings home $25 as "my contribution towards making Father comfortable, and bringing him home" (210).

As Madelon Bedell suggests, the scene is tremendously complex, "too richly suggestive to yield up a single meaning."[8] We can begin to understand it, however, by noticing that while Jo's act is dramatic, it serves no direct purpose. Her mother tells her twice that "there was no need of this" and that "it was not necessary" (211). And, in fact, the money is not used; her father brings it back

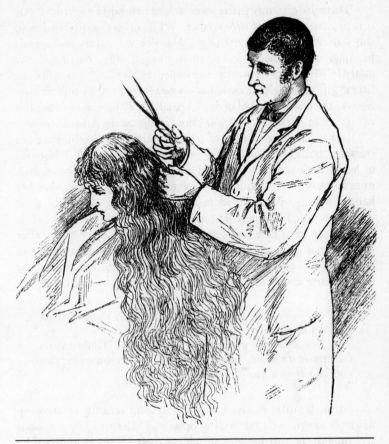

Frank T. Merrill for *Little Women* (Boston: Roberts Brothers, 1869).

with him (286). In other words, Jo's sacrifice, while touching, is largely an extravagant and gratuitous gesture.

Its extravagance is evident when, by means of hyperbole, Jo melodramatically likens her haircut to mutilation. In terms reminiscent of Tom Sawyer's exaggerated visions of himself as a martyr, Jo seems to imagine herself as a wounded soldier who has sacrificed his body to the cause: "I felt queer when I saw the dear old hair laid out on the table. . . . It almost seemed as if I'd an arm or leg off" (214). Even if readers are sympathetically disposed to accept Jo's pathetic portrait of herself, what can't be forgotten is that this "wound" was not only unnecessary but self-inflicted.

There are certainly many motivations behind Jo's gesture,[9] but it is primarily an act of *self*-sacrifice. While others' contributions to the war effort involve time (e.g., Marmee volunteers and spends her days making bandages) or money (e.g., Meg contributes her salary to pay the rent now that her father is absent), Jo's sacrifice is a literal gift of herself. If Bedell is on target when she observes that hair is "the classic symbol of one's sexuality,"[10] we can add that Jo's neutering of herself for the war effort is almost an Amazonian act.

Her act is also a sacrifice of self in another war. Jo thinks of her tresses as both her "one beauty" and her "bosom enemy." Mindful of her father's advice to his daughters (to "fight their bosom enemies bravely, and conquer themselves"), she rationalizes that her haircut will provide an antidote to her selfishness: "It will be good for my vanity; I was getting too proud of my wig" (211).

But the scene does not quite end there. Later in the night, after everyone has gone to bed, Meg hears muffled sobbing and asks Jo whether she is crying about her father. Jo says, guiltily, that she is not thinking about him, but about herself. She is crying because of

> "My—my hair!" burst out Jo, trying vainly to smother her emotion in her pillow. . . .
> "I'm not sorry," protested Jo, with a choke. "I'd do it again tomorrow, if I could. It's only the vain, selfish part of me that goes and cries in this silly way." (215)

So the familiar situation of *Little Women* returns: of knowing what one *should* feel, but feeling otherwise. Despite Jo's strenuous attempts to conquer herself and achieve the selflessness idealized by her father, in the end guilty individualism resurfaces. The child who has sacrificed her "one beauty" still feels bad about being less than completely willing to do so. In the midst of all this self-effacement, in other words, there still appears the damnable "selfish part," which is so confoundedly contrary and recalcitrant in its unwillingness to completely sacrifice itself for its Maker.

Here is the familiar and central emotional state of *Little Women*. What we see is a *mentalité* that Hegel called the "Contrite Consciousness," a "mindset" that is conflicted, both dualistic and idealistic.[11] On the one hand is the Fickle Self sicklied o'er with selfish individuality; hence Jo's condemnation of the "vain, selfish part of me." On the other hand is the Absent Ideal of selflessness, a selflessness approved of by the March girls' Absent Father. The Contrite Consciousness, Hegel observes, is an acute awareness of the discrepancy between these two, and it issues in the kind of persistent self-criticism and constant awareness of faults evident in Jo's and her sisters' frequent condemnation of themselves and their "bosom enemies." As that last phrase suggests, in Alcott's novel we see another kind of Civil War: the self at war with the self.

As Hegel observes, the only way to win this kind of war is, paradoxically, to lose. To move toward the ideal of selflessness is to make the self into naught. But herein lies the contradiction: if the self, itself, is used as the engine of deliverance, every conscious or deliberate attempt at self-negation brings fresh evidence of the individuality that is abhorred.

This is precisely the double bind in which Jo finds herself. *She* chooses to have her hair cut. *She* engages in self-mutilation. *She* is a self-made martyr making glamorous but gratuitous gestures of self-effacement. For this reason, in the midst of all her self-abnegation, the damnable "selfish part" still arises. There is no repose. In this irresolvable and remorseful agon, the girl constantly condemns herself as "wrong"—as Alcott, according to her sister, often condemned herself.

Deliverance from this double bind *is* possible, but it must come from outside. If victory comes from being vanquished, if selflessness is achieved by making the self into naught, the self must be humbled not by itself in extravagant acts of self-martyrdom, but my circumstances apart from it. And so, in *Little Women,* humbling circumstances are welcome—even invited.

Humbling Circumstances

The Alcott family seems to have always been impressed by the New Testament notion that the exalted shall be humbled and the humble exalted. They welcomed poverty and criticism and mischance as proof of their righteousness, or in anticipation of the eventual turning of the tables. Reading about their lives, one finds it difficult to escape the conclusion that—in following to its ultimate

conclusion the notion that the first shall be last and the last shall be
first—they were sometimes engaged in a pell-mell race for last
place.

To a certain extent, this attitude came from the head of the
household. Bronson Alcott was a famous minister-cum-philosopher
who often mistook his eccentricities for high-minded principles
and whose principled stands often reduced the family to an abject
poverty in which they depended on handouts and loans from friends
and relatives. Ralph Waldo Emerson lived nearby and was frequently obliged to help the Alcotts. Emerson sized up his hard-
luck and righteously idealistic neighbor by noting that Alcott
never considered the possibility that he was wrong, but "took his
rejection by this world as proof of his popularity in the next."[12]

Implicit here—and everywhere evident in *Little Women*—is a
doctrine of paradoxicality. The last and the first exchange places;
humiliation is welcome as a prelude to eventual exaltation; wealth
and happiness are inversely proportionate. *Little Women* is full of
inverse ratios. There may be no other book in the world so full of
the language of contraries:

> It was a comfortable old room, *though* the carpet was faded and
> the furniture very plain. (14)

> She was not elegantly dressed, *but* a noble-looking woman. (18)

> It was uninteresting sewing tonight, *but* no one grumbled. (23)

> "I don't believe fine young ladies enjoy themselves a bit more
> than we do, *in spite of* our burnt hair, old gowns, one glove
> apiece, and tight slippers." (51)

> Each tried to be cheerful *in spite of* wintry weather. (55)

> "*Though* she was poor, she was a great deal happier." (66)

> On the other side was a stately stone mansion, plainly betoken-
> ing every sort of comfort and luxury. . . . *Yet* it seemed a
> lonely, lifeless sort of house. (67–68)

> "They will have a hard time, I'm afraid; *but* . . . it will do
> them good." (147)

If the humble shall be exalted, then, by this law of contraries,
we can say that Alcott's March family is fortunate to be impoverished. But what is more important is the other side of this doc-

trine of paradoxicality. If the exalted shall be humbled, then the Marches are also fortunate to encounter one degrading episode after another, and they welcome these humiliations when they occur. For example:

- Amy goes through her "Valley of Humiliation" when she is caught misbehaving at school and publicly shamed. But this humbling does her good.

- At the Moffats' party, Meg behaves in a way that makes her ashamed when she later confesses her errors to her mother.

- When Marmee is dejected because her husband is away at the war, she chances to meet a man who gave four sons to the army (two have been killed, another is a prisoner, another sick). This meeting puts Marmee in the wrong, and she is grateful: "He spoke so cheerfully, looked so sincere, and seemed so glad to give his all, that I was ashamed of myself. I'd given one man, and thought it too much, while he gave four without grudging them. . . . [I] gave him some money, and thanked him heartily for the lesson he had taught me" (65).

Alcott is always contriving events like these to put her characters in the wrong. In this, she does something different from Clemens in *Tom Sawyer*. In Clemens's novel, humor arises from Tom's contrivances to create situations that put others in the wrong, to create Pietàs in which others are smitten with remorse and regret. In *Little Women*, the author, herself, contrives these occasions, and there is nothing comically contrived about the guilt-inducing Pietàs she presents. Henry James, in fact, reckoned this a fatal habit of Alcott when he reviewed her first novel, *Moods*, and complained about the facile way she has her heroine "put her husband and everyone else in the wrong by dying the death of the righteous."[13]

This willful perversity is also present in *Little Women*. If Dickens is always accused of inventing incredible coincidences that work to the benefit of his heroes, Alcott might be accused of always contriving coincidences that pull the rug out from underneath her characters to leave them abject:

- When Jo's writing begins to appear in the newspaper and she becomes reasonably proud of her success, Beth suddenly falls ill and Jo is pulled down from the heights and humbled. Beth, alone, has gone and cared for the Hummels' sick baby and contracts scarlet fever. This puts Jo in the wrong, and she reproaches herself for being a "selfish pig, to let you go, and stay writing rubbish by myself" (230).

- When Mrs. March is, reasonably, despondent because of her husband's absence, a man happens along who has sacrificed more. Her melancholy now seems self-indulgence.

- When the girls are feeling disagreeable and irritated on a gloomy November day, by chance a telegram arrives from Washington saying that their father is gravely ill. Their moodiness is made to look shabby.

- When Amy destroys the only copy of a book of stories that Jo has been writing for years, Jo is, reasonably, angry. But then Amy falls through the ice, nearly drowns, and is brought home and put to bed. This "accident" creates the familiar Pietà, the deathbed scene of the expiring ephebe that leaves all those gathered around in the wrong and filled with remorse and regret: "'If she should die, it would be my fault,' Jo [said, as she] dropped down beside the bed, in a passion of penitent tears, telling all that happened, bitterly condemning her hardness of heart" (109).

These are only some of the incredible coincidences and instances of bad luck that befall the members of this hapless family. Even in happier circumstances, Alcott hunts for and delivers the cloud in every silver lining that ensures that her characters will be left miserable:

- After the girls have sacrificed their Christmas dinner to a poor family, they are rewarded by Mr. Laurence, who sends ice cream over to their house. But just as they are about to sit down to enjoy this rare treat, they start to feel guilty and sad as they remember that their father is at the front and not enjoying such luxuries.

This dizzying array of humbling episodes reveals a wonderworking author relentlessly intent on arranging events so that they end on the downbeat, so that her characters are beaten down and abased. What motivates this?

Certainly the abundance of unfortunate coincidences and occasions for heartache makes more touching this melodrama, which Alcott once thought of titling "The Pathetic Family." Certainly, too, this compulsion to abase her characters reflects the neurotic nature of an author who—to recall again her sister's observation—"always seems to feel the moment she is having a good time that she is doing wrong and that her duty in life consists in doing exactly what she doesn't wish to do." But perhaps this impulse to denigration is best understood as the logical consequence of the doctrine of paradoxicality and Alcott's modification of her Protestant heritage.

If the last shall be first, if the humble shall be exalted, then abjectness becomes a desirable condition. If victory comes through being vanquished, if the ideal of selflessness is achieved by making the self into naught, then martyring circumstances are welcome—or, in the case of Jo's sacrificial haircut, deliberately sought.

While not exclusively religious,[14] this *mentalité* has a long tradition in Protestant thought. It may have been best articulated in Luther's comment on Paul's Epistle to the Romans, when Luther speculates about Paul's and God's intentions:

> The whole purpose of the apostle, as of his Lord, is to humble the proud, to teach them their need of grace, to destroy their own justice, and drive them in humility to Christ, that they may confess themselves sinners, receive grace and be saved. . . . Unless a man learns to listen freely to that which goes against him, unless he rejoices to have his own intent thwarted and reproved, . . . he cannot be saved. . . . Therefore to be despised, reviled and rejected is the way of security.[15]

This notion (that occasions for denigration should be welcomed) is implicit everywhere in Alcott's novel, in which opportunities to be thwarted and humbled abound and are relished. Still, we should understand that in Alcott's novel these occasions serve no religious purpose. Instead, *Little Women* secularizes this *mentalité* and enlists humbling circumstances not as a means to salvation, but as goads to character formation.

Little Women is a secularized book, as if *Pilgrim's Progress* had been rewritten by a modern-day counselor for girls.[16] Instead of sin and the wiles of Satan, the March sisters battle negative emotions—anger, envy, pride, vanity, and the like. Instead of salvation, the book concerns maturation and character growth. Instead of morality, Alcott's subject is personality. And instead of Christ, we have (as one critic has observed) the girls' almost heavenly Father, whose approval they seek.[17]

The result is a remorseful book, an inner melodrama taking place entirely within the Theater of Feelings. To understand Alcott's intentions in *Little Women,* then, we need only rephrase Luther's remarks in secular terms: For Alcott, the whole purpose of an author is to contrive situations to humble her characters, to destroy their righteousness, that they may confess themselves in the wrong, mend their ways, and thereby conquer their "bosom enemies," so that, ultimately, they may be worthy of their father's praise when he calls them "little women."

9

✣ ✣ ✣ ✣ ✣ ✣ ✣
Bread and Circuses
Toby Tyler

One of the many chastening moments in *Little Women* occurs when Amy falls through the ice. Angry at her sister for having destroyed her prized book of writings, Jo has not paid attention to her sibling's safety, and Amy nearly drowns. What follows is a *Tom Sawyer*–like Pietà. At her sister's bedside, worried that Amy may die, Jo is filled with remorse and bitterly condemns her "bosom enemy," her anger, which brought this to pass.

Jo turns to her mother for advice about how she can "conquer" this fault, "control" it, "check" her bosom enemy (109–13). Her mother confesses that for forty years she, too, has been troubled by this problem of anger but that she has learned to repress that emotion under the wise tutelage of her husband, who secretly signals when she is in danger by putting a finger to his lips. At that moment, both Pietà and lesson in repression, Jo learns "not only the bitterness of remorse and despair, but the sweetness of self-denial and self-control" (113).

That gesture of putting a finger to the lips provides a good symbol of the subject of *Toby Tyler, or Ten Weeks with a Circus* by James Otis Kaler (writing under the pseudonym James Otis). Its subject is repression, self-denial, self-control. But instead of anger or some other glamorous emotion contested in the Theater of Feelings, the "bosom enemy" of Kaler's novel is one of the most elemental: hunger.

Toby Tyler is a book obsessively devoted to hunger. Toby says about himself: "I'm an awful eater, an' I can't seem to help it. Somehow I'm hungry all the time."[1] And that seems to be the case. On nearly every other page, mention is made of Toby's prodigious feats at the dinner table, his gargantuan appetite, the menu of his meals, his strategies for being first in the eating line, his hunger pangs and anxieties about starving. His best friends in the circus company are, notably, the Fat Woman and her husband, the Living Skeleton. With surprising frequency, conversations deal with the problems of and cures for choking or stomach aches brought on by overeating, or with the mysteries of why some people who eat a great deal remain thin and why others who eat little still grow fat.

What accounts for this obsession? Bernard Wishy has detailed the special concern of nineteenth-century American pediatrics with the connection between virtue and food.[2] Other American children's books of this period also described juvenile miscreants in terms of their eating habits. In his Preface to *The Story of a Bad Boy,* Thomas Bailey Aldrich begins to explain his title by saying, "I call my story the story of a bad boy, partly to distinguish myself [from other boys who have appeared in Sunday school books]. . . . I was an amiable, impulsive lad, blessed with fine digestive powers. . . . I failed to send my little pocket money to the natives of the Feejee Islands, but spent it royally in peppermint-drops and taffy candy." Likewise, Samuel Clemens introduces his own Bad Boy in the opening paragraphs of his novel by showing Tom Sawyer raiding the pantry and wantonly feasting on purloined jam.

Toby Tyler goes further than this in its oral preoccupations. Since the novel reads like a dieter's nightmare, it is unfortunate that we cannot discover more about its author—whether, for example, Kaler had problems with his weight. The most detailed entry on his life appears in *Something About the Author* and consists of two slender paragraphs of biographical information, followed by five pages listing Kaler's 175 books.[3] One piece of relevant information, however, comes from Kirk Munroe (Kaler's editor), who, in his Foreword to later editions of *Toby Tyler,* described how the story came to be published:

It happened one morning, in the early 'eighties, while I was the editor of *Harper's Young People,* that a shabbily clad stranger, unwashed and unkempt, appeared, unannounced, at my office door. . . . [The stranger demanded to see the editor and explained,] "I am desperately in need of a little ready money. Two weeks ago I was the editor of a bankrupt American paper in London. At the final smash I had barely enough to pay for a steerage passage home. I have here a story that I wrote on the way over, working at it night and day; and it is a bang-up yarn, if I do say so. Now if you will just let me read it to you—" . . .

[Munroe explained it was the custom to leave manuscripts to be read at a later date, and continued,] "Now if you will excuse me, I am about to go to lunch."

"Lunch!" repeated the stranger. "That generally comes after breakfast, doesn't it?"

"Generally," I laughed. Then, noting the hunger lines on the man's face, I added, "If you have no other engagement, won't you join me?" . . .

A few minutes later we were installed in one of the small diningrooms of the old Astor House. Here a waiter had no sooner taken our order and departed than my surprising companion again produced his MS. and, without apology, began to read aloud the story of *Toby Tyler, or Ten Weeks with a Circus.* He utterly ignored the waiter's return and the placing of food on the table, together with my suggestion that he defer his reading until we had eaten.

Munroe was entirely won over by the story and found a way, at Kaler's insistence, to pay him immediately. Two days later, the stranger returned—"neatly dressed, clean shaven, and well fed"— and Kaler became "a regular contributor [to the magazine] and one of the most popular American writers of juvenile fiction."[4]

Certainly, some explanation for the obsessions of *Toby Tyler* can be found, then, in the fact that it was written by a hungry and impoverished author traveling in steerage to America. But what is interesting in the anecdote is that Kaler, despite his presumably acute hunger, put off eating until he had read and secured payment for his story. This is a kind of temperance nearly impossible for Toby Tyler, and it exhibits a kind of maturity that psychologist Bruno Bettelheim would approve of.

In his analysis of "Hansel and Gretel," Bettelheim argues that the proof of the two children's maturity appears at the end of the tale when they leave the witch's house and take jewels instead of food.[5] "Hansel and Gretel" is a tale about hunger, from the beginning when there isn't enough food, through the children's voracity when they encounter the Gingerbread House. This gluttony, Bettelheim suggests, exhibits an immature concern with immediate pleasure. To mature and become independent, the children must accept the reality principle: they must repress the desire for immediate pleasure, exercise forethought, and make plans for longer-lasting rewards, symbolized by the jewels—or, in Kaler's case, the royalty payment.

Toby Tyler likewise deals with a childhood eating disorder, and shows how Toby gradually matures and tames his oral greed. Like Hansel and Gretel, Toby's problem is his obsession with oral gratification. To solve that problem he must learn repression, acquire self-discipline, master thrift and forethought. Maturing in this fashion, in a process analogous to weaning, he ends his dependence on parental benefactors and becomes a provider. His achievement is signaled by his shift of attention from acquiring food to acquiring savings and is accompanied by the death of the monkey Mr. Stubbs.

Kaler's novel does not, however, present a smooth transition to maturity. Instead, Toby proceeds by fits and starts and with some backsliding. This progress is easiest seen if the novel is divided into five parts, each associated with the characters Toby comes to know.

Uncle Daniel and Job Lord

Toby Tyler opens with the boy cadging food from the owner of the circus's food concession. When the vendor, Job Lord, makes general inquiries about who the boy is, Toby confides: "I'm an awful eater, an' I can't seem to help it. I'm hungry all the time" (3). In the first three pages, Toby's oral greed is introduced, and it is established by repetition in succeeding pages: it takes a great deal to satisfy him (32); he eats a great deal and a long time (32); he can eat anything if given the chance (29); and he astonishes others by the amount of food he consumes (31).

It is not difficult to find the cause for Toby's incredible appetite and to discover that there is "some connection between his heart and his stomach" (21). Toby is a foundling. When the vendor asks the boy, "Didn't you ever get enough to eat?" Toby replies: "I suppose I did; but you see Uncle Dan'l he found me one mornin' on his hay, an' he says I was cryin' for something to eat then, an' I've kept it up ever since" (3). Even a timid psychologist could not fail to see the origin of Toby's acute hunger in this moment when he was abandoned. Bettelheim's description of "Hansel and Gretel" seems apt here: it is the story of "a small child . . . threatened by complete rejection and desertion, which he experiences in the form of fear of starvation."[6]

If the cause is easily identified, the results of Toby's oral greed are equally recognizable. He suffers from low self-esteem: "I don't seem to amount to much as the other fellers do, an' I guess it's because I'm always hungry" (19). His behavior is obsessive: he can't, for example, prevent his feet from straying toward the Edenic temptations of Job Lord's candy stand (9). And his monomania makes him dangerously manipulable: Job Lord bribes the boy into joining the circus by plying him with peanuts and candy sticks, and Toby accepts the proposal because he believes that as a member of the troupe "you get all you want to eat" (22).

While these are significant problems, a greater one is his dependence on others for food and the guilt that arises because he is only a consumer and not a provider. Uncle Daniel complains, Toby says, because "I eat four times as much as I earn" (3); and he confesses, "I don't like to work as well as a feller without any father and mother ought to. I don't know why it is, but I guess it's because I take up so much time eatin' that it kind of wears me out" (5). Joining the circus would seem to be a step in the direction of becoming independent and providing for himself; but instead the problem reappears in a new guise. When Job Lord offers Toby a job, he relates a story about his former helper:

> "Here I was just like a father to him . . . and I gave him his board and lodging and a dollar a week besides."
> "Could he do anything he wanted to with the dollar?"
> "Of course he could. I never checked him, no matter how extravagant he was, an' yet I've seen him spend his whole week's

wage at this very stand in one afternoon. And even after the money had all gone that way, I've paid for peppermint and ginger out of my own pocket just to cure his stomachache. . . . Yet that boy was ungrateful enough to run away." (6–7)

Oral greed, lack of self-control, dependence, ingratitude—these are the themes sounded in this anecdote, and they suggest how Toby will be similarly entrapped. But the tale also foreshadows what will occur when Toby returns home and prepares to run away from his own benefactor, Uncle Daniel. Then, Toby is so troubled by the ingratitude of his contemplated action that—to Uncle Daniel's astonishment—the boy is unable to eat. Eating would, of course, put him further in debt to his kindly guardian; and in Toby's eat-or-be-eaten world, he is consumed by guilt.

The parallels between the anecdote that Job Lord relates to Toby and the events that transpire between Uncle Daniel and the boy suggest a link between the two adults. Both are father figures. Just as Uncle Daniel cares for Toby like a father, Lord says of his relationship with the other boy that "I was just like a father to him." That Lord comes to see his eventual relationship with Toby in a paternal fashion is suggested later by his "fatherly" gestures (130) and by his telling Toby "I've learned to look on you as my own son" (139). In fact, Job Lord's very name suggests paternalism: it signals Toby's dependence because Job Lord is Toby's "chore boss"; moreover, the religious connotations, especially of the surname, recall that Uncle Daniel is a church deacon who prays to "Him who is ever a father to the fatherless" (183).

But if the text makes clear that Job Lord is a double for Uncle Daniel, it also indicates that he is a "dark" double, a "bad" father. Initially, the candyman appears kindly and generous. But like the witch in the Gingerbread House of "Hansel and Gretel," he changes the next morning into a demanding and cruel creature who has complete control over Toby and who occasionally whips the boy with an India-rubber cane. As guardian of the food stand, he also gives food to Toby or withholds it; and after his first disappointment with his helper, Lord tells the boy he has had his Last Supper.

Old Ben and the Treats

In terms of the familiar childhood split of parents into "good" and "bad" parent figures, Toby has a "bad" father in Job Lord and a "good" father in his confidante Old Ben, the wagon driver. Ben's paternal role is clear throughout the book in his solicitous care for the boy and in such statements to Toby as "Think of Old Ben, an' remember that his heart beats for you as if he was your father" (147). And that he is a "good" father and something of an antidote to the "bad" father is evident in the way he protects Toby from Job Lord's beatings and in the fact that he provides Toby with food when they first meet.

Old Ben also provides Toby with valuable advice concerning his eating problems, but the immature boy does not comprehend it. As Toby wolfs down doughnuts, Ben warns him of the dangers of eating: "You're too small to eat so fast. . . . Some time you'll . . . choke yourself to death." Toby turns aside the caution, replying "I'll never choke. . . . I'm used to it" (20). Noting that circus fare can be meager, Ben also advises: "Whenever we strike a new town, you find out at the hotel what time they have the grub ready, an' you be on hand, so's to get in with the first. Eat all you can, an' fill your pockets" (22). But Toby misses the point, says he always does that anyway, and mistakes Ben's counsel about prudence and thrift as further encouragement for his oral greed and food hoarding.

Toby also gets advice when he acquires a set of "good" parents in Mr. and Mrs. Treat. They are the Jack Sprat and his wife of the circus sideshows: he is the Living Skeleton, and she is the Fat Woman. Besides exaggerating the oral nature of the novel to freakish dimensions, the Treats also serve as guardians and benefactors to Toby. Like Old Ben, they are a warm and hospitable antidote to Job Lord: they, too, protect the boy from his employer's beatings, and they provide him with food.

Toby appreciates them most in this latter capacity. When his boss has denied him his supper, Mrs. Treat brings Toby a plate piled high with an assortment of pie, cake, bread, and meat. Earlier in the book, Toby had observed, "Uncle Dan'l says I'd eat till I was sick, if I got the chance; but I'd like to try it once" (4). In a kind of wish fulfillment, Toby gets that chance when the Fat Woman

TOBY GETS HIS SUPPER

W. A. Rogers for *Toby Tyler* (New York: Harper and Brothers, 1881).

invites him to gorge himself: "You shall eat as much as you want to; an' if you get a stomachache, . . . I'll give you some catnip tea" (47).

While Mr. Treat also provides Toby with food, the ample Mrs. Treat has a much larger role as the source of Toby's meals. She is, in a fashion, a figure for the Dream Mother, the all-good mother of infancy, the food provider. This is clear whenever she is seen in the novel, bringing her "son" huge trays loaded with food and encouraging him to eat his fill. And whenever this bountiful "mother" emerges from the steam and cooking odors of her kitchen, she is also lavish with her hugs and kisses. For a foundling like Toby, dimly aware of "some connection between his heart and his stomach" (12), these embraces are as important as the food.

Like Old Ben, the Treats offer Toby advice about eating. Grown-ups seem grown-out to Toby, and he confusedly describes Mrs. Treat as a "great" woman. In his eat-or-be-eaten world, Toby believes that "if I was as big as her . . . I wouldn't be afraid of anybody" (45). Mr. Treat gently tries to correct him by explaining that "it hain't so much the size" that makes a person "great" or fearless, but Toby doesn't quite comprehend. Later, Mrs. Treat also offers a lesson by noting that there is no direct relation between consumption and physical growth: her husband eats all the time but remains the Living Skeleton, while she "don't eat enough to keep a chicken alive, an yet I grow fatter and fatter every day" (47).

Toby cannot be said to grasp the subtle advice he is offered. But with Ben and certainly with the Treats, he gets the attention and affection otherwise missing from his cheerless life as an employee of Job Lord; and when the latter deprives him of meals, Toby can count on others to provide for him. With his anxiety about starving ameliorated, he has a basis from which to begin his maturation. That he begins to see a way out of the guilt he feels for being dependent is suggested in the thanks he offers the Treats, a courtesy that combines gratefulness with a notion of maturity: "You're awful good to me, an' when I get to be a man, I'll give you lots of things" (46).

Mr. Stubbs and the Savings

From his first days with the circus, Toby has struck up a friendship with an old monkey, which he calls Mr. Stubbs because of the animal's resemblance to a neighbor in Toby's hometown. Mr. Stubbs is Toby's confidant, and the boy pours out his troubles to the creature, who seems to understand and sympathize. But Mr. Stubbs is not only Toby's Secret Sharer, he is also a double for Toby. When Ben and the boy are arguing about whether monkeys can understand, their dispute is settled by a gesture: Mr. Stubbs reaches through the bars of his cage for a doughnut, and "the action seemed so natural, so like a hungry boy who gropes in the dark pantry for something to eat," that there no longer seems any point to arguing (55). In another striking passage, Toby has a dream in which he and Mr. Stubbs exchange identities (85).

Mr. Stubbs's role in the novel is complex, but he largely represents the "animal" side of Toby—his orality and desire for immediate pleasure, his childishness. At the same time, the gradual rise of Mr. Stubbs as an important character *apart* from Toby suggests a first step in the boy's maturation, since the duality implies a splitting off of that side of his personality.

Another important sign of Toby's maturation occurs after the wreck of a circus wagon, when the troop of monkeys escapes. Toby emerges as the savior of the circus. Instead of giving in to his desire to run away with them, Toby assumes responsibility and leads the monkeys back. For this act he is widely praised, and, in gratitude, the owner of the circus gives Mr. Stubbs to Toby. The fact that Toby is given control over the monkey, and later has to discipline the creature when it wants to play, suggests Toby's growing mastery over the animal side of his own personality.

Another indication of Toby's growing maturity appears when the Treats live up to their name and arrange a huge Sunday dinner to honor the boy. While Toby is delighted by the incredible spread of turkey and all the fixin's, it is almost too much and he feels a bit smothered by both the ample fare and the affection of Mrs. Treat, who enfolds him in hugs. He also begins to notice, for the first time, some negative aspects of eating. Significantly, it is the circus' sword swallower who seems unusually greedy and who bounds to the table "with the most unseemly haste. The others, more especially Toby, proceeded in a more dignified manner" (79). Polite conversation is impossible, Toby observes, until people have taken the edge off their appetite by eating at least one plateful. Mr. Treat worries everyone by choking and has to be rescued. Finally, Mr. Stubbs behaves badly and embarrasses Toby by scampering about during the banquet.

That Toby recognizes these untoward aspects of orality signals the beginning of a change in him. After he leaves the Sunday orgy of gluttony, he encounters Ben returning from church and wishes he had gone to church himself. The next Sunday Toby does go, after declining an invitation to another meal with the Treats because, as the author observes, "he hardly cared to go through the ordeal of another state dinner" (94).

Toby's maturation is not complete, however. He occasionally backslides. Although he has declined dinner with the Treats to go to church, he accepts an invitation for a supper with them later in the day. And then, he seems to go on a binge:

> Mr. and Mrs. Treat were not only very kind, but so attentive that he was actually afraid he should eat so much as to stand in need of the catnip tea which Mrs. Treat had said she gave to her husband when he had been equally foolish. The skeleton would pile his plate high with turkey bones from one side, and the fat lady would heap it up, whenever she could find a chance, with all sorts of food from the other, until Toby pushed back his chair, his appetite completely satisfied, as if it had never been so before. (97)

It is at this point that Toby begins to make plans with the Treats for his escape from the circus and Job Lord. He must secretly run away because his employer, wanting to retain the small candy salesman who brings in so much money, has contrived a way to put Toby in debt and will not release him until he has paid for all he has eaten. Significantly, Toby cannot begin to make plans, and consider what provisions must be made, until *after* he is "completely satisfied" by the Treats' meal. He cannot, in other words, repress his oral desires in order to engage in forethought; goal-directed behavior is possible only after these desires are sated. At this point in his maturation, Toby wants, in a fashion, to have his cake and eat it too.

Later that night, Toby resumes making plans and asks Ben what amount of money would be needed for the escape. Ben coun-

sels thrift: "If you go spreadin' yourself all over creation, as boys are
very apt to do, your money won't go very far; but if you look at your
money two or three times afore you spend it, you ought to get back
and have a dollar or two left" (99–100). Toby must not, in other
words, be "foolish," as he had been earlier in the evening, when he
had considered eating to such a foolish extent that catnip tea would
be required.

Like the jewels in "Hansel and Gretel," money represents the
opposite of food. Toby's savings require thrift and prudence in the
face of his desires for immediate pleasure and oral gratification.
Significantly, Toby has acquired money by exchanging it for food:
he has worked for the candyman Job Lord at a food stand and
hawked lemonade and candy inside the big top.

By these means, Toby acquires a small fund that will be needed
for his escape. But he is not completely prudent and circumspect.
One night, Toby falls asleep on top of the circus wagon and with
Mr. Stubbs in his arms. The monkey rummages through Toby's
clothes, finds the small bag of money, and proceeds to toss the coins
onto the road as the wagon travels along. The money is irretrievably
lost.

In a sense, it is appropriate that Mr. Stubbs should be the agent
for the tragic loss of Toby's funds. Money constitutes a kind of
threat to what the monkey represents. And Ben has warned Toby
about foolish boys who give in to their "animal" desires and throw
their money away.

Mr. Castle and Riding the Animal

Delaying his departure for home and lengthening his stay with the
circus, the loss of the money is a genuine tragedy for Toby and it
unleashes a flood of sorrow and tears. Ben offers the sobbing boy
some advice, which is repeated at such length that its importance
becomes evident: "Don't take on so. . . . You must kinder brace
up an' not give way so about it. . . . You must try to take it like
a man. . . . You must keep a stiff upper lip, even if it does seem
hard at first" (102–3). The narrator observes: "This keeping a stiff
upper lip in the face of the trouble he was having was all very well
to talk about, but Toby could not reduce it to practice, or, at least,

not very soon. . . . Toby knew the advice was good, and he struggled manfully to carry it to execution, but it was very hard work" (103–4).

The phrases "like a man" and "manfully" suggest the part this episode plays in Toby's maturation. When Ben counsels Toby "not to think about" or "not to talk about" the lost money, when he urges the boy to buckle down and earn the savings once again, he is encouraging a trait noticeably absent in Toby: self-discipline. Repression is, in fact, a cornerstone of maturity—the ability to plan for the future instead of thinking always of the immediate. Toby gets an opportunity to increase that self-discipline when he goes to work for Mr. Castle.

Mr. Castle is in charge of the circus's equestrian acts and persuades Job Lord to release Toby for a few hours each day so that he can be trained as a performer. In a sense, Mr. Castle is another Job Lord: a hard taskmaster who warns Toby that if he thinks the beatings he receives from his employer are bad, he can expect worse from Mr. Castle's whip if he fails to measure up. Toby is crestfallen to find himself now under a harder master than Job Lord. But what genuinely confuses Toby is that Ben and the Treats do not offer pity for his new plight, but encourage the boy to make the most of his opportunity.

The enthusiasm of Ben and the Treats for Toby's training under Mr. Castle suggests that there is a benign aspect to this apprenticeship. In fact, under Castle, Toby acquires self-discipline and a skill by which he can become self-supporting and end his dependence on Job Lord. And it is entirely appropriate that Toby should learn to be an equestrian; in an image as old as Plato's *Phaedo,* controlling horses has been a symbol for disciplining animal-like emotions. Equally relevant is the fact that as Toby grows more skilled and disciplined as an equestrian, his animal friend Mr. Stubbs seems to withdraw from him and become less communicative (116).

From this point on, signs of Toby's growing maturity become more frequent. In the absence of Mr. Stubbs, Toby befriends a girl his own age, Ella, another circus equestrian, who gives him his first and subsequent kisses and with whom he is being trained to ride around the ring "arm-in-arm." Toby also becomes more preoccupied with earning and saving money so that he can not only escape, but also "amount to something" (138). Indeed, what frequently appears in his conversations now is the phrase "when I get to be a man" (122, 129, 151, 153).

Toby's development is signaled in a variety of other ways: in the skilled performance he eventually presents to an approving circus audience and to the warm congratulations of his friends; in his postponement of his escape so as not to disappoint Ella, who hopes to perform in the ring with him; in his recognition that, as a celebrated performer, he is no longer in the employ of Job Lord but free to do as he pleases; and in his relief when the Treats don't invite him to one of their dinners, "which he had learned to fear rather than enjoy" (127). This is a new Toby Tyler, and this new identity is symbolically suggested by his being given a new circus name (Monsieur Ajax) and by his being presented with a costume by his friends.

Despite his notable successes, Toby still does some backsliding. After riding well during one show, he adjourns to a meal and "performed quite as great wonders in the way of eating as he had in the afternoon in the ring" (143). In uncontrolled cupidity, he follows that meal with another binge with the Fat Woman in which he bolts down doughnuts.

At this meeting with the Treats, Toby tells them of his plan to run away that night. They are surprised. After his successes, they thought the boy might stay on with the circus. Readers may be surprised, too: Toby has triumphed and become accomplished and independent. While it will soon appear otherwise, Toby's plan to return to Uncle Daniel seems like a regressive wish to return to dependence. And the glee Mr. Stubbs shows, when Toby tells the monkey of their imminent escape, might also seem to suggest a retreat to self-indulgent immaturity.

The Young Man and Shooting the Monkey

After a successful evening performance and a farewell to his friends, Toby steals away from the circus to return home. He does so in secret because he has been advised that Job Lord and Mr. Castle will pursue him, not wanting to lose the boy in whom they have a vested interest. This journey is a test of Toby's newly acquired maturity, and this is made more evident by the fact that Toby travels with Mr. Stubbs. The question is how Toby will deal with his animal nature, with his childlike orality and desire for immediate pleasure, with the monkey on his back.

The proofs of Toby's maturity are immediately evident. He takes great pains to calculate the amount of food and money necessary for the trip. He represses the desire to flee immediately (which would make him more noticeable to his pursuers), opting instead to spend some days hiding in the woods until the circus has traveled on. And, remembering what had happened before, he takes special precautions to place his provisions out of Mr. Stubbs's reach.

Toby's maturity is also evident in his dealings with the monkey, who gives no thought to the morrow and indulges in present pleasures and who comes to represent, even more dramatically, the childlike nature that impedes his master's progress. Toby cannot, for example, persuade Mr. Stubbs to wash:

> The old monkey would hardly have been troubled if they had not had their faces washed for the next month to come, but he grinned and talked as Toby trudged along, attempting to catch hold of leaves as they were passed and in various other ways impeding his master's progress, until Toby was obliged to give him a most severe scolding in order to make him behave himself in anything like a decent manner. (158–59)

Toby also has to scold the monkey for his rapacious eating habits: "'Now look here, Mr. Stubbs!' said Toby sternly, 'You can have all you want to eat, but you must take it in a decent way, an' not go cuttin' up any such shines'" (161).

Boy and monkey travel only a little way before they are lost in the dark woods—a familiar transitional period in fairy tales. Toby faces the situation "manfully" and "resolutely" (166). He sits down and tries to calculate time and direction. He also realizes that if they eat the food he has brought, they will become thirsty, and no water is at hand. So he resolves, in an act of temperance unusual for Toby, that "we've got to have something to drink or else we can't eat all these sweet things, an' I'm so tired that I can't go any farther. Don't let's eat dinner now, but let's stay an' rest an' then we can keep on looking for water" (167).

Toby does take a rest but fails to take precautions. Mr. Stubbs gets to the food, tears it into small shreds, and scatters it irretrievably. Toby wakes to this tragedy. Angered by the waste, he sees the monkey as a real threat to his well-being: "Now you've killed us Mr. Stubbs. . . . We never can find our way out of here. An' now we haven't anything to eat and by tomorrow we shall be starved to death" (168). When the monkey seems to pretend innocence and invite tolerance for his childish antics, Toby won't indulge him.

At this point in the novel, Toby comes face to face with his deepest fear: starvation anxiety. Shadowing it is another fear; in Toby's eat-or-be-eaten world (where he wishes, for example, to be as big as Mrs. Treat so he needn't be afraid of anybody), he also worries about being eaten by wild beasts. But the hint of a resolution appears when Toby determines, "I can get along one day without eating anything." And then he finds blackberries and begins "to believe that he might possibly be able to live, perhaps for weeks, in the woods solely upon what he might find growing there" (170).

This is an important moment: no longer able to depend on food given to him by the motherly Fat Woman, Toby begins to think it possible that he might be able to provide for himself. It is a situation akin to weaning, and it leads to the turning point of the novel:

> Just when he was feeling the most sad and lonely, and when thoughts of death from starvation were most vivid in his mind, he heard the barking of a dog, which sounded close at hand. His first thought was that at last he was saved, and he was just starting to his feet to shout for help, when he heard the sharp report of a gun and an agonizing cry from the branches above. And the old monkey fell to the ground with a thud that told he had received his death wound. (171–72)

The shooting of Mr. Stubbs by a young man out hunting is certainly, as John Seelye suggests, the most memorable scene in the novel.[7] At a very simple level, the death of Mr. Stubbs also serves the exigencies of the plot; as much as every boy might want to have a monkey as a pet, Mr. Stubbs would be out of place in Guilford when Toby returns home and, by grim necessity, he has to be gotten out of the story. But the shooting of Mr. Stubbs is more significant and complex than this.

Most notable is the fact that Mr. Stubbs's death occurs at precisely the moment when Toby feels "the most sad and lonely" and his fears of starvation are "most vivid," and when he believes that "at last he was saved." The death of Mr. Stubbs is, in fact, a salvific tragedy. And no matter how pathetic, it also constitutes something salutary.

At its simplest level, the death of Mr. Stubbs represents the death of childlike immaturity in Toby, the sad but necessasry end of childhood. At a deeper but more ambiguous level, the event brings with it a constellation of symbols connected to Toby's dependence on parent figures.

Perhaps the easiest way to begin to understand these issues is to note the remarkable similarity between this scene and another in a later work, Edgar Rice Burroughs's *Tarzan of the Apes* (1914). Tarzan is suckled and raised by his ape mother, Kala, and the bond between them is unusually strong and enduring. Kulonga, a black native and hunter, kills Kala by sending an arrow into her breast. Tarzan tracks Kulonga, slays him in revenge, puts on the native's jewelry, and takes his knife; from that point forward, the motherless child becomes an adult and a fearsome hunter who eventually earns the title of Lord of the Jungle.

Read in a psychological fashion, the events in Burroughs's novel can be said to represent an important step in the maturation of a child: "cutting the apron strings," "leaving the nest," the assertion of individuality that ends a child's dependence on the mother. That this step begins with, and is analogous to, weaning is ever so slightly suggested by the fact that the ape mother dies from an arrow to her breast. A child's reluctance to make this break with a parent, or the worry that this assertion of individuality might seem like ingratitude toward the parent, is often answered by having some outsider engage in symbolic matricide. But in some unconscious way, Burroughs makes clear that Tarzan and Kulonga are the same person: Tarzan, the author states, is the son of an English lord, and Kulonga is the son of the king; moreover, after he kills the native, Tarzan puts on his victim's jewelry and knife, and takes on the other's identity by becoming a fierce hunter as well.

Toby's monkey is also shot in the breast by "a young man, whose rifle and well-filled bag of game showed that he had been out hunting" (174). In a sense, this "young man" is an image of the new Toby Tyler, a double for the future Toby, a self-provider whose "well-filled bag of game" echoes what Toby had postulated when he found the blackberries and realized that he might be able to survive in the woods by finding food for himself. It is the "young man" who replaces or does away with the "monkey" in Toby. That the boy hates him—"You've killed all I ever had in this world of my own to love me" (175)—is to be expected. The transition to adulthood is painful and marked by separations, from the "tragedy" of weaning through the various forms of parricide often performed by others and doubles. Nonetheless, these events remain salvific tragedies.

In another way, equally submerged and ambiguous, the death of Mr. Stubbs addresses Toby's relations with the fathers of his childhood. Mr. Stubbs dies in Toby's arms, with the boy telling the monkey how grateful he has been and saying what he has longed to say to Uncle Daniel: "Forgive me for ever being bad to you" (172).

Toby buries his childhood when he buries Mr. Stubbs and his circus costume. Likewise—in another image of repression and one that recalls Ben's advice to Toby when he is brooding about his lost savings—the "young man" encourages Toby to put the events of the day behind him and not think any more about the monkey. And the young man provides Toby with a steamboat passage so that he can not only return home, but elude those old fathers of childhood. These pursuers are scouring the countryside to catch and entrap him once again in the double bind of dependence and ingratitude. The very names of his circus employers, Lord and Castle, suggest that (like the episodes involving the Duke and the King in Huckleberry Finn) this is a story of America breaking free from the fatherland.

Toby does return home, and he begs forgiveness from Uncle Daniel, as he had from Mr. Stubbs. But he is a new Toby Tyler. Uncle Daniel says to him: "Stay here, Toby, my son, and help support this poor old body as it goes down into the dark valley of the shadow of death, and then, in the bright light of the glorious future, Uncle Daniel will wait to go with you in the presence of Him who is ever father to the fatherless" (183).

Now their roles are exchanged. Toby will care for Uncle Daniel. Like Hansel and Gretel, the boy returns home as a provider. He has matured, outgrown the oral compulsions and dependence on his childhood. And he has found a way, at last, to be both independent and grateful.

FOUR

✣ ✣ ✣ ✣ ✣ ✣ ✣

The Gospel
of Optimism

10

✢ ✢ ✢ ✢ ✢ ✢ ✢

Sunny Land, Angry Waters
Hans Brinker

The internal lives of children are the subject of the contrived melo-dramas in *Tom Sawyer,* in which the boy luxuriates in self-pity over the way he imagines he has been mistreated; of the episodes of contrition in *Little Women,* in which the March sisters wrestle with those negative emotions they call their "bosom enemies"; of the numerous scenes in *Toby Tyler,* in which the runaway suffers pangs of hunger. While Tom indulges his feelings in Clemens's comic novel, more often than not the subject of these books is the control of feelings: how the March sisters learn to check their anger, vanity, envy, and shyness; how Toby learns to repress his hunger.

Mary Mapes Dodge's *Hans Brinker; or, The Silver Skates* (1865) is also concerned with feelings and their control; this is, as we will see, the subtext of the novel's famous incident about the boy who sticks his finger in the leaking dike. But there is also something else at work in the novel. What distinguishes the title character is not only his ability to control his feelings, his stiff upper lip, but his unfailing cheerfulness; and, in this regard, *Hans Brinker* would establish a tradition in American children's books that would reach its apogee in the cheerfulness of *Pollyanna.* After a fruitless morning of looking for work to feed his needy family, without a morsel in the house, Hans still holds up his chin and whistles as he resolutely heads out the door to mend matters.

This incident fairly describes the particular emotional tone of the novel and the personality that Hans inherited from his creator. Like many other writers of American juvenile literature, Mary Mapes Dodge was a scribbling widow. Her husband, William Dodge, committed suicide in 1859 after a bout of melancholy, drowning himself in the Atlantic and leaving behind a wife and two sons. Mrs. Dodge's response, apparently, was to tuck up her skirt and roll up her sleeves and put all that behind her with a briskness that concealed her wounds. She returned to her father's house, began writing magazine articles, and then turned out *Hans Brinker*—a novel involving a mother whom the townspeople call "Widow Brinker" and two children who lost their father during an oceanic storm but later recover him.

Dodge's other novels were forgettable, but that fact did not diminish her influence on American literature. After stints on other juvenile magazines, Dodge became in 1873 the editor of America's premier periodical for children, *St. Nicholas,* and remained there until her death in 1905. The list of people she befriended and persuaded to write for the magazine reads like *Who's Who:* Louisa May Alcott, Frances Hodgson Burnett, Jack London, Mark Twain, Rudyard Kipling, Robert Louis Stevenson, William Cullen Bryant, Henry Wadsworth Longfellow, Helen Hunt Jackson, Frank Stockton, Lucretia P. Hale, Susan Coolidge, Howard Pyle, Joel Chandler Harris, Edna St. Vincent Millay, and Kate Douglas Wiggin.

Some observations about *St. Nicholas* might be in order because the magazine reflected Dodge's personality, which, in turn, shaped the emotional tone of *Hans Brinker.* First there is the title. Dodge revered Christmas. Her first publication was "A Song of St. Nicholas," and her subsequent work, especially in *St. Nicholas,* was full of talk of Santa and Christmas. *Hans Brinker* is no exception. The events of the novel occur during the holiday season. Stories about and songs to St. Nicholas abound. An extended glimpse of a Dutch family's Christmas is provided. And a lengthy discussion of the difference between Dutch and American ways of celebrating begins with a reference to Clement Moore's poem: "We all know how, before the Christmas tree began to flourish in the home life of our country, a certain 'right jolly old elf,' with 'eight tiny reindeer,' used to drive his sleigh-load of toys up our house-tops.''[1]

Part of the emotional tone of *Hans Brinker* is this holiday feeling. School is out, and every child is on skates. Their flights on the ice induce a vacation mood not unlike that of the river life in *Huckleberry Finn*—but with one difference. Dodge could never abide the frivolity of Twain's character, with his bare feet trailing in the water; she condemns one of her characters because "she was never in earnest. . . . A pleasant heart, a pleasant manner— these only last for an hour" (85). Beneath the good cheer, then, must be an earnestness.

Part of Dodge's personality was a kind of no-nonsense matter-of-factness. This was perhaps most evident, a biographer notes, in the editorial policies she adopted at *St. Nicholas*:

> Two things to which Lizzie stuck firmly and forever were good-ness and reality—even her fairies were good and real, and noth-ing deep, esoteric or subtle passed her test—an iron-bound pol-icy based on personal conviction against . . . allegory and the suggested. She wanted her tales to convey to stalwart and intel-ligent young Americans, stalwart and intelligent facts—she fed them oatmeal deliberately, and if a fairy popped into the cereal, she must be a real fairy and not a symbol. It was Europeans who indulged in the subterranean meaning: the hidden underlying the visible; the delicate handling and subtlety such as that of Lang and Anderson and Kingsley, or the macabre and terrify-ing . . . of the Brothers Grimm.[2]

And, indeed, though she became a good friend of George Mac-Donald, Dodge never solicited or published anything by him be-cause his work was deep rather than straightforward.

Dodge was a logical positivist when it came to enchantment. This, too, shapes the emotional tone of *Hans Brinker*. Fairies are people like Peter Van Holp's sister and Annie Bouman, who earn that epithet simply because they are charming. Hans and Gretel Brinker are the down-to-earth namesakes of their Grimm ancestors. And when Gretel is called the Goosegirl, it is not because the children have seen her resemblance to the character in the Grimm fairy tale, but because she tends geese.

Holland serves Dodge in the same way. In her eyes, the great virtue of the country was that it was a real place, yet as fascinating as any land of enchantment: "Holland is one of the greatest countries under the sun. It should be called Odd-land or Contrary-land, for in nearly everything it is different from other parts of the world" (14). Because the lowlands are surrounded by dikes, ships can be seen floating higher than the rooftops, gardens are kept on canal boats, houses are built on stilts, and windmills are everywhere. This netherland offered Dodge something as close to a fairyland as she could come within her realistic guidelines. Indeed, what she knew about Holland came from encyclopedias, almanacs, and Dutch friends; at the time the novel was published, Dodge had never traveled to Europe.

Besides factuality, Dodge also apparently felt an imperative for a robust healthy-mindedness. Describing the ideal juvenile magazine before the premier of *St. Nicholas,* she would use such words as "stronger," "truer," "bolder," "uncompromising," "cheer," "freshness," "heartiness," "life," and "joy." At one point in *Hans Brinker* the Dutch poet Jacob Cats comes off better in a comparison with Shakespeare (who, it is conceded, wrote very good plays): "Cats sees no daggers in the air, he has no white woman falling in love with dusky moors; no young fools sighing to be a lady's love, no crazy princes mistaking respectable old gentlemen for rats. No, no. He writes only sense" (57). Dodge was a literary version of Teddy Roosevelt, who would have told Bartleby the Scrivener to do calisthenics and put the melancholy Hamlet in jogging shoes. Her sunny work in *Hans Brinker* is robust and healthy-minded, all pink cheeks and ice-skating.

The atmosphere of her novel, then, is one of peremptory cheerfulness. When, for example, Peter Van Holp leads his company of boys on their skating expedition from their homes in Broek to The Hague, they get only halfway before they discover that Peter has lost the purse containing their funds for the trip. When the boys grow sullen and finally surly, Peter proposes that they make "the best of a bad business and go back pleasantly, like men," and the boys cheer; Peter proposes that "we may as well make up our mind there's no place like Broek, after all," and the boys cheer; Peter proposes that they put on their skates and head home, and the boys leave with their faces "nearly as bright" as they had been a half-hour before (78).

It is as if no trouble can descend in this novel without the author sweeping in with a rosy glow on her cheeks and her sleeves rolled up, seizing the child on the brink of a blue funk, and hurrying him along with a snatch of the tune "Pack Up Your Troubles in Your Old Kit Bag." This seems to explain the briskness of the novel, the constant motion of children and the streaking of skaters, the transience of events and the hurry of errands, and the contest of the silver skates "For the Fleetest." But troubles swept away can also be troubles swept under the rug. Despite the novel's gregariousness, the fact that this is a wounded and defensive *joie de vivre* is evident in darker ways—in a suspicion of moodiness, an emphasis on watchfulness, and a preoccupation with the danger of broken dikes.

Leaks and Dikes

The most famous anecdote in *Hans Brinker* is the story of the boy who stuck his finger in the leaking dike. That boy, incidentally, is not Hans; the story "The Hero of Haarlem" is something Dodge inserted into her novel as an account of Holland being read by English schoolchildren while her Dutch characters are exploring the country and its customs. The story is also not a piece of Dutch folklore; Dodge herself invented it. [3] But the fact that this story is so widely remembered, and that it almost seems to have taken on a life of its own, suggests its importance. This opinion is shared by the Dutch characters of the book when one says, "That little boy represents the spirit of the whole country." And, indeed, the story provides clues to understanding the larger story of the novel.

The actual tale "The Hero of Haarlem" is easily told. It is about a sunny-haired boy whose father works on the dikes as a sluicer. The boy knows the importance of "strong dikes or barriers" without which the surrounding country would be inundated, how "constant watchfulness is required" to keep the ocean in its place, how "a moment's neglect of the sluicer's duty may bring ruin and death to all" (101). One day he sets out to deliver cakes to a blind man, and on his return he glances out at the stormy ocean beyond the dikes. The day grows darker, he feels lonely and remembers mursery tales about orphans lost in the woods, and then he spots the leak. Into the hole goes his chubby finger: "The angry waters must stay back now! Haarlem shall not be drowned while *I* am here!" (103). During the night he fights off cold and sleepiness and controls his emotions, and in the morning the little hero is found and the dike repaired.

This story is but one indication of the importance the novel attaches to dikes. Among the thousand emblems of life in Holland—tulips, for example, or windmills or wooden shoes—Dodge is most preoccupied with these barriers or boundaries. She also leaves the impression that her Dutch share this preoccupation and that every second thought of theirs concerns the safety of the dikes; as a nation, they seem to live in a mild but constant paranoia: "Holland is often in a state of alarm. The greatest care is taken to prevent accidents. Engineers and workmen are stationed all along [the dikes] in threatened places and a close watch is kept up night and day" (21). Finally, Dodge suggests that "leaks" come in various forms when she says the boy who sticks his finger in the dike "represents the spirit of the whole country. Not a leak can show itself anywhere, either in politics, honor, or public safety, that a million fingers are not ready to stop it at any cost" (104).

Hans Brinker is a novel full of threats and varied forms of protection. "Leaks" and "floods" come in different shapes, as well as the need for "dikes." But, as Robert Frost said, "Before I built a wall I'd ask to know / What I was walling in or walling out."

Among all other things, the danger Dodge seems to fear on the other side of the dikes is the flood of emotions, what Freud called "the oceanic," the loss of ego when overwhelmed by the wildness of feelings. Emotions are suspect in this novel. One of the most revealing statements in the book occurs when Hans turns away as his sister Gretel starts to cry: "He had a true Dutch horror of tears, or emotion of any kind" (30). The message of Dodge's *Hans Brinker* is control your feelings.

This message can be perceived in a scene involving music, because music has the power to evoke a flood of emotions that can threaten the dikes of self-control. When Peter Van Holp and his party of boys are on their expedition, they happen to stop at St. Bavon's just as the celebrated organ of that church begins to play:

> Louder it grew until it became like the din and roar of some mighty tempest, or like the ocean surging on the shore. . . . The storm broke forth again with redoubled fury—gathering its distant thunder. . . . At last an answer came—soft, tender,

loving, like a mother's song. The storm grew silent; hidden birds sprang forth filling the air with glad, ecstatic music, rising higher and higher until the last faint note was lost in the distance. . . . In the glorious hymn of thanksgiving that now arose, one could almost hear the throbbing of the human heart. . . . It seemed that the angels were singing. [The boys'] eyes grew dim and their souls dizzy with a strange joy. At last, as if borne upwards by invisible hands, they were floating away on the music, all fatigue forgotten, and with no wish but to hear forever those beautiful sounds—when suddenly Van Holp's sleeve was pulled impatiently and a gruff voice beside him asked:

"How long are you going to stay here, captain—blinking at the ceiling like a sick rabbit?" (91–92)

This terminating question is the psychic version of *coitus interruptus*. This kind of moment happens frequently in the novel. Whenever emotions rise dangerously close to flood stage, Dodge finds the need and occasion to bring them under control, to shore up the dikes against ruin, to keep the oceanic within bounds. Her battery of facts about Holland serves her well in this regard, as part of her fervid assertion of the reality principle. Immediately after the boys nearly lose themselves in the ecstasy of the organ music, Dodge dampens the mood by shoveling in such facts as the height and width of the organ and the number of pipes, stops, and keyboards.

This suspicion of emotions includes a similar apprehension about another state in which the dikes of self-control are weak. Sleep seems dangerous in this novel. Early in the book, Hans's mother tells a story about three sons who depart from their father and stay at an inn, where they are murdered in their sleep by the landlord. Some pages later, Peter and his traveling companions stay at the Red Lion Inn, and while they sleep a knife-bearing robber enters their room. On the same trip, one of the boys, Jacob Poot, grows cold and tired and falls asleep outdoors; everyone endeavors to wake him because they know that sleeping in the snow leads to death. Something similar happens to Gretel. When Dr. Boekman begins to operate on Raff Brinker, Gretel goes outside, becomes hysterical, and then drops off to sleep; fortunately, her friend Hilda van Gleck sees the child crumpled in the snow and energetically forces Gretel to wake up.

Wakefulness and watchfulness are, consequently, praiseworthy postures. This is what is commendable about Dame Brinker as she keeps a sleepless vigil over her invalid husband in the fear that the man may go berserk or drift from sleep to death. It is what is commendable about the boy who fights off sleepiness and self-pity to keep his finger in the dike. The dikes must be manned against the oceanic, those conditions that threaten to swamp the ego.

Dr. Boekman also exhibits emotional control. He was deeply wounded when his son Laurens abandoned him after a misunderstanding. To protect his feelings so they cannot be hurt again, Dr. Boekman adopted a defensive posture and earned the reputation of "being the crossest man in Holland" (82). The control of feelings is so important to him that before he operates on Raff Brinker, he insists that the females leave the house (because of their inclination to cry or faint); and he dispassionately discusses the success of a colleague's operation, ignoring the fact that the patient died.

As in *Little Women* (with its scene of Jo learning to repress her anger by the gesture of putting a finger to the lips), above all other emotions in *Hans Brinker,* the one that must be controlled is anger. It is mentioned in the story of the boy who puts his finger in the dike when the boy begins to muse: "He thought of his father's brave gates and felt glad of their strength for, thought he, 'If *they* gave way, where would his father and mother be? These pretty fields would be all covered with the angry waters—father always calls them the *angry* waters; I suppose he thinks they are mad at him for keeping them out so long'" (102). If this passage is interpreted psychologically, the boy's question is: Without the strong gates or dikes of the father, without the protective father of childhood, where would this family be? The answer is: Drowned in the angry water, drowned in the waters the father thinks are mad at him. Without the protective father, the family is in danger of being drowned by "madness at the father."

This is the secret of the novel and the key to the Brinkers' name. After his accident, Raff Brinker (who was once a brave and strong dike keeper) is no longer the protective father; in fact, he is a threatening father, since he occasionally goes berserk.[4] On one occasion, for example, he turns into a hysterical madman who tries to push his wife into the fire while his children look on helplessly. This has created a dangerous situation where the family might easily be destroyed by a tidal wave of madness at the father. But the Brinkers resist. Although they live on the brink of a dangerous situation, they man the dikes against this emotion.

There is, however, an occasional leak. In a moment of free-thinking reverie, Gretel acknowledges that there is something else beneath her surface affection for her father. She wonders

> whether it was very wicked to care more for one parent than for the other—and sure, yes, quite sure that she dreaded her father, while she clung to her mother with a love that was almost idolatry. "Hans loves the father so well," she thought, "why cannot I? . . . If this sickness [of the father] lasts we shall never skate any more. . . . Hans and I will not see the race," and Gretel's eyes that had been dry before, grew full of tears.
>
> "Never cry, child," said her mother soothingly. . . .
>
> Gretel sobbed now. "Oh, mother, . . . you do not know at all—I am very, very bad and wicked!" . . . Gretel looked up . . . and said in a trembling voice: "The father tried to burn you—he did—I saw him, and he was *laughing!*"
>
> "Hush, child!" The mother's words came suddenly and sharply. (87–89)

Raff Brinker stands in the way, and, despite her mother's sharp injunction to control her emotions, Gretel's anger against her father sometimes leaks through. All the other children of the novel have lives full, Dodge says repeatedly, of fun and frolic; but Gretel's life is poor and unhappy because, unlike her neighbors, she comes from a "broken home." For all the other children, the Silver Skates to be won in the great race are like visions of sugarplums. For Gretel, they are "treasures passing hopelessly out of her reach" as her father's illness grows worse (84).

There is only one exception in the host of juvenile dreamers: "the vision of the Silver Skates failed to appear" to Hans Brinker (84). Like Gretel's, Hans's life is different from those of the other children of the novel; while Peter Van Holp and his company of well-to-do boys skate off on their expedition, Hans is busy locating a doctor, trying to find work, and discovering ways to provide food because his father is ill. Unlike his sister, though, Hans does not give in to anger and resentment toward his father. He mans the dikes and controls his emotions. In the darkest times, he maintains his cheerful and even disposition. He does not even long for the Silver Skates, much less see his father as an obstacle to winning them.

"Don't cry." Thomas Nast for *Hans Brinker; or, the Silver Skates*
(New York: James O'Kane, 1865).

Like the boy who saves the dike, Hans is self-sacrificing, duty's child. In the absence of the protective father, he becomes the protector and child-savior. Hans sees to the recovery of his father, the reconstitution of the family, and the restoration of their savings. Even more than the hero of Haarlem, Hans Brinker can be seen as the representative of a country ever on guard against leaks.

Hans, then, is a particular kind of hero. Compared with Huck Finn, Little Lord Fauntleroy, or Rebecca of Sunnybrook Farm, he is dull and ordinary. But these are his virtues in Dodge's novel. The fact that he is undramatic is proof that he can control his emotions. Not only does he have no feelings of resentment, but he must turn away when he sees his sister about to cry and is stunned when his mother affectionately uses the familiar form and addresses him as "thee." Hans controls his feelings. He is a strong individual who creates his ego out of the ocean of id and maintains this "Holland" against the threats of uncontrolled passions.

There may well be autobiographical roots in this endorsement of Hans Brinker. Perhaps after the suicide of her husband, Dodge, too, felt a "madness at the father" and anger that her husband had left her a widow and her two sons without a father. Perhaps she discovered that the undramatic and rigorously maintained cheerfulness and even temper of Hans Brinker was best. Or perhaps the fact that her husband drowned himself in the ocean after being overcome by melancholy led her to see the importance of maintaining dikes against powerful emotions.

Teasing for Tears

Whatever the case, it should be noted that the result is a contradictory novel. While the book advocates the control of emotions, Dodge uses every conceivable trick of the sentimental novel to create a tear-jerker. The clearest example of this occurs in the story of the hero of Haarlem, which, it must be remembered, is being read by children in their school. In the passages Dodge puts in brackets, the classroom readers are urged to control their emotions, while the story they read employs every possible trick to set them blubbering:

["Now, Henry," said the teacher, nodding to the next little reader.]

"Suddenly the boy looked around in dismay. . . . It was growing dark, he was still some distance from home, and in a lonely ravine . . . and with a beating heart recalled many a nursery tale of children belated in dreary forests. . . . He looked up and saw a small hole in the dike. . . . His chubby finger was thrust in almost before he knew it. . . .

"But the night was falling rapidly; chill vapors filled the air. Our little hero began to tremble with cold and dread. He shouted loudly; he screamed 'Come here! Come here!' but no one came. The cold grew intense, a numbness, commencing in the tired little finger, crept over his hand and arm, and soon his whole body was filled with pain. He shouted again, 'Will no one come? Mother! Mother!' . . . He tried to whistle, perhaps some straggling boy might heed the signal; but his teeth chattered so, it was impossible. Then he called on God for help; and the answer came, through a holy resolution—'I will stay here 'til morning.'"

["Now, Jenny Dobbs," said the teacher. Jenny's eyes were glistening, but she took a long breath and commenced:]

"How can we know the sufferings of that long and fearful watch—what falterings of purpose, what childish terrors came over the boy as he thought of the warm little bed at home, of his parents, his brothers and sisters, then looked into the cold, dreary night! . . . He was not sure of living. What did this strange buzzing mean? and then the knives that seemed to be pricking him from head to foot? . . ."

["Jenny Dobbs," said the teacher, rather impatiently, "if you cannot control your feelings so as to read distinctly, we will wait until you recover yourself."] (102–3)

The voice of the teacher who chides the emotional child-reader is that of Mary Mapes Dodge. But Dodge is also the author of the tale the child reads, a story that attempts to evoke the child's emotion.

In a sense, this is what Dodge does throughout the novel: she creates emotional situations and then urges control over the emotions. When Raff Brinker undergoes a perilous operation and is brought back to his senses and family, she asks that no tears fall on the page; when Dr. Boekman is reunited at long last with his estranged son Laurens, she asks that no lump form in the throat; when Gretel finally gets her wish and enters the great race and wins the Silver Skates, she asks that no heart flutter; and when Hans shivers in the cold and wonders where to get work or food, she asks that the reader feel no pangs of pity. Obeying these requests is, of course, close to impossible.

In this way, Dodge creates an almost unbearable tension. She imposes a taboo and, at the very same time, supplies elaborate occasions to sin. She provides abundant temptations to test her readers' resolve and seduces them to abandon it, thereby creating the juvenile version of the romance novel. Contemplated adultery, Denis de Rougemont says in *Love in the Western World*,[5] is the heart of the romance because it creates that kind of exhilarating tension seen in the legend of Tristan and Iseult, in which the two lovers lie down with a sword between them as a symbol of the boundary they must not cross, though they long to do just that. In *Hans Brinker*, Dodge teases for tears but at the same time condemns tears as leaks, as emotional adultery that jeopardizes not a marriage, but a family.

This is what Dodge condemns. But we should also pay attention to what she advocates. Unfailing cheerfulness, optimism, positivity—these provide a magical way to restore the broken home and family. This is characteristic of *Hans Brinker*, and is even more so of *The Secret Garden* and *Pollyanna*.

11

✢ ✢ ✢ ✢ ✢ ✢ ✢
Positive Thinking
The Secret Garden

Much of Frances Hodgson Burnett's *The Secret Garden* (1911) can be understood from the way it is remembered. With surprising frequency, readers mention that they first came to know the book when they were sick and home from school, showered with attention and soup by a ministering mother, and read or had this story read to them during their convalescence.[1] *The Secret Garden* is, certainly, a sickroom book, a novel about illness and cures. Indeed, Burnett's novel might be reckoned one long convalescence.

The Secret Garden is concerned with two ailing children, Mary Lennox and her cousin Colin Craven, but it must be noted that their medical problems are essentially mental ones. Mary, when she first appears, is a sickly and jaundiced child because her "mind was full of disagreeable thoughts . . . which affected her liver and her digestion and made her yellow and tired."[2] Later, Colin is introduced; because he has "shut himself in his room and thought only of his fears and weakness," he is a "hysterical, half-crazy little hypochondriac" (282).

Writing about psychological issues, then, Burnett faced a familiar authorial problem: how to make invisible mental problems (and their cures) visible, how to make the "meta" physical. In *Hans Brinker*, Mary Mapes Dodge found a solution in her conceits, among them the vision of the dike as a barrier against oceanic feelings. In *The Secret Garden*, Burnett's solution was to present totemic places that mirror the psychological states of her characters: the garden and the mansion.

Mary is associated with gardens several times in the book before she actually enters the Secret Garden. When Mary is first seen in India, she is creating a make-believe garden with dirt and blossoms, and in her Edenic play her only companion is a snake. Later, when the orphan stays briefly with the family of an English clergyman, Mary again heaps up dirt and makes paths for a garden. There, the clergyman's children find her such a prig that they taunt her with the nursery rhyme "Mary, Mary, quite contrary, / How does your garden grow?"[3]

When the orphan comes to live with her uncle, she is lonely and bored and passes her time by wandering about Misselthwaite Manor and looking for the "secret garden" that the servants have mentioned. It was the favorite place of Mary's uncle and his wife, but when she died it was sealed up and forgotten. One day, by chance, a robin alights near a buried key and a gust of wind blows back a mat of vines exposing a door.[4] In this way, Mary enters the Secret Garden, which "no one else has [been] inside [of] for ten years": "Ten years was a long time, Mary thought. She had been born ten years ago" (64).

That link is important. Mary's life has been the exact parallel of the Secret Garden's concealment. She was born when the garden was closed. Since then, both of them have been forgotten, hidden away, neglected, unloved. More important, Mary's and the garden's futures are linked.

In succeeding days, Mary visits the garden every chance she gets, weeds and digs, and (with the help of her friend Dickon) brings it back to life. This new interest and physical activity not only improve the garden, but also improve her health and her disposition. By means of this cathexis, in other words, she works her own regeneration. She gets better as the garden does, and vice versa. Their regeneration is simultaneous and mutual.

Besides her discoveries outdoors, Mary also explores "indoors." Ever since coming to Misselthwaite Manor, she has been bothered (like Jane Eyre) by a particular sound: nocturnal cries issuing from somewhere deep inside the mansion and the scurry of hurrying feet.[5] This has provoked her curiosity: "She felt as if she must find out what it was. It seemed even stranger than the secret garden and the buried key" (122).

Heretofore, on rainy days and at night, Mary has tentatively explored the sealed rooms and corridors of the many-roomed mansion. Like the explorations of the narrator in Poe's "The Fall of the House of Usher," Mary's wanderings in the gothic mansion have an intramental quality; she keeps wondering whether "she was in a real place or if she had fallen asleep and was dreaming without knowing it" (123). In a psychological sense, Mary is probing the unconscious and seeks the darkest, most remote, and most deeply hidden secret of the House of Craven—which, as in Poe's tale, is a name for both the mansion and the family.

Even deeper than her daytime discoveries about herself (that she is lonely, for example, or that she does not like herself), these dreamlike and often nocturnal explorations of the labyrinth of corridors and rooms lead her past memories: galleries where portraits of her ancestors hang and a room full of ivory miniature elephants that recall her days in India. Eventually, however, at the end of her searches, in the remote and most deeply hidden room in the mansion, she confronts herself, her Doppelgänger, her cousin Colin.

Colin's history is notable. His father, Archibald Craven, bears a grudge against the boy because his wife died while giving birth to Colin, and Mr. Craven is hysterically convinced that his son will become a hunchback like himself.[6] Mr. Craven gave up on Colin, concluded it would be better if the child died, and instructed his staff that Colin was to be confined to a distant room in the mansion, was not to be talked about, and was to be treated as the invalid he would inevitably become—a conviction that came to be shared by the hypochondriacal boy. "My mother died when I was born," Colin explains, "and it makes [my father] almost wretched to look at me. . . . He almost hates me." "He hates the garden, because she died," Mary replies—adding one more link to the chain of resemblances in the novel (126).

This linking continues as Mary talks to the irritable but pathetic boy:

> "How old are you?" he asked.
> "I am ten," answered Mary, forgetting herself for a moment, "and so are you."

"How do you know that?" he demanded in a surprised voice.

"Because when you were born the garden door was locked and the key buried. And it has been locked for ten years." (128)

Not only the same age and cousins, they seem to be twins. Colin's history is a replication of Mary's, is a replication of the garden's: both born when the Secret Garden was closed, both forgotten and neglected like the garden, both getting better as the garden is brought back to life.

This multiple echoing is made even more extensive when Colin's room is added. We are to understand Mary's discovery of Colin's room as paralleling her discovery of the Secret Garden. Both are secret domains: the door to Colin's room hidden behind a tapestry; the door to the garden, behind a curtain of ivy. What is more conspicuous is how Colin's room is the opposite of the garden: a dark chamber with shades drawn, not an arena of sunlight; a claustrophobic place of disease and decay, not a sheltered place of growth and fertility. This totemic place also has to be regenerated and—just like Mary's restoration of and in the garden—its regeneration is synchronous with the regeneration of Colin. As Mary continues to visit the bedridden boy and brings news of her work outdoors, and when Dickon begins to accompany her and brings a bevy of animals (a fox, a crow, two squirrels, a newborn lamb) to his room, Colin's spirits are lifted, the shades opened, and the sickroom converted into a place more like the garden.

To complete his recovery, Colin really needs to go to Lourdes itself, and his youthful co-conspirators soon find a way to acquire a wheelchair and smuggle him into the Secret Garden.[7] There, Colin is finally cured. Tossing his lap rugs aside in a climactic scene, he rises from his wheelchair and hazards his first steps.

Positive Thinking

I am selling my Lourdes stock and buying Christian Science trust. I regard it as the Standard Oil of the future.

Mark Twain, quoted in Justin Kaplan,
Mark Twain and His World

Much time is devoted in *The Secret Garden* to Mary's and Colin's curative regimens—which include breathing in the moor's fresh air, nourishing themselves with the right kind of food (potatoes, milk, porridge), and a system of Charles Atlas–like muscle exercises that Dickon learned from a local wrestler and teaches Colin. There is nothing unique about this. Mary and Colin are examples of a generation of literary juveniles who might be styled "fresh-air kids." It was a craze. Debunking the era's pediatric enthusiasms, Clemens would describe Aunt Polly in *The Adventures of Tom Sawyer* as simple-minded and easily hoodwinked because "she was a subscriber for all the 'Health' periodicals. The 'rot' they contained about ventilation, . . . and what to eat, and what to drink, and how much exercise to take, and what frame of mind to keep one's self in . . . was all gospel to her" (92–93).

Of all the remedies Clemens mentions, the last—mental health, keeping one's self in the proper frame of mind—is the *via regia* to a cure in Burnett's novel. And it was all "gospel" for Burnett as well. *The Secret Garden* belongs in every Christian Science reading room.

Burnett was intimately familiar with the Church of Christian Science. Between 1882 and 1884, she lived in Boston and summered in Lynn, Massachusetts—then a center of the movement, since Mary Baker Eddy began her organizational efforts there in 1879. During this period, Burnett was treated for migraines by mind-healers. Later, her son Vivian became an administrator in a Long Island branch of the church. Still, Burnett always insisted she was not a Christian Scientist, but someone sympathetic to their ideas.[8] That secret sympathy is one of the secrets behind *The Secret Garden*.

Like Colin and Mary, (Mary) Eddy was a sickly child. She, too, was kept out of school (because her father had been told she had a brain too large for her body). Eddy claimed to have cured herself of her childhood sicknesses by reading Scripture and by positive thinking. In *Science and Health* (1875), she developed the doctrine that all of existence is a divine brain without a body: there is no matter; the eternal Mind is the source of all being. Eddy and her followers emphasized mind-healing in the conviction that disease is caused by incorrect thinking.

Colin, the hypochondriac, likewise cures himself of his medical problems through positive thinking. First, Mary tells him to avoid negative thoughts about his problems; as Burnett comments, "It was the best thing she could have said" (146). Then, when he steps from the wheelchair and tries his first steps, the atmosphere is thick with encouraging thoughts—like The Little Engine That Could, Mary, for example, is in the background puffing, "You can do it! You can do it! I told you you could! You can do it! You *can!*" (226). And he does.

This experience leads Colin to assert that there is an animating force at work in the world. He does not use Eddy's terms and call it "God" or "the Divine Mind." Instead, he refers to this force as "Magic." Moreover, like Eddy, Colin believes that this doctrine is verifiable by "scientific experiment." He proposes that we can "get hold of [this force] and make it do things for us—like electricity and horses and steam," and "perhaps the beginning is just to say nice things are going to happen until you make them happen." Turning to his companions in the garden, he tells them, "I am going to try a scientific experiment. . . . Every morning and evening and as often in the daytime as I can remember I am going to say, 'Magic is in me! Magic is making me well!'" (236–39).

Magic works its magic, and positive thinking has its effect. Colin becomes a healthy boy. Explaining this phenomenon in the concluding chapter of *The Secret Garden,* Burnett offers her secret paean to Christian Science, without ever directly mentioning the church:

> In each century since the beginning of the world wonderful things have been discovered. . . . One of the new things people began to find out in the last century was that thoughts—just mere thoughts—are as powerful as electric batteries—as good for one as sunlight is, or as bad as poison. To let a sad thought or a bad one get into your mind is as dangerous as letting a scarlet fever germ into your body. . . .
>
> So long as Mistress Mary's mind was full of disagreeable thoughts . . . , she was a yellow-faced, sickly, bored, and wretched child. . . . When her mind gradually filled itself with [other, more positive thoughts], . . . there was no room left for disagreeable thoughts which affected her liver and her digestion and made her yellow and tired.
>
> So long as Colin shut himself in his room and thought only of his fears and weakness . . . , he was a hysterical, half-crazy little hypochondriac. . . . When new, beautiful thoughts be-

gan to push out the old, hideous ones, life began to come back to him, his blood ran healthily in his veins, and strength poured into him. . . . Much more surprising things can happen to anyone who, when a disagreeable or discouraged thought comes into his mind, just has the sense to remember in time and push it out by putting in an agreeable, determinedly courageous one. (281–83)

In Loco Parentis: *Magical Restoration of the Family*

If we could X-ray *The Secret Garden,* we would find, beneath the flesh of the story and the musculature of its advocacy of positive thinking, that basic skeletal structure which we have been describing as "The Three Lives of the Child-Hero."

To begin with, Mary and Colin are "orphans": both of Mary's parents have died, while Colin's mother has died and his father has abandoned him. Both children are also victims of parental neglect. In fact, this neglect is the main cause of their emotional problems. When Mary Lennox is first encountered in the novel, she has been abandoned in a house in India during an outbreak of cholera. This abandonment is not new to her:

> Her father . . . had always been busy and ill himself, and her mother had been a great beauty who cared only to go to parties and amuse herself with gay people. She had not wanted a little girl at all, and when Mary was born she handed her over to the care of an Ayah, who was made to understand that if she wished to please the Mem Sahib she must keep the child out of sight as much as possible. . . . Nobody wanted her. (1–7)

This neglect has made Mary a sickly and jaundiced child with a dictatorial and repugnant personality. When her parents die in the cholera outbreak and the orphan is sent to live with her uncle in England, there is little reason to think she will improve since her new guardian, Archibald Craven, is a moody recluse and, according to his housekeeper, not likely to ever want to see the child.

Colin's situation is similar. When he was born, his mother died. Harboring a grudge against the child, his father never wanted to see him and consigned the boy to a distant, secret room in the mansion. This neglect has made Colin a sickly and bedridden youngster with a personality as repugnant and dictatorial as Mary's.

Opposite Mary and Colin, we should note, is another child of about their same age: Dickon, a robust and kindly boy, surrounded by animals and knowledgeable about nature, part Pan and part Yorkshire St. Francis.[9] He has been shaped by his warm and attentive mother, Mrs. Sowerby, who seems the paragon of parenthood (her opinions on child raising are often sought and quoted by others). She stands in stark contrast, in other words, to Archibald Craven, who is the exemplar of parental neglect in the way he pays no attention to his orphaned niece and ignores his own son, to the detriment of both children.

Of these three children, however, our attention needs to be focused almost exclusively on Colin because, by the middle of the novel, *The Secret Garden* has largely become Colin's book. Dickon remains an extra, and the earlier story of Mary (it eventually becomes clear) merely introduced themes that are subsequently taken over by Colin's story. Once Mary has been cured, early in the novel, her presence becomes less noticeable and she takes on a largely supportive or maternal role as attention shifts to the recovery of the woebegone boy.

In Colin, we can trace the gradual unfolding of the remainder of "The Three Lives of the Child-Hero." Colin comes from a dysfunctional or "broken" family, and this has made him sick in body and spirit. When he makes the short journey to the secondary world of the garden, he joins a surrogate family. Recalling how the March sisters act in much of *Little Women* once their parents are absent, Burnett's children—in their parents' absence—form their own all-child, substitute family in the garden. Under the tutelage of the maternal Mary and the preternaturally wise Dickon, Colin matures. Through the cathexis of the garden and the Magic of positive thinking, Colin restores himself. But what is also interesting is how he also magically restores his missing family life.

Colin's problems are oedipal in nature. This theme is only hinted at in the beginning, when we are told the reason behind the boy's "broken" family: how he came between his parents, how his birth separated husband from wife. It really becomes manifest later in the story, when we see Colin's strong bonds of affection with mother figures and when we see him working through his troubled relations with father figures.

The best way to begin an examination of these issues may be to consider the actual garden that seems to have inspired *The Secret Garden*. Burnett's own father died when she was four years old. Although her British family had been prosperous and middle class, this calamity reduced them to paupers. They were forced to move in with relatives in the working-class neighborhood of Islington. There, perhaps out of grief and in compensation, the little girl spent her time in back of the house, building make-believe gardens in a ruined garden that had become an ash pit. [10]

This activity recalls a fairy tale that was important to Burnett—"Cinderella," or "Ash Daughter" (as the Grimms' version is called). [11] In Grimm, Cinderella's mother, before her death, promises always to watch over her daughter. Afterward, the impoverished Cinderella goes daily to tend her mother's grave, making it into a kind of garden where a tree grows and birds come to its branches. The tree and the birds, the tale makes clear, are associated with the mother and the means by which the dead mother's promise is fulfilled.

The Secret Garden seems a similar place. The children tend it almost daily. Likewise, a prominent feature of the garden is a tree associated with Colin's dead mother; a falling branch from this tree struck her, bringing on his birth and her death. Birds, too, nest in this place and play a significant role in this story; a mother robin hatches her eggs there, the same robin that magically befriended Mary and pointed to where the key to the garden was buried. There is yet another suggestion that, Cinderella-fashion, the garden serves *in loco parentis* for the motherless Colin. As he gets well in this magical place, others seek an explanation, and Dickon offers his Yorkshire opinion that Colin's mother is "many a time lookin' after Mester Colin, same as all mothers do when they're took out o' th' world. They have to come back, tha' sees. Happen she's been in the garden an' happen it was her set us to work, an' told us to bring him here" (217).

All that remains, perhaps, is to make this *genius loci* corporeal, and one day that occurs. Through positive thinking, Colin continues his progress toward health begun in the Secret Garden when he first rose from his wheelchair and walked. Eventually, on one particularly epiphanic day, he realizes how far he has come, "realized something to the full," and shouts: "I'm *well*—I'm *well!*" It is a moment of "rapturous belief and realization," and in gratitude

" 'PRAISE GOD FROM WHOM ALL BLESSINGS FLOW' "

Unknown illustrator for *The Secret Garden*
(New York: Frederick A. Stokes, 1911).

those assembled in the garden spontaneously break into song and sing the Doxology: "Praise God from whom all blessings flow. . . ." (271–73).

In this joyous moment, in the midst of the quasi-religious ceremonials in the garden, something else happens. God, Herself, seems to visit:

> "Who is coming in here?" [Colin] said quickly. "Who is it?"
>
> The door in the ivied wall had been pushed gently open and a woman had entered. She had come in with the last line of the song and she had stood still listening and looking at them. With the ivy behind her, the sunlight drifting through the trees and dappling her long blue cloak, and her nice fresh face smiling across the greenery she . . . seemed to take everything in. . . . Unexpectedly as she had appeared, not one of them felt she was an intruder at all. . . .
>
> "It's mother—that's who it is!" [Dickon] cried. (274–75)

It's Dickon's mother, Mrs. Sowerby, to be specific, but the circumstances are so epiphanic, so reverential, that it seems as if Cinderella's fairy godmother or the Earth Goddess herself has come to visit. All the ceremonials in the garden, the fervent believing and positive thinking, have evoked what is missing. And by a kind of sympathetic magic, what has been evoked is a Mother.

Mrs. Sowerby is the book's Incarnation of Motherhood. Throughout the book, the quotable Mrs. Sowerby is thrown up as the ideal parent, and her opinions on child raising are taken as scripture. Although she is Dickon's mother, this benign peasant woman also takes a special, maternal interest in the lives of both Mary and Colin—wishing them well, providing skip ropes, nurturing them with gifts of food. And when Mrs. Sowerby visits, what she talks about is Mother, telling Colin and Mary how much they resemble their dead mothers.

But this maternal visitation, this Second Coming, seems especially intended as an answer to the wishes of the motherless boy. Colin catches the hem of Mrs. Sowerby's cloak and, with "adoration" in his eyes, says to her: "You are just what I—what I wanted. . . . I wish you were my mother!" "Dear lad," the Yorkshire woman replies, "Thy own mother's in this 'ere very garden, I do believe. She couldna' keep out of it. [And now] Thy father mun come back to thee—he mun!" (279–80).

And so he does. But as we turn to that other side of the oedipal triangle, we note (not surprisingly) that the reconstitution of a father–son relationship is far more involved. For Colin, it involves a two-step process: first triumphing over a father figure (Dr. Craven), and then transforming his own father (Mr. Craven) so that the family can be restored.

Dr. Craven is Colin's physician and a mysterious, confusing character in the novel. On the one hand, his genuine concern with the boy's health makes him seem a benign partner to the maternal Mrs. Sowerby; for example, Chapter 24 begins with Mrs. Sowerby saying about the children, "Let them laugh," and it ends with Dr. Craven saying the same. On the other hand, according to Colin, the physician is the boy's rival and has little interest in his patient's recovery, since, Colin observes, if he were to die, Dr. Craven would become heir to Misselthwaite Manor. In truth, this negative characterization seems to be Colin's own extravagant fantasy and not at all consonant with the facts, since the physician seems to genuinely care for the boy without reservations or darker motives. It seems, in other words, an oedipal fantasy, with Dr. Craven having been assigned the role of the rivalrous Bad Father. In terms of this fantasy, the physician is the dark double of Colin's father: Dr. Craven and Mr. Craven are cousins, and (if we credit Colin's suspicions) they are equally shameful in their neglect of the boy.

But Colin thwarts and humbles this paternal surrogate, this Bad Father. He improves on his own, with no help from Dr. Craven, and he conceals his recovery from the physician, pretending to be still infirm and "getting the better" of the man through his imposture. Colin spites Dr. Craven, in other words, and he takes some pleasure in doing so.

As is the case with other literary heroes in the second of the Three Lives of the Child-Hero, this oedipal triumph over a parental surrogate paves the way for the Third Life and the reconstruction of the original family. First, however, Colin must become a savior.

While the children have been prospering in the garden, Colin's moody, Byronic father has been wandering the Continent, visiting sites known for their remote, sublime, and romantic beauty. Still grief-stricken by the loss of his wife, he has given no thought to the son he would just as soon forget. But one day in the Austrian Tyrol, while staring at (significantly) a patch of blooming forget-me-nots, he feels within himself a change, a shift to the positive, and the beginning of a recovery from his melancholy. Months later he discovers that, *at this very hour* (Burnett's emphasis), Colin had cried out in the garden, "I'm *well*—I'm *well!*" At this moment (as if a pulse of positive mental energy had been bounced off a satellite and communicated to him), Mr. Craven feels the start of regeneration within himself.

By this dreamlike synchronicity, Burnett would have us understand that Colin is responsible for curing his woebegone father. As we have seen, a child's redemption of a misanthropic adult is a familiar theme: Rebecca of Sunnybrook Farm warms the hard heart of Aunt Miranda; Little Lord Fauntleroy converts his mean-spirited grandfather; Hans Brinker melts the icy manner of Dr. Boekman; and Pollyanna saves curmudgeons right and left. But we might observe that in no other novel (except, perhaps, one influenced by Christian Science) can this regeneration be said to occur by such extraordinary means—by telepathy.

This psychic experience is followed by another. Mr. Craven has an unusually vivid dream in which his dead wife appears. When he asks her where she is, he receives an answer that haunts him: "In the garden." This experience and a letter from Mrs. Sowerby prompts him to return home, and on the way "he found himself thinking of his boy as he had never thought in all the ten years past" (289). Arriving at Misselthwaite Manor, Mr. Craven asks where Colin might be found and in answer hears once again the haunting phrase: "In the garden." Approaching the garden, he is surprised when a boy (engaged in a footrace and winning) bursts through the door and into his arms. "Who—what?" he asks. "Father," the boy replies, "I'm Colin" (295).

In other American childhood classics, the winning of a race, often enough, precedes recognition of the child. When Cedric Errol wins a footrace, his grandfather's lawyer is present and observes, "So, this is Little Lord Fauntleroy." After Gretel Brinker wins the competition for the Silver Skates, her father's amnesia passes and he recognizes his children. Colin's triumph in the footrace leads, in a similar fashion, to a reunion with and acknowledgment by his father. This recognition is carried further in the last pages of the novel when Archibald Craven and his son march up the lawn to the house to meet the servants so that the father can introduce them to their new master—"Master Colin." It is a Recognition Ceremony, an acknowledgment of the true heir, that recalls many others in the conclusions of America's children's books.

An American Advocacy

Our illumination of the skeletal structure of *The Secret Garden* reveals that ur-plot, "The Three Lives of the Child-Hero," which we have found in so many other American childhood classics. At the same time, as we have been suggesting throughout this study by means of comparisons, this ur-story can sometimes be found in other national literatures—in, for example, the tales of Oedipus and of Hansel and Gretel. Our point, consequently, has not been that this ur-story is "American," but that what is notable is how—given a panoply of other possible archetypes available to writers for children and for reasons of their own—American authors were drawn to this particular pattern. But with *The Secret Garden* we can now move on to observe how Americans gave this particular ur-story a particularly American "spin."

In the variations that American authors play on this ur-story, a distinctive national characteristic is the advocacy of positive thinking. For the most part, this feature seems largely absent from Children's Literature of other countries; it would be difficult to say, for example, that the aim of *Peter Rabbit* or *Wind in the Willows* or *Pinocchio* is to offer a clarion call for mental optimism.[12] This is even true of tales that share the ur-story featured in American children's books; few readers would say, for example, that the point of the stories of Oedipus and of Hansel and Gretel is to champion upbeat attitudes.

The mental nature of American children's books is signaled in their preoccupation with feelings. As we read pages of detailed accounts of the March sisters' struggles with their "bosom enemies," as we witness Tom Sawyer's continual creation of tableaus in which others wring their hands in troubled remorse, it is difficult to escape the impression that these stories really unfold elsewhere, in some internal world, in that place we have been calling the Theater of Feelings. And more than the Children's Literature of other countries, it seems, American children's books tell us of the inner lives of children: not only in the copious descriptions of, say, Jo's wrestlings within herself in her own internal civil war, but also in the lengthy passages describing the mental state and troubled anxieties within Clemens's pauper or the profuse accounts of the pangs of hunger and struggle for self-control within Toby Tyler.

Bad feelings, negative emotions, "bosom enemies," wrong thoughts—these are the problems in such books as *Toby Tyler, Hans Brinker, Little Women,* and *The Secret Garden.* Not surprisingly, positive thinking is their cure. "Believe in yourself!"— that is the lesson the Wizard gives to Dorothy and her three companions, so full of personal misgivings. "Believe in others!"—that is the lesson in *Little Lord Fauntleroy,* as the little boy's innocent trust in others remakes the world and they become as good as he thinks they always were. "Believe!"—that is the lesson of *Tom Sawyer* when the boy persuades his friends to whitewash the fence and what seemed like work is actually turned into play. Keeping bad thoughts in check and emphasizing positive thinking—that is an American theme also evident in the stalwart personality of Hans Brinker and the endorsements of *The Secret Garden.* These advocacies are even more apparent in *Pollyanna.*

12

✢ ✢ ✢ ✢ ✢ ✢ ✢

Radical Innocence
Pollyanna

Published near the end of the Golden Age of Children's Literature, Eleanor Porter's *Pollyanna* (1913) can be seen as representative of the American childhood classics we have been discussing. At the same time, no book besides *Pollyanna* so clearly indicates the American preoccupation with the emotional lives of children and the American advocacy of positive thinking—from Hans Brinker's efforts to maintain his sunny disposition against the tidal assaults of oceanic feelings, to *The Secret Garden*'s secret endorsement of Christian Science. But no discussion of the novel can proceed without reckoning first with the book's reputation as a saccharine story about empty-headed optimism.

The history of *Pollyanna*'s popularity is remarkable. Following publication, the novel appeared on adult best-seller lists for the next two years. It spawned a sequel in 1915 that was a year-long best seller. After selling a million copies in the United States, the novel was issued in editions in France, Germany, Holland, Poland, Czechoslovakia, Norway, Sweden, Brazil, Switzerland, Scotland, and Japan. By 1920 it had gone through forty-seven printings. By 1946 the book had become a series, with twelve titles by four authors, and had given birth to clubs, a play, several films, and an entry in dictionaries. Then, suddenly, the novel fell out of favor and, until very recently, was virtually unavailable from American publishers.[1]

Pollyanna seems, in our own time, to be a book few people have read but everyone dislikes, largely because of its reputation. "Pollyanna" has become a noun that *The American Heritage Dictionary* defines as "a foolishly or blindly optimistic person." Contemporary reference books describe Pollyanna Whittier as "possibly the most exasperating heroine in fiction. . . . She seems the epitome of everything that is priggish and sentimental in the fiction of a half century ago."[2]

That wasn't the feeling when the novel first appeared. As one scholar explained, "The publication of the story in 1913 was only less influential than the World War. White Mountain cabins, Colorado teahouses, Texas babies, Indiana apartment houses, and a brand of milk were immediately named for the new character."[3] Recogni∴ing a sure thing, Mary Pickford paid the then-astronomical sum of $115,112 for rights to produce a silent-screen version of the book.

Porter's publisher had asked for a cheerful book, and the author responded by inventing the Glad Game and a girl who preaches the gospel of Gladness. Living out West with her impoverished missionary father, Pollyanna wishes for a doll. When the barrel from the missionary society arrives, however, it contains only crutches; but Pollyanna consoles herself by finding that she can at least be glad that she doesn't need the crutches.

Orphaned by her father's death, Pollyanna moves to Beldingsville, Vermont, and into the house of her hard-bitten aunt. In the next hundred pages, this evangelical girl and juvenile social worker persuades the whole town to play the Glad Game. Cranky Mr. Pendleton, the bedridden Mrs. Snow, the dispirited Reverend Ford, the forlorn Dr. Chilton, and (finally) her sclerotic aunt succumb to the power of positive thinking and begin to hunt for and find things in their lives to be glad about.

After the novel's appearance, American editorial writers reached for hyperboles: "It is probably not putting the case too strongly when we state that it is the greatest game ever discovered since the foundation of the world."[4] Testimonials to the book's transformative power poured in from stockbrokers, clergy, missionaries, millionaires, dowagers, file clerks, and a sobbing Philadelphia newspaperman. "To the list of those who have done something to make the world more joyous," the *Boston Transcript* enthused, "must be added the names of Pollyanna and Eleanor H. Porter."[5]

Americans began to sport enameled buttons showing a smiling girl to indicate that they were members of Glad Clubs—which included the Glad Kids, a group of prisoners in a penitentiary whose ages ranged from thirty-two to seventy-six. By 1947, however, things had changed. Then, a writer would lament: "Almost nobody plays the Glad Game any more. . . . [It] seems to belong to a more innocent time."[6]

The novel's fall from grace is not hard to explain. Some found Pollyanna's unbounded optimism a bit much when, for example, she consoles a gardener stooped by arthritis that he should be glad that he doesn't have so far to bend over, or when the girl herself is crippled and brightly concludes that she can be glad that she had the use of her legs "once." Other readers seemed to share the exasperation of Pollyanna's aunt when she says, "Will you stop using that everlasting word 'glad'! It's 'glad'—'glad'—'glad' from morning until night until I think I shall grow wild!"[7] Importuned, perhaps by members of the Glad Clubs, a cartoonist pictured a girl involved in an accident and lying in the street underneath the wheels of an automobile; the caption read: "I'm so GLAD it was a limousine!"[8]

An attempt was made to resuscitate Pollyanna in 1960 when Disney Studios released a movie based on the book. *Time, Newsweek,* and other major reviewers agreed that such an enterprise promised to be a disaster—a tear-jerker of a story presented by the master of schmaltz. To the surprise of the critics (whose opinions were unanimous), it was Disney's best live-action film ever.[9] But few had reckoned with the curse of the book's by-then smarmy reputation. When the movie failed to bring in half of the $6 million that was expected, Disney opined: "I think the picture would have done better with a different title. Girls and women went to it, but men tended to stay away because it sounded sweet and sticky."[10]

Shortly thereafter, American publishers let the book drift out of print. What is surprising is that this wasn't true in other parts of the world. My own British copy of the book, for example, a Penguin paperback, lists this publishing history: "1969. Reprinted 1970, 1972, 1973 (twice), 1974 (twice), 1975 (twice), 1976,

1977, 1978." In America, however, few people have been willing to read the book because of its unfortunate reputation for bubble-headed optimism.

That reputation is largely undeserved and has become something of an unthinking reflex whenever the book is mentioned. Porter herself recognized that fact: "I have been made to suffer from the Pollyanna books. I have been placed often in a false light. People have thought that Pollyanna chirped that she was 'glad' about everything. . . . I have never believed that we ought to deny discomfort and pain and evil; I have merely thought that it is far better to 'greet the unknown with a cheer.'"[11]

These days, only an open-minded reader, ready to go beyond received opinion, will open the book. And only a skillful reader will recognize that Pollyanna is not as naive as she might seem at first. She is, instead, one of the most cunning tricksters to appear in American children's books since Tom Sawyer persuaded his friends to whitewash the fence for him.

Pollyanna's Cunning

Only brief reference can be made to other motifs which seem to be loosely related to [these ur-stories]. Such themes include that of playing the fool, which [seems] . . . the universal childhood attitude towards grownups.

Otto Rank, "The Myth of the Birth of the Hero"

It is, perhaps, too easy to underestimate Pollyanna. When she first appears in the novel, she seems a dithery eleven-year-old, chattering along in an incessant way, a kind of juvenile Lucille Ball. Her innocence seems witless, as well, when this orphan meets her spinster aunt for the first time and learns that she is forbidden ever to mention her late father's name. Aunt Polly detested Pollyanna's father, but the child hastily presumes that her aunt's motives are benign and that the woman merely wants Pollyanna to get over her grief more quickly.

Moments such as these have seduced superficial readers to make superficial observations. "Pollyanna is stupid," Mary Cadogan and

Patricia Craig say, an example of "imbecile cheerfulness. . . . [The novel reduces] the doctrine of making the best of things to the level of complete absurdity" and "makes no demands on the reader's ability to think."[12]

To the surprise of some, the novel is far more complex than that. Pollyanna is only playing the fool. If Tom Sawyer manipulates adults by playing the martyr, Pollyanna is more clever. She gets her way by being glad—and such innocent gratitude seems not only above reproach, but invulnerable to suspicion.

Take the circumstances that lead to Pollyanna's acquiring more reasonable accommodations in her aunt's house. Aunt Polly is only doing her "duty" when she takes in her orphaned niece, and her reluctance to do so is evident when she places the child in a hot and dusty attic room with bare furnishings—a choice of quarters that even the maid finds inexcusable. Having already suffered from abject poverty in the West, Pollyanna had anticipated better circumstances when she came to the mansion of her wealthy aunt, but she makes the best of what she finds. When her aunt happens to visit her one day in that room, Pollyanna chatters away and, in the midst of her volubility, offers her gratitude to her aunt: "I just love this room, even if it hasn't got the carpets and curtains and pictures that I'd been [wanting]" (71). The absence of a mirror, she explains, makes it impossible to see her dreaded freckles. The absence of pictures is compensated by the lovely view through the window. "You've been so good to me," Pollyanna finally says to her aunt (71–72). The girl's gladness and negative rhetoric shames the woman, and Pollyanna is given a more comfortable room.

This gladness also disarms the aunt whenever she tries to punish the child:

- When Pollyanna is late for dinner, Aunt Polly tells her that, regrettably, she must be disciplined and can have only bread and milk, and must eat with the maid. Pollyanna replies, "I like bread and milk, and Nancy too. You musn't feel bad about that one bit" (36).

- When Pollyanna leaves her window open, her aunt sends her to her room to read a pamphlet about the diseases carried by flies. Pollyanna later thanks her aunt for the opportunity for such interesting reading.

- When, one hot evening, Pollyanna crawls out her window to sleep on the porch and wakes up the household, Aunt Polly, to chastise the girl, tells her she must sleep the night in the aunt's room. The girl's delight at this prospect unnerves her guardian: "For the third time since Pollyanna's arrival, Miss Polly was punishing Pollyanna—and for the third time she was being confronted with the amazing fact that her punishment was being taken as a special reward of merit. No wonder Miss Polly was feeling curiously helpless" (51).

Call her a genius at "reverse psychology." In the way Pollyanna disarms her aunt she is anything but stupid. This is readily apparent, as well, when she teaches the bedridden Mrs. Snow how to play the Glad Game. This is a challenge, another character explains, because "Nothin' what ever *has* happened, has happened right in Mis' Snow's eyes. Even the days of the week ain't run ter her mind. If it's Monday she's bound to say she wished it 'twas Sunday; and if you take her jelly you're pretty sure ter hear she wanted chicken—but if you *did* bring her chicken, she'd be jest hankerin' for lamb broth" (54–55).

Pollyanna does take the invalid some food, but, before presenting it, asks her what she wants. This flummoxes Mrs. Snow: "She had so long been accustomed to wanting what she did not have, that to state offhand what she *did* want seemed impossible—until she knew what she had" (67). Finally, Mrs. Snow asks for lamb broth, and Pollyanna produces it from behind her back. Having second thoughts, Mrs. Snow wishes she had asked instead for chicken, and Pollyanna produces that, too. Instead of these, Mrs. Snow finally concludes she wished she had calf's-foot jelly, and Pollyanna startles her by producing that as well.

As the narrator notes, Pollyanna's clever gambit undermines something habitual in Mrs. Snow: "The sick woman seemed to be trying—mentally—to find something she had lost" (67). This leads to a recognition that is the first step in a reorientation of the woman's outlook on life: she "had lived forty years and for fifteen of those years she had been too busy wishing things were different to find much time to enjoy things as they were" (57). Through Pollyanna's indirection, Mrs. Snow finds things to be glad about, ceases to be a grumpy invalid, rises from her bed, regains her health, and rejoins the community.

Pollyanna, in other words, is not a simple-minded waif. In the way she manipulates Mrs. Snow, wins herself a better room in the mansion, and defuses her aunt's punishments, it is clear that she uses optimism as a tool. Moreover, as the incidents surrounding Jimmy Bean make clear, she is not above blackmail.

Although others know Aunt Polly as a hard-hearted spinster, Pollyanna considers her "a kind protector and angel of mercy" because she adopted her (76), and Pollyanna sings her aunt's praises throughout the town. Pollyanna, consequently, brings home stranded kittens and a dog under the expressed conviction that her aunt is so kind that she will take in creatures when others wouldn't. This is a species of blackmail: how can her aunt gainsay her? The girl's benign presumptions shame the aunt and leave her in the grip of "the curious helpless feeling that had been hers so often since Pollyanna's arrival" (76). The limits are reached, however, when Pollyanna uses the same ploy to argue that Aunt Polly should adopt Jimmy Bean, a waif from a nearby orphanage.

Aunt Polly refuses to adopt the boy, so Pollyanna turns to the local Ladies Aid Society and again uses benign presumptions to effect. She explains that, having been helped by a Ladies Aid Society in the West, she knows of their goodwill and is sure that someone in the society will be glad to adopt Jimmy. She is told, in turn, that this group in Beldingsville has earned a national reputation for supporting orphans in India. This leads to another benign presumption on her part: that the society would be even more eager to care for a local orphan. The discussion that follows, however, before the motion is tabled, puzzles the girl: "Some of what was said at this time Pollyanna thought she could not have understood, for it sounded as if they did not care what the money *did,* so long as the sum opposite the name of the society in a certain 'report' 'headed the list'—and of course that cannot be what they meant at all!" (87).

In a moment like this, it is easy to see why a review in the *New York Sun* would describe *Pollyanna* as "a book for grown-ups who will understand the criticism of convention."[13] In a similar vein, Grace Isabel Colbron would observe in a 1915 issue of *Bookman* that Pollyanna is "the supreme non-conformist [who refuses] to accept the artificial dicta of the grown-up world."[14]

Representative Novel: The Ur-Plot Redux

> [Pollyanna *is an example of*] *a genre much favored by writers in the three decades before the First World War, and grew out of the evangelical story on which most of them would have been reared and their parents before them, the story of the child who spoke heavenly truths and converted its hard-hearted elders and wayward contemporaries. After* Little Lord Fauntleroy (1886), *whom Pollyanna much resembles, this genre became secularized; Pollyanna and her kind tame the crabby and melt the hearts of the obdurate by no heavenly message, merely by their own buoyant spirits.*
>
> Gillian Avery, "Porter, Eleanor H.," in
> *Twentieth-Century Children's Writers*

As Avery suggests, the resemblances between *Pollyanna* and *Little Lord Fauntleroy* are difficult to miss. Change the gender of the child-hero and a summary of *Fauntleroy* sounds like a recapitulation of Porter's book. *Fauntleroy* is the story of a boy who travels to the mansion of a wealthy and disagreeable relative who reluctantly takes the child in. The child, nonetheless, is optimistic and good-hearted and assumes the best about its relative. After a period of philanthropy, the child melts the heart of its curmudgeonly antagonist.

More specific resemblances, however, can be detected between *Rebecca of Sunnybrook Farm* (1903) and *Pollyanna* (1913). Both are stories of a lively girl who travels to the New England home of a spinster aunt who is more prosperous yet reluctant to take the child in, who is rigid and fixed and irritated by the spontaneous child. While both girls have opposite-sex adult friends (bachelor "uncles"), an antagonism exists between the girl and the aunt. Nonetheless, both girls become favorites of the town because of their philanthropy, and both represent their aunts at a meeting of the church aid society. Finally, the hearts of both curmudgeons are eventually melted, and the aunts express affection for the girl.

Besides *Little Lord Fauntleroy* and *Rebecca of Sunnybrook Farm,* *Pollyanna* has uncanny resemblances to *The Secret Garden* (1911). When Burnett's Mary Lennox arrives at Misselthwaite Manor, she encounters a maid and a close-mouthed gardener who will befriend her; likewise, Pollyanna meets the amiable Nancy and the taciturn Old Tom (who, like Burnett's gardener, describes the child's late mother as a departed angel present in the garden). Likewise, *Pollyanna* is a story full of secrets: there is a mystery to be puzzled out (the earlier love affair between Aunt Polly and Dr. Chilton), and there is Mr. Pendleton's "skeleton in the closet" (that he was once in love with Pollyanna's late mother). While Pollyanna discovers this "skeleton" when she explores the eerie mansion of Mr. Pendleton, Mary Lennox finds another skeleton in the closet when she explores her uncle's Gothic mansion and encounters Colin. Mary redeems Colin, encourages him to open the curtains and let light into his room, urges him to get out of bed and go outdoors, persuades him to surrender his hypochondria for a more positive attitude. Pollyanna does the very same thing with Mrs. Snow. Likewise, just as *The Secret Garden* turns to a great extent on Colin's leaving his wheelchair and learning to walk, much of *Pollyanna* deals with legs and mobility: the Glad Game is invented when Pollyanna receives crutches she doesn't need; Mrs. Snow is a bedridden invalid until Pollyanna cheers her up; Mr. Pendleton breaks his leg, and Pollyanna nurses him to health; and (in the conclusion) Pollyanna is struck by a car and unable to use her legs but (in the very last pages) is on the mend and makes use of those previously unneeded crutches to take her first steps in the hospital.

Numerous other resemblances might be noticed between these three novels and *Pollyanna*.[15] But numerous resemblances might also be noted between *Pollyanna* and the other eight works that we have been examining. When Porter's novel is seen in context, in other words, we encounter once again the startling uniformity of American children's books of the Golden Age. Like these others, Porter's novel plays variations on that ur-story we have been calling "The Three Lives of the Child-Hero."

THE FIRST LIFE

True to the structure of the three lives outlined in the Introduction to this study, *Pollyanna* is the story of an *orphan;* both her parents have died before the novel opens. Unlike some of her literary kin, she is not a victim of parental *neglect;* her father was loving and devoted. Instead, like others, she is a victim of *poverty;* because her father "was the pastor of [a] small mission church, and had a very meager salary," they lived on donations sent by the missionary society, and when he died, "he left practically nothing else save a few books" (9). Given her American milieu, Pollyanna is not an example of *dispossessed royalty;* instead, her golden past takes the form of the *vanished happy time:* when she comes to live with her irritable aunt, she brings with her the memory of a happier time with a poor but loving father who always found something to be glad about in the darkest situations. At the same time, like other American literary children, Pollyanna was born after a *violation of a marriage prohibition:* Pollyanna's mother had wed the impoverished minister over the objections of her family.

With these a priori conditions in place, the American children's story begins, and the transition is marked by a *journey.* Pollyanna's mode of transport is not as dramatic as Dorothy Gale's gale, or as luxurious as Little Lord Fauntleroy's ocean liner, or as pedestrian as that of Twain's peripatetic prince, or as adventurous as Huck's raft and Toby Tyler's circus wagon. It is more on the order of Rebecca's stagecoach ride from Sunnybrook Farm to her aunts' house. When her father's parishioners are unwilling to care for the orphaned eleven-year-old, Pollyanna is railroaded into living with her Yankee aunt; put on a train and shipped from a small town in the West to Beldingsville, Vermont.

THE SECOND LIFE

Recalling the castles and mansions that are the destinations of America's other literary heroes, Pollyanna comes to her own *big house*—the mansion with servants of her well-to-do aunt. Like other locales, outside her aunt's home is the *great outdoors,* the township of Beldingsville, where Pollyanna can do as she pleases, where there are hills to climb and fields for philanthropy. In this new place, Pollyanna is *adopted into a second family* headed by her wealthy Aunt Polly, a *surrogate parent of a different social rank.* Her aunt, who is put off by the lively girl and harasses her whichever way she turns, is her *same-sex antagonist.* But Pollyanna has the aid of two bachelor "uncles," Mr. Pendleton and Dr. Chilton, who are *opposite-sex helpers* and whose encouraging interest in the girl offers an alternative to her aunt's harshness.

By means of her gladness, however, Pollyanna wins many battles with her aunt (obtaining a better room, defusing Aunt Polly's punishments, getting her way) until the campaign is won. Pollyanna's *triumph over the antagonist* is clear when her contrite aunt asks the girl to teach her the Glad Game. Just as Dorothy aids her friends and liberates the people enslaved by witches in the kingdoms surrounding the Emerald City, just as Twain's prince and pauper improve the lots of those in the kingdom surrounding London, Pollyanna is likewise a *child who emerges as a savior.* Just as Hans Brinker persuades Dr. Boekman to help and cure his father, just as the March sisters serve as nurses to a community suffering from everything from colds (Laurie) to scarlet fever (Beth and the Hummels), Pollyanna is a medical wonder-worker who visits and aids invalids all over Beldingsville (from the bedridden Mrs. Snow to Mr. Pendleton with his broken leg). But she is more social worker than nurse, and (like Rebecca or Fauntleroy) her primary object is to melt the hard hearts of curmudgeons.

THE THIRD LIFE

In the end, Aunt Polly (who, in the earlier parts of the novel, would like to believe that Pollyanna has had only one parent and forbids the child ever to speak of her father) humbly asks the girl to teach her the Glad Game (which Pollyanna learned from her father and which is his legacy to her). In this way a taboo is lifted, Pollyanna is acknowledged as the offspring of both a father and a mother, and *issues of identity are resolved.* This resolution is brought on by the accident in which Pollyanna is struck by a car, loses the use of her legs, and is confined to bed. Expressions of sympathy and testimonials to the girl's transformative power pour into Aunt Polly's house from all over town: from Mr. Pendleton, Mrs. Snow, and Tom the gardener; from two widows consoled by the girl; from a woman who had contemplated leaving her husband. In *Pollyanna*'s own version of the *recognition ceremony,* virtually the entire population of Beldingsville become well-wishers, assembled on the lawn outside the invalid's bedroom because they recognize that "the whole town is wonderfully happier—all because of one little girl" (195). On the one hand, the resolution of questions of identity reintroduces information about the child-hero's First Life; on the other hand, the recognition ceremony acknowledges just how much the child-hero has done in her Second Life.

Now some *accommodation between the two lives* must be struck. Some heroes, like Tarzan and Jo March, get stuck on the threshold of choice. Others choose between: while Huckleberry Finn opts for his Second Life, prodigals Dorothy Gale and Toby Tyler return to their families and their First Lives in Kansas and Connecticut. The return to the family is, in fact, the most common gambit in the resolutions of these novels. Some children have their First Life given back to them when the father is restored: when Raff Brinker recovers from his cranial operation and becomes once again the head of the household; when Mr. March parades home from Washington; when, apologetic, Mr. Craven comes to the Secret Garden. In another group of stories, however, the family is restored in some imaginative way by the creation of new domestic arrangements: not choosing between the Motherland and the Fatherland, Fauntleroy invites all his American friends to England to join him in an extended family presided over by both his mother and his paternal grandfather; Rebecca invites her mother and siblings from the penury of Sunnybrook Farm to the distant home of her aunts, which she has inherited, and the book ends with a proclamation of a *vita nuova* for the Brick House. *Pollyanna* also ends with this kind of domestic innovation. The girl's accident brings together two estranged lovers, her Aunt Polly and Dr. Chilton, and the orphan is given a family once again when they marry at her bedside.

Representative Novel: Oedipal Meaning

While the striking unanimity of these stories might be explained in various ways, we have been employing a psychological methodology in this study because, quite simply, such an approach yields more. Instead of generating piecemeal observations about parts of these novels, this means of interpretation provides a comprehensive understanding of more of their shared particulars and offers an explanation for their consistent syntax, their uniform arrangement in a shared ur-plot.

Since, as we have observed, many of these books conclude with the reconstruction of a family, it isn't surprising that a backward glance indicates that the major problem presented for resolution in these novels is domestic disharmony. At the same time, when the friendly and unfriendly adults who take a parental interest in the child are grouped by gender, the exact nature of this "family problem" comes into focus. These various works treat in symbolic terms the disruption of family peace that comes when the child, quite naturally, asserts its individuality. The recurrent scene of the reconstruction of a family can be said to portray the restoration of domestic harmony once a child has worked through a period of oedipal estrangement.

Understood in these terms, *Pollyanna* is like these other books in its account of oedipal development. Like many of America's other literary orphans, Pollyanna's "angelic" mother, the mother of infancy, dies before the story opens. She is replaced not by Cinderella's cruel stepmother, but by her familiar incarnation in the girl's books—the hardhearted aunt.

As might be expected, adult males in the story are unusually kind to the girl. In the case of Pollyanna, Mr. Pendleton and Dr. Chilton can be regarded as father figures because the former offers to adopt the child and the latter does so. Notable as well is the fact that both these men are bachelors.

Equally revealing is the hostile relationship that exists between Aunt Polly and Pollyanna's various "fathers." Like Jo, who does not care for Mr. Brooke because he would marry Meg and thereby break up the March family, Aunt Polly harbors ill feeling toward Pollyanna's father because he took her sister away, and, as another character observes, "Miss Polly—young as she was—couldn't never forgive him" (171). For this reason, she forbids her niece ever to speak of her father. This antagonism toward Pollyanna's father is also widened to include Pollyanna's father figures: Aunt Polly is not on speaking terms with either Mr. Pendleton (because he also courted Pollyanna's mother) or Dr. Chilton (because of a disagreement that arose between them when they were sweethearts).

This condition of "parental" estrangement does not seem to be something Pollyanna is responsible for. Instead, she inherits this situation when she enters the novel. Still, these circumstances might be more accurately seen as a disguised reflection of Pollyanna's own oedipal emotions:

- In the oedipal situation, children feel, quite naturally, both affection and hostility toward their parents. Because they sometimes feel guilty about their feelings, the principals in these psychic dramas are disguised so that instead of mother and father, the villains and favorites are recast as uncles, aunts, grandfathers, witches, stepmothers, and the like.

- This disguising is continued through the projection of these feelings. Instead of the *child* feeling affection for one parent and hostility toward the other, those feelings are attributed to others. In the case of Pollyanna, it is her *aunt* who is hostile toward her and her *"uncles"* who are affectionate.

- A final form of disguise appears in the way the child's rivalrous feelings are projected and reappear as antagonistic feelings of the parent figures toward each other. This antagonism is seen as the result of events that took place before the child appeared on the scene; thus the child is not responsible for them. The *child* does not prefer one parent over the other; instead, through projections, the *"parents,"* themselves, seem engaged in a rivalry for the child. These "parents" seem to require the child to choose between them.

This final state does eventually appear in Porter's novel. Pollyanna's friendships with and her affection for Dr. Chilton and Mr. Pendleton alarm and threaten her aunt. Then, in an episode that seems unmistakably oedipal, she is asked to choose: Mr. Pendleton tells Pollyanna of his love for her late mother, tells the child he has likewise fallen under her spell, and invites her to come and live with him. Mr. Pendleton, of course, has in mind adoption, not marriage; but the fact that he sees the eleven-year-old as the reincarnation of his former sweetheart and Pollyanna's mother makes this distinction seem murky. Moreover, Mr. Pendleton makes clear that this invitation to move to his house is extended only to Pollyanna; if they were to set up housekeeping, Aunt Polly would be left behind. Seeming to sense that this is an incorrect oedipal solution, and unwilling to abandon her aunt, Pollyanna declines.

This oedipal issue remains essentially unresolved until the novel's penultimate scene, when the necessity for choosing is eliminated. Late in the book, Pollyanna is removed from the competition when she is struck by an automobile and crippled. When testimonials to the child's influence and the power of her Glad Game flow in from around the town, her aunt wonders what this is all about. This provides Nancy, her maid, with the occasion to

"BORNE, LIMP AND UNCONSCIOUS, INTO THE LITTLE ROOM
THAT WAS SO DEAR TO HER."

Stockton Mulford for *Pollyanna* (Boston: Page, 1913).

explain to Aunt Polly that she was not told about the Glad Game because it was associated with Pollyanna's late father, and Aunt Polly had forbidden the child to speak of him. Learning this, Pollyanna's aunt runs to the child's bedside, says she too will play the Glad Game, and thereby removes the taboo regarding the girl's father, which had been the stumbling block.

Aunt Polly's acknowledgment of Pollyanna's father paves the way for rapprochements with the girl's father figures. Through shared concern for the girl, Aunt Polly meets first with Mr. Pendleton, and then with Dr. Chilton. In this way, parental estrangement is brought to an end. In the final episode, Aunt Polly and Dr. Chilton marry at the child's bedside, and Pollyanna gets once more a mother and father.

In this dreamlike fashion, then, a child's solution of its own oedipal problems is symbolized—in a manner that leaves the child entirely blameless. At the beginning of the book, the even-tempered Pollyanna is the recipient, not the author, of both hostility and affection—emotions that emanate from capricious adults. In Beldingsville she encounters a longstanding antipathy between her parent figures for which she is not responsible. She does not prefer one "parent" over another; instead, adults require her to choose them as sole guardian, and she endeavors to avoid such choices. Finally, the guileless Pollyanna does not deliberately resolve these oedipal problems; instead, unintentionally, her accident provides the occasion for these parent figures to resume a harmonious relationship and to restore the "family."

Pollyanna is a complex novel, then, replete with disguises. It is not only the story of an innocent optimist who is really a cunning trickster for the good, but also a series of oedipal extrapolations that convert Pollyanna from agent into blameless victim and unwitting savior. Behind this tissue of psychological fictions, however, is a recognizable process, whose own consistency explains the consistencies of its representation in various American children's books.

Representative Novel: Revising the Pietà

The novel's wonderfully pictorial conclusion can serve as a convenient benchmark of change in American Children's Literature. *Tom*

Sawyer poked fun at the Protestant Pietà of earlier Children's Literature in Tom's self-indulgent fantasies of martyrdom. *Little Women* modified that Pietà by having similar episodes (for example, when Amy has fallen through the ice and the family gathers at her bedside) lead not to religious reformation, but to bouts of self-recrimination that are a prelude to character development. *Pollyanna,* too, offers a new kind of Pietà.

Gone is the Protestant version of earlier American Children's Literature, with the dying child in its sickbed, preaching heavenly truths to those huddled around. In its place is the secularized version of *Pollyanna*'s conclusion, in which there are wedding bells and an invalid girl presiding in her hospital room over a marriage that can be reckoned a symbol of her own developmental progress. The difference between these Pietàs suggests just how much these later works substituted medical and psychological issues for spiritual ones.

Now, concerns are more temporal, and doctors are more likely to be in attendance than ministers: Beth March in her sickbed suffering from scarlet fever and surrounded by her family and the family physician; the bedridden hypochondriac Colin Craven being visited daily by his peers and Dr. Craven; and Pollyanna, after her injury, attended to by Dr. Chilton and well-wishers from all over town. Now, instead of a fallen world tainted by Original Sin, these new secularized novels seem to offer a vision of the world as sick ward: an England full of maimed and scabrous paupers that Clemens's prince resolves to help, a Massachusetts town where the March family is called on to nurse wounded soldiers and contagious immigrants, and a Vermont village in *Pollyanna* that seems to be populated almost entirely by invalids. Finally, now in the conclusions, children are not transported to the Pearly Gates but, more often, attain a terrestrial reward: Beth gets better; Colin rises from his wheelchair and walks; and Pollyanna, on the last page, is at last able to hazard her first tentative steps after the accident.

The thrust of these earlier religious tales and their Pietàs was to prompt remorse and reformation in the hardhearted sinners surrounding the sickbed of an exemplary and expiring ephebe. In these latter-day tales, however, reformation is inspired in those who are simply hardhearted: Rebecca melts her Aunt Miranda, making her into as warm a person as she can possibly become; the ever-sunny Hans Brinker, in his own icy world, arranges events that finally bring happiness, especially to the otherwise cheerless physician Dr. Boekman; Fauntleroy, all innocence and naiveté, redeems his grumpy grandfather; and Pollyanna's gladness transforms an entire community of miscellaneous misanthropes. In these secularized tales, then, sin is replaced by dourness. Adults are "born again," but in a psychological rather than religious fashion. And salvation often comes through optimism.

These secularized novels, then, substituted emotional problems for their religious equivalents. The "bosom enemies" of the March sisters, for example, are not the Seven Deadly Sirs, but negative emotions like anger. Hans Brinker is not a young Christian soldier righteously resisting evil, but a stalwart youth maintaining his cheerfulness against the tidal assaults of untoward emotions. Toby Tyler does not suffer from the sin of cupidity, but from the psychological problems of his unchecked appetite: he is tempted not by the devil, but by devil's food cake. Negative Thinking, not Original Sin, hobbles Dorothy's unself-confident companions in Oz—invalids like those in *The Secret Garden* and *Polllyanna* who must embrace positive thinking. In the American children's books of the Golden Age, in other words, we depart from religious venues and enter the secular world of the Theater of Feelings, where we are concerned not with spiritual well-being, but with good spirits and mental health.

Still, looking backward, we can see the religious roots of these stories. Pollyanna's optimism is, sub rosa, religious in origin. Like *The Secret Garden*'s secret endorsement of Christian Science, Pollyanna's message is a slightly disguised evangelical one. This explains the extraordinary enthusiasm of clergy for the book when it first appeared, as well as the circumstances of its first publication as a serial story in the *Christian Herald*.[16] There is no mistaking the fact that Pollyanna is a "savior." Her mother is frequently called an "angel." Her late father, it is often said, is in heaven. And when Pollyanna is missing from her room, other characters react as if encountering the empty tomb of Jesus: "that blessed child is gone, . . . vanished right up into heaven where she come from" (31). If "a child shall lead them," Pollyanna assumes that role, curing the sick and acquiring disciples who spread the Word about the Glad Game. It was her minister father who taught her the game, and, in a sense, Pollyanna is always "about her father's business" as she spreads her message of "good news."

The evangelical message, however, is "secularized." Pollyanna is not a spiritual savior, but a social one, and her gospel is an inoffensive one of positive thinking. Literary historians, in fact, might regard the taboo that Aunt Polly places on her niece about never speaking of her late father as the equivalent of the restraints under which writers like Porter composed their works: abjured by a secular age to make little mention of the heavenly "Father," authors resorted to analogy.

But analogizing is a two-way process. Like new wine in old wineskins, the attempt in *Pollyanna* and these other novels to secularize the earlier religious tradition also created unprecedented forms and rendered religious tropes vestigial. Looking forward, we can glimpse rough intimations of more modern pediatric paradigms.[17] Gone is the Original Sin and the Fall; in its place we begin to see oedipal rebellion and the loss of domestic peace. Gone is a vision of a heavenly paradise and the recovery of a happiness once felt in Eden; in its place is the promise of a post-oedipal bliss and the restoration of a family harmony known in early childhood. Gone is Adam and his apple; in its place is adolescence and the increasingly prominent adam's apple of puberty.

Radical Innocence: The American Theme

"I've seen her get into a trolley car that was full of cross-looking men and women, and whimpering children, and in five minutes you wouldn't know the place. The men and women have stopped scowling, and the children have forgot what they are cryin' for."

Eleanor Porter, *Pollyanna Grows Up*

"Before I shipped that young fellow, my forecastle was a rat-pit of quarrels. . . . But Billy came; and it was like a Catholic priest striking peace in an Irish shindy. Not that he preached to them or said or did anything in particular; but a virtue went out of him, sugaring the sour ones."

Herman Melville, *Billy Budd*

In his study *The American Adam*, R. W. B. Lewis argues that for the past two centuries American literature has divided into three camps: the parties of Hope, Memory, and Irony. Lewis makes his argument by means of Melville: there is, respectively, Billy Budd (the innocent optimist), his nemesis Claggart (driven by contrariness to a cynic disdain of innocence), and Melville himself (who pits the two characters against each other in his story and, by distancing himself, suggests the tragedy of preferring one over the other). In modern times, Lewis suggests, the Party of Irony has been ascendant—dismissing innocence as irredeemably naive and cynicism as the regrettable legacy of a pessimistic religious tradition.[18]

This was all phrased in humbler terms in a magazine quiz in a recent issue of *Seventeen* entitled "Are You a Pollyanna or a Pessimist?" Teenage girls were asked to evaluate themselves by answering such questions as how they feel when the alarm clock rings or when someone arranges a blind date for them. Among the possible answers were "Good morning, world!" or "Another day so soon?" and "[I know] he'll be Mr. Right" or "If he's so great, why doesn't she date him?" The correct response, we are led to believe, is not to be a Pollyanna who thinks that everything is "peachy-keen" or a Melancholy Baby, but someone in between—"a levelheaded realist."[19]

The norms advocated by modern sensibility or by adults writing for youths who read *Seventeen* need not, however, be taken as the last word. And Pollyanna needn't be seen as a failure. She can also be viewed as a representative of a countertradition present in other American childhood classics, a subversive alternative to maturity—if "maturity" means a surrender to "things as they are," ironic resignation, and "level-headed realism." In the world of America's children's books, change for the better is still possible. Life doesn't have to be taken as given. We are still free to make of it what we will.

This freedom to see life as we choose is one of the major verities of American children's books. It is ultimately the point of the famous scene in *Tom Sawyer* when Tom presents the whitewashing of the fence to his friends not as a chore, but as a delicious opportunity afforded to only a few. "That put things in a new light," Clemens writes, using the phrase by which he will signal Tom's other discoveries about the principle of subjectivity.[20] What Tom learns on this occasion is "a great law of human action"; the difference between "work" and "play" is determined by the way a given activity is imaginatively conceived.

Much of *Pollyanna*, it should be clear, is also about forcible shifts in perspective, techniques for seeing things differently. And this is true of many other American childhood classics. They are full of scenes like the one in *The Wizard of Oz* in which Dorothy and her companions put on green glasses before entering Emerald City, and then marvel at how green everything looks. In *Pollyanna*, however, the equivalent image is, significantly, not rose-colored glasses, but the prism. When the girl hangs dozens of these in the windows of Mr. Pendleton's house, we see something more than her transformation of his gloomy room into a rainbow-spangled place. We see how she has changed him in her prismatic shifts of perspectives. It is her pointing to a spectrum of possibilities, her reminding him of his freedom to choose, which leads Mr. Pendleton to conclude that Pollyanna is "the very finest prism of all" (128).

As this study has suggested, this is the very specific way in which the ur-story found in American children's books is "Americanized." Although this ur-story can be found in other national literatures, the "spin" that Americans, particularly, give to it is a dramatic emphasis on the power of thinking—whether it is seen in the lessons about self-confidence that Dorothy's companions eventually learn after they have believed themselves deficient, or the advocacies and healing praxis of *The Secret Garden*, or the decided composure of Hans Brinker, or the conviction of Toby Tyler and the March sisters that their "bosom enemies" can be conquered, or the infectious benignity of Little Lord Fauntleroy and Rebecca of Sunnybrook Farm that remakes cynical curmudgeons, or the "gladness" of Pollyanna. Here, too, is an explanation of the particularly "interior" nature of American children's books, with their visions of struggle in the Theater of Feelings and their accounts of intramental transformation.

What is conspicuous about the conclusions of many of America's children's classics, in other words, is not an inevitable surrender to "things as they are," a sensible resignation to level-headed realism and maturity. Instead, we have the very opposite. Adults are made child-like, made to realize that they are free to choose how they see life, and readmitted to the Party of Hope. In American Children's Literature, in particular, the oedipal victory over parent figures is also construed into a refusal to surrender to "maturity," if that means accepting life as it is. These books are about nonconformists. They speak of the endurance of hope. And they suggest, even more than *Billy Budd,* that it is possible to remain innocent without being ignorant.

Pollyanna is clearly an example of this, a benign trickster who is only "playing the fool." When she speaks to the missionary society and assumes that it will support a neighborhood orphan rather than spend money in other ways to look good on the national report, when she expresses gladness for the shabby room she has been given and thereby shames her aunt into giving her more reasonable accommodations—in these and a hundred other ways Pollyanna engages in what Ihab Hassan has called "radical innocence."[21]

Unwilling to accept life on defeatist terms, Pollyanna looks for (and assumes she will find) goodness, and her presumptions constitute a critique that manipulates others until they become as good as they can be. Jacques Maritain might have been describing her when he wrote in *Reflections on America:* "Deep beneath the anonymous American smile there is a feeling that is evangelical in origin—compassion for man, a desire to make life tolerable. This symbolic smile is a kind of anonymous reply of the human soul, which refuses to acknowledge itself vanquished."[22]

The same might also be said about a plucky girl from Kansas or a wily boy on a Mississippi odyssey, about heroines not daunted by dour aunts or heroes who overcome Old World patriarchs, about a boy with a finger in a leaking dike or another in a wheelchair in the Secret Garden. As their stories and as their enduring popularity attest, they are all audacious kids who refuse to be vanquished.

✢ ✢ ✢ ✢ ✢ ✢
Afterword

Was the Golden Age of American Children's Literature, from 1865 to 1914, a historical accident, a "blip" in this country's literary history? Its importance is undeniable, and it certainly cast long shadows; but are we ever likely to see again a period when best-seller lists were headed by children's books that were read by young and old alike, an era when authors of the caliber of Samuel Clemens saw writing for children as their work and would (without embarrassment and with encouragement from their society) pen masterpieces for the young? Are we ever likely to see again an age when Children's Books was the very center of publishing houses, rather than some satellite department, a time when the field was solidly in the mainstream, rather than a genre with separate but (not quite) equal status in national book reviews?

During the last decade and a half, something has been occurring that bears noticing. As I write this, magazines and newspapers have been discussing an extraordinary phenomenon in publishing that has been styled "The Boom in Kiddie Lit":

- In 1980 children's books were a $200 million business, with sales strong enough to subsidize losses by publishers in their adult divisions. Frank Scioscia, sales manager of Junior Books at Harper & Row, reported, "The children's book business has enjoyed a consistent increase in sales" and added, "The young may be paying the rent in many bookstores." Looking over 1980 sales figures, Jack Artenstein of Simon & Schuster observed, "The children's book business is stronger this year than any other year I've seen." Terence Daniels of Little Golden Books predicted, "This is a growth business."

- The figures were even more striking ten years later. Since 1982, sales of children's books across the country have very nearly quadrupled. And circulation figures for 1990 from the children's sections of public libraries indicate that book borrowing is up 54 percent from the already high figures of the year before.

- While others were lamenting new statistics which indicated that television-viewing time by children had increased, Theodor Geisel (Dr. Seuss) noted that while television "certainly detracts from time to read books, the paradox is that good kids' books are selling more than ever." Surveying the world of publishing, Anita Dore, chair of the Children's Book Committee at New York's Bank Street College, observed, "There's no question that children's books is growing faster than any other category."[1]

This recent enthusiasm for children's books has often been explained by the fact that the great postwar demographic bulge known as the baby-boom generation is now having children and creating a population boomlet. They're buying books for their kids, and that accounts, we're told, for the dramatic rise in sales. And that is certainly true. At the same time, however, the explanation is more complex than that.

Strangely enough, this growing interest in children's books is occurring at a time when the actual number of children in the population has decreased. While sales of children's books nearly quadrupled between 1982 and 1990, in 1985 the number of children aged five to thirteen reached a twenty-five-year low, and 1987 births were 58 percent of what they had been in 1957. Moreover, the number of childless couples and single-person households has risen considerably.[2] What these paradoxical facts suggest, of course, is that (in addition to baby-boom purchases) there is considerable *adult* interest in children's books.

Several years ago, writer James Marshall told me that marketing studies done by publishers indicated that one-third of all illustrated children's books are purchased by adults who don't plan to pass them along to children. Recent events seem to suggest this is true. In 1981, for example, Harper & Row simultaneously announced Maurice Sendak's new picture book *Outside Over There* on both their adults' and children's lists—tacitly acknowledging the public's growing recognition of Sendak's artistic genius, no matter what was originally reckoned to be his audience. Two of Dr. Seuss's recent books—his 1984 parable about the arms race, *The Butter Battle Book,* and his 1986 geriatric fable, *You Only Grow Old Once!*—have also appeared on adult best-seller lists.

While presenting less dramatic evidence, recent events in the field of fiction suggest a widening interest in the kind of book Randall Jarrell described as "half for children, half for grown-ups."[3] Following the lead of Jarrell and E. B. White, established writers have been less reluctant to address themselves to children. Isaac Bashevis Singer provides an example. Russell Hoban provides another; although Hoban's works for adults (e.g., *Riddley Walker*) may win awards, he is better remembered by others of all ages for his children's books (e.g., *The Mouse and His Child*). In this era, Hoban has said, "Books in a nameless category are needed—books for children and adults together."[4]

Even more dramatic evidence of this enthusiasm for a "shared" literature is apparent in the fairly recent interest among adults in the classic fairy tales long beloved by children: an interest both in the tales themselves and—through works as diverse as Anne Sexton's *Transformations* (1972), Stephen Sondheim's *Into the Woods* (1986), and Robert Bly's *Iron John* (1990)—in the subjects they raise. The considerable popularity of Bruno Bettelheim's celebrated study of fairy tales, *The Uses of Enchantment* (1976), is also notable. Serious scholarship and literary criticism, Bettelheim's work nonetheless appealed to the generally educated reader, was excerpted in *Ladies' Home Journal* and the *New Yorker,* and won a National Book Award.

Another measure of this renaissance of interest in Children's Literature may be seen in changes in American higher education.

For many years, Children's Literature seemed beneath college English departments and was regarded as a suitable subject only for "methods" courses offered to would-be schoolteachers by Education departments. Once the field began receiving its scholarly imprimaturs, however, opinions changed. These days, by my count, more than 200 American universities—including Dartmouth, Cornell, Princeton, and the universities of Washington, North Carolina, and Florida—now regard Children's Literature as literature and have offered or regularly offer courses on the subject in their English departments.

Given the chance, students have poured into these courses. In fact, like publishers' reports of the dramatic surge in sales of children's books, it seemed as if the floodgates were suddenly opened. At the University of Connecticut, a class devoted to this subject regularly enrolls 300 students each term. In other places across the country, enrollments are likewise measured in hundreds.

My own experience has been no different. In 1982 I offered a course in Children's Literature at UCLA, and 325 students signed up; since then, my classes elsewhere have routinely enrolled 200 or more. In higher education, these are sizable shifts of interest, and it is worth considering what motivates them. My students tell me that they take the course in order to read the books they weren't given a chance to encounter in childhood.

Besides the extraordinary sales figures from bookstores, besides the growing popularity and interest in a literature adults and children can share, and besides the great sea changes in enrollments when classes finally were made available to university students, the recent renaissance of interest in Children's Literature has also been occurring in literary scholarship. In fact, on the face of it, this American interest in Children's Literature seems so logical, so inevitable, that the only question might be: Why has it taken so long? As Leslie Fiedler observed in 1959, "There is a real sense in which our prose fiction is immediately distinguishable from that of Europe, though this is a fact difficult for Americans to confess. The great works of American fiction [e.g., *Adventures of Huckleberry Finn, The Last of the Mohicans,* the tales of Poe, *The Red Badge of Courage*] are notoriously at home in the children's section of the library."[5]

We might note that this "fact difficult for Americans to confess," this embarrassment that Fiedler speaks of, is peculiar to the

United States. In Great Britain, for example, the field of Children's Literature has long enjoyed respectability among scholars, possibly because a number of authors for children were also Oxford dons: Lewis Carroll, C. S. Lewis, and J. R. R. Tolkien. In Germany the situation is similar: following the Grimm brothers, the study of Children's Literature has been regarded seriously because of its connection with folkloric pursuits. Until very recently, however, American scholars had not regarded their nation's Children's Literature as a serious subject and, in general, abandoned the field to librarians, educators, and antiquarian book collectors.

That situation has begun to change. Until recently, however, literary histories of the Golden Age were likely to concern themselves with the "high art" of, for example, William Dean Howells' *The Rise of Silas Lapham* or Henry James's *The Ambassadors* (as well they should), but in such an exclusive fashion that little or no mention was made of such works as *The Wizard of Oz* and *Little Women* (which were dismissed, to use evaluative synonyms, as "popular" or "low art").[6]

Emblematic of the change that has begun to take place in the United States is the history of the leading scholarly journal in the field: once privately printed by an enthusiast, Dr. Francelia Butler, and called *The Great Excluded,* it has since been retitled *Children's Literature* and is now published by Yale University Press. Professional organizations and other scholarly journals have sprung up. University presses have begun routinely to publish monographs in what they regard as a "coming" field. Prestige has been accorded by international bodies like the Modern Language Association, which raised Children's Literature from a discussion group to the status of a division. And the National Endowment for the Humanities has begun regular funding for institutes devoted to the study of Children's Literature. Indeed, among those who champion a widening of the "canon," the successes of the field have often provided occasions for celebration.

What this amounts to in the United States, in other words, is belated recognition that this country's Children's Literature is not marginal, but squarely within our central literary tradition. Indeed, it might be argued, this has always or especially been the case in the United States. To quote Leslie Fiedler again: the single most important characteristic of our national literature and the way "our prose fiction is immediately distinguishable from that of

Europe"—now that we are no longer embarrassed to acknowledge
this fact—is that "the great works of American fiction are notoriously at home in the children's section of the library."

And why shouldn't this be so? As this study has suggested, the
recurring story of maturation in American children's books em-
bodies and speaks directly to our own particular cultural experience
and to America's vision of itself: as a young country, always making
itself anew, rebelling against authority, coming into its own, and
establishing its own identity.

Considering this, remembering how the field has long been
slighted by native scholars embarrassed by their ephebic patri-
mony, and only now encountering studies like this one and other
belated acknowledgments of the importance of Children's Literature in America, a thoughtful person might reasonably conclude
with some impatience: "It's about time." This attitude, too, be-
speaks a "renaissance."

Notes

PREFACE

1. Best sellers from 1865 to 1914 are listed in Frank Luther Mott, *Golden Multitudes* (New York: Bowker, 1947), 309–13.

2. Graham Greene, *The Lost Childhood and Other Essays*, quoted in Jim Trelease, *The Reading Aloud Handbook* (New York: Penguin, 1985), 1.

3. See Sarah Crichton, "What We Read as Youngsters: Top Editors Recall Their Favorite Childhood Books," *Publishers Weekly*, 26 February 1982, 121–24; an unpublished survey conducted in 1977 by the Public Library of Mobile, Alabama; Bernice Cullinan and M. Jerry Weiss, eds., *Books I Read When I Was Young: The Favorite Books of Famous People* (New York: Avon, 1980); Evelyn B. Byrne and Otto M. Penzler eds., *Attacks of Taste* (New York: Gotham Book Mart, 1971); Jerry Griswold, "Young [Ronald] Reagan's Reading," *New York Times Book Review*, 30 August, 1981, 11, 21; Jerry Griswold and Amy Wallace, "What Famous People Read," *Parade Magazine*, 13 March 1983, 21–25.

4. Henry Steele Commager, Introduction to the First Edition, *A Critical History of Children's Literature*, ed. Cornelia Miegs, rev. ed. (New York: Macmillan, 1969), xvi.

5. Leslie Fiedler, *Love and Death in the American Novel* (New York: Dell, 1966), 24.

6. G. T. Stubbs and L. F. Ashley, Preface to the First Edition, *Only Connect,*

ed. Sheila Egoff, G. T. Stubbs, and L. F. Ashley, 2nd ed. (Toronto: Oxford University Press, 1980), xix.

7. Russel Nye, *The Unembarrassed Muse* (New York: Dial Press, 1970), 425.

INTRODUCTION

1. Marcus Cunliffe, "Mark Twain and His 'English' Novels," *Times Literary Supplement*, 25 December 1981, 1503–4; Albert Bigelow Paine, "The Prince and the Pauper," *Mentor* 16 (December 1928): 8–10.

2. Irwin Porges, *Edgar Rice Burroughs* (Provo, Utah: Brigham Young University Press, 1975), 368.

3. Alison Lurie, *Don't Tell the Grown-ups: Subversive Children's Literature* (Boston: Little, Brown, 1990).

4. Perry Nodelman, "Progressive Utopia: Or, How to Grow Up Without Growing Up," in *Proceedings of the Sixth Annual Conference of the Children's Literature Association,* ed. Priscilla Ord (Villanova University, 1980), 146–54.

5. Nina Baym, *Woman's Fiction* (Ithaca, N.Y.: Cornell University Press, 1978).

6. Vladimir Propp, *Morphology of the Folktale,* trans. Laurence Scott, ed. Louis Wagner and Alan Dundes (Austin: University of Texas Press, 1968); Joseph Campbell, *The Hero with a Thousand Faces* (Princeton, N.J.: Princeton, University Press, 1947); Otto Rank, "The Myth of the Birth of the Hero," trans. F. Robbins and Smith Ely Jeliffe, in *The Myth of the Birth of the Hero and Other Writings,* ed. Philip Freund (New York: Random House, 1964), 3–96.

7. A more convoluted form of mitigation appears in some children's novels in which pairs of same-sex parent figures appear: the friendly and unfriendly aunts of *Rebecca of Sunnybrook Farm,* Aunt Em and Elvira Gulch in the movie *The Wizard of Oz,* Judge Thatcher and Injun Joe in *Tom Sawyer.* As in some fairy tales in which fairy godmothers vie with witches, these pairs seem to be another way of treating the child's simultaneous feelings of affection and hostility toward the parent. In all these cases, it is also noticeable that the "good" twin is less powerful than the "bad" twin, who is the object of the child's antagonism.

8. Quoted in George Forgie, *Patricide in the House Divided* (New York: Norton, 1979), 98.

9. See Forgie, *Patricide in the House Divided;* Christopher Looby, "'The Affairs of the Revolution Occasion'd the Interruption': Writing, Revolution, and Conciliation in Franklin's *Autobiography,*" *American Quarterly* 38 (1986): 72–96; Michael Grossberg, *Governing the Hearth: Law and Family in Nineteenth-Century America* (Chapel Hill: University of North Carolina Press, 1985), 7; Philip Greven, *The Protestant Temperament: Patterns of Child-Rearing, Religious Experience, and the Self in Early America* (New York: Meridian, 1979); Norman O.

Brown, *Love's Body* (New York: Random House, 1966), 3–31; Winthrop D. Jordan, "Familial Politics: Thomas Paine and the Killing of the King, 1776," *Journal of American History* 60 (September 1973): 294–308; Peter Shaw, *American Patriots and the Rituals of Revolution* (Cambridge, Mass.: Harvard University Press, 1981), 177–203 and passim; Edwin G. Burrows and Michael Wallace, "The American Revolution: The Ideology and Psychology of National Liberation," *Perspectives in American History* 6 (1972): 167–308.

10. Looby, "'The Affairs of the Revolution,'" 74.

11. Shirley Samuels, "The Family, the State, and the Novel in the Early Republic," *American Quarterly* 38 (1986): 385.

12. Samuel Osgood, "Books for Our Children," *Atlantic Monthly*, December 1865, 724.

13. Anne Thwaite, *Waiting for the Party* (New York: Scribner, 1974), 107–8.

14. William Dean Howells, Review of *The Prince and the Pauper*, *New York Tribune*, 26 October 1881, 6, quoted in Everett Emerson, *The Authentic Mark Twain: A Literary Biography of Samuel L. Clemens* (Philadelphia: University of Pennsylvania Press, 1984), 110.

15. Charles Darwin, *The Descent of Man* (New York: Appleton, 1897), 142.

16. Humphrey Carpenter, *Secret Gardens* (Boston: Houghton Mifflin, 1985). Cf. Roger Lancelyn Green, "The Golden Age of Children's Books," in *Only Connect*, ed. Sheila Egoff, G. T. Stubbs, and L. F. Ashley, 2nd ed. (Toronto: Oxford University Press, 1980), 1–16.

17. Jason Epstein, "'Good Bunnies Always Obey': Books for American Children" in Egoff, Stubbs, and Ashley, *Only Connect*, 75. Cf. Felicity Hughes, "Children's Literature: Theory and Practice," *ELH* 45, no.3 (Fall 1978): 542–61.

18. Quoted in Mary Lynn Stevens Heininger, "Children, Childhood, and Change in America, 1820–1920," in *A Century of Childhood*, ed. Mary Lynn Stevens Heininger (Rochester, N.Y.: Margaret Woodbury Strong Museum, 1984), 3.

19. Lloyd deMause, "The Evolution of Childhood" in *The History of Childhood*, ed. Lloyd deMause (New York: Psychohistory Press, 1974), 3.

20. Quoted in Heininger, "Children, Childhood, and Changes," 2.

21. Quoted in Harvey Green, "Scientific Thought and the Nature of Children in America, 1820–1920," in Heininger, *Century of Childhood*, 133.

22. Jay Martin, *Harvests of Change* (Englewood Cliffs, N.J.: Prentice-Hall, 1967), 184.

1. *THE WIZARD OF OZ*

1. See Fred Erisman, "L. Frank Baum and the Progressive Dilemma," *American Quarterly* 20 (Fall 1968): 616–23. See also Edward Wagenknecht, "Utopia Americana" and "Utopia Americana: A Generation Afterwards"; Marius Bewley,

"The Land of Oz: America's Great Good Place"; S. J. Sackett, "The Utopia of Oz"; and Henry M. Littlefield, "The Wizard of Oz: Parable on Populism," in *The Wizard of Oz,* The Critical Heritage Series, ed. Michael Patrick Hearn (New York: Schocken Books, 1983). Hearn's casebook reprints many other interesting essays and is a convenient source for secondary materials on Baum and his book.

2. See Selma Lanes, *Down the Rabbit Hole* (New York: Atheneum, 1976), 96–101.

3. Teenager Edgar Rice Burroughs had a job at the World's Fair driving guests around in a battery-powered car (an invention Baum had speculated about some years before, when he was a newspaperman in South Dakota). Burroughs enjoyed his job because it allowed him to visit Karl Hagenbeck's Wild Animal Show, and that enthusiasm later found its way into his Tarzan books. Frances Hodgson Burnett, a few years after the success of *Little Lord Fauntleroy,* wrote her own travelogue about the fair called *Two Little Pilgrims' Progress: A Story of the City Beautiful* (1895). Like *Little Women* by Burnett's friend Louisa May Alcott, this is a secularized version of Bunyan's allegory. See Francis J. Molson, "Two Little Pilgrims' Progress: The 1893 Chicago Columbian Exposition as Celestial City," *Markham Review* 7 (Spring 1978): 55–59. More interesting is the possibility that this book may be the origin for Baum's own presentation of Aunt Em as someone who thwarts Dorothy's playful nature; in *Frances Hodgson Burnett* (Boston: Twayne, 1984), Phyllis Bixler describes the novel in this fashion: "Through her portrayal of the children's aunt, concerned only with the success of her farm and her growing bank account, Burnett shows that a devotion to work alone shrivels the imagination and keeps one from enjoying life's many pleasures" (58). As his essay "Modern Fairy Tales" indicates, Baum was familiar with Burnett's work and her use of fairy tales. See L. Frank Baum, "Modern Fairy Tales," *Advance,* 19 August 1909, 236–37, reprinted in Hearn, *Wizard of Oz,* 137–40.

4. Anne Thwaite, *Waiting for the Party* (New York: Scribner, 1974), 149.

5. Jordan Brotman, "A Late Wanderer in Oz," *Chicago Review,* December 1965, reprinted in *Only Connect,* ed. Sheila Egoff, G. T. Stubbs, and L. F. Ashley, 2nd ed. (Toronto: Oxford University Press, 1980), 157; Jerry Griswold, "A Man Too Far Ahead of His Time," *Los Angeles Times Magazine,* 27 July 1986, 6, 8.

6. Michael Patrick Hearn, *The Annotated Wizard of Oz* (New York: Potter, 1973), 28. I am indebted to Hearn's masterful scholarship in a variety of ways.

7. Quoted in Karl Keller, "L. Frank Baum: The Wizard of Coronado," *San Diego Seacoast* or [title varies] *Southern California Seacoast* 2 (February 1981): 53.

8. Baum, "Modern Fairy Tales."

9. See Allen Eyles, *The World of Oz* (Tucson, Ariz: HP Books, 1985), 65–91; Conrad Phillip Kottak, "Structural and Psychological Analysis of Popular American Fantasy Films," in *Researching American Culture,* ed. Conrad Phillip Kottak (Ann Arbor: University of Michigan Press, 1962), 87–98; Jerry Griswold, "Return to Oz," *Los Angeles Times Book Review,* 8 September 1985, 10.

10. L. Frank Baum, *The Wonderful Wizard of Oz* (New York: Dover, 1960), 12–13. Subsequent references to pages of this work appear in parentheses.

11. Quoted in Eyles, *World of Oz*, 53.

2. *ADVENTURES OF HUCKLEBERRY FINN*

1. Leslie Fiedler, "Come Back to the Raft Ag'in, Huck Honey!" *Partisan Review* 15 (June 1948): 664–71.

2. William Dean Howells, *My Mark Twain,* ed. Marilyn Austin Baldwin (Baton Rouge: Louisiana State University Press, 1967), 144–45.

3. Interview with Clemens, in *The Art of Authorship,* ed. George Bainton (New York, 1890), quoted in Susan Gilman, *Dark Twins: Imposture and Identity in Mark Twain's America* (Chicago: University of Chicago Press, 1989), 33–34.

4. Walter Blair, *Mark Twain and Huck Finn* (Berkeley: University of California Press, 1960).

5. Samuel Clemens, *Selected Mark Twain–Howells Letters, 1872–1910,* ed. Frederick Anderson, William M. Gibson, and Henry Nash Smith (Cambridge, Mass.: Harvard University Press, 1967), 212.

6. Samuel Clemens, *The Autobiography of Mark Twain,* ed. Charles Neider (New York: Harper and Brothers, 1959), 265.

7. Mark Twain, *Adventures of Huckleberry Finn,* ed. Walter Blair and Victor Fischer (Berkeley: University of California Press, 1985), 104. Subsequent references to pages of this work appear in parentheses.

8. Allan B. Ellis and F. André Favat, "From Computer to Criticism: An Application of Automatic Content Analysis to the Study of Literature," in *The General Inquirer,* ed. Philip J. Stone et al. (Cambridge, Mass.: MIT Press, 1966), 628–38.

9. Karol Kelley, "*Huckleberry Finn* as Popular Novel," *Proteus* 1, no.2 (1984): 19–26. Cf. three articles by Robert Sears et al.: "Content Analysis of Mark Twain's Novels and Letters as a Biographical Method," *Poetics* 7 (1978): 155–75; "Episodic Analysis of Novels," *Journal of Psychology* 85 (1973): 267–76; "Episodic Analysis of Mark Twain's Novels: A Longitudinal Study of Separation Anxiety," in *Literary Criticism and Psychology,* Yearbook of Comparative Criticism 7, ed. Joseph P. Strelka (University Park: Pennsylvania State University Press, 1976), 198–206.

10. Kenneth S. Lynn, "Huck and Jim," *Yale Review* 47 (March 1958): 421–31; Lynn, *Mark Twain and Southwestern Humor* (Boston: Little, Brown, 1959), 195–213 and passim. One scholar has suggested that Lynn's view of Jim as a father figure gained early currency because critics sought a psychological interpretation of Huck and Jim's relationship that offered an alternative to Leslie Fiedler's identification of homoeroticism. See Jesse Bier, "'Bless You, Chile': Fiedler and 'Huck Honey' a Generation Later," *Mississippi Quarterly* 34 (Fall 1981): 456–62.

11. José Barchilon and Joel S. Kovel, *"Huckleberry Finn:* A Psychoanalytic Study," *Journal of the American Psychoanalytic Association* 14 (October 1966): 775–814; Scott Donaldson, "Pap Finn's Boy," *South Atlantic Quarterly* 36 (May 1971): 32–37; Ronald Dorris, "Paternal Relationships in *Huckleberry Finn,"* *Proteus* 1, no.2 (Fall 1984): 57–61; Keith M. Opdahl, " 'You'll Be Sorry When I'm Dead': Child–Adult Relations in *Huck Finn,"* *Modern Fiction Studies* 25 (1979–1980): 613–24; William Power, "Huck Finn's Father," *University of Kansas Review* 28 (Winter 1961): 83–94; Robert Shulman, "Fathers, Brothers, and 'the Diseased': The Family, Individualism, and American Society in *Huck Finn,"* in *One Hundred Years of Huckleberry Finn,* ed. Robert S. Sattelmeyer and J. David Crowley (Columbia: University of Missouri Press, 1985), 325–40; Eric Solomon, *"Huckleberry Finn* Once More," *College English* 22 (December 1960): 172–78; C. K. Tirumulai, "Father–Son Relationships in *Huckleberry Finn,"* *Exercise Exchange* 12 (November 1964): 22–23; Ray Browne, "Huck's Final Triumph," *Ball State Teachers College Forum* 6 (Winter 1965): 3–12; Keith Coplin, "John and Sam Clemens: A Father's Influence," *Mark Twain Journal* 15 (Winter 1970): 1–6.

12. Jay Martin, "The Genie in the Bottle: Huckleberry Finn in Mark Twain's Life," in Sattelmeyer and Crowley, *One Hundred Years of Huckleberry Finn,* 56–81.

13. See Bruno Bettelheim, *The Uses of Enchantment* (New York: Knopf, 1976), 159–66.

14. Lynn, *Mark Twain and Southwestern Humor,* 211; cf. Martin, "Genie in the Bottle," 60–61.

15. See Martin, "Genie in the Bottle," 62.

16. The minor role of father figures in *Tom Sawyer* should be taken not as a sign of their unimportance, but quite the opposite. This is the case, for example, in the story of another fatherless boy, "Jack and the Beanstalk," the fairy tale *Tom Sawyer* most resembles. Paternal issues may be introduced at the beginning of the novel in the grave-robbing scene in which Doc Robinson is killed by Injun Joe and Muff Potter. This choice of locus might be the result of the most traumatic moment in Twain's childhood, when he surreptitiously watched a doctor perform a post mortem on his father (see note 30). The three characters who are present can be seen as representative paternal types in Twain's novels. Doctors (along with colonels, lawyers, judges, and the like) are facets of the High-born Kind Father. Injun Joe (along with Pap, John Canty in *The Prince and the Pauper*) are variations on the Low-born Father. Muff Potter is an embodiment of an interesting, intermediate type (the Low-born but Kind Father seen later in the Welshman in *Tom Sawyer,* in Miles Hendon in *The Prince and the Pauper,* in Jim and perhaps Boggs in *Huckleberry Finn*).

17. See Coplin, "John and Sam Clemens," 6.

18. Robert Regan, *Unpromising Heroes* (Berkeley: University of California Press, 1966), 113–14.

19. Twain had once considered Pap as a possible accomplice to Injun Joe in

Tom Sawyer. See Michael Patrick Hearn, ed., *The Annotated Huckleberry Finn* (New York: Potter, 1980), 80, n.12; Martin, "Genie in the Bottle," 62.

20. Quoted in Dixon Wecter, *Sam Clemens of Hannibal* (Boston: Houghton Mifflin, 1952), 67.

21. Clemens, *Autobiography*, 68.

22. Lynn, *Mark Twain and Southwestern Humor*, 210.

23. Martin, "Genie in the Bottle," 59.

24. Ibid., 63.

25. See Peter G. Biedler, "The Raft Episode in *Huckleberry Finn*," *Modern Fiction Studies* 14 (Spring 1968): 11–20; William R. Manierre, "On Keeping the Raftsmen Passage in *Huckleberry Finn*," *English Language Notes* 6 (November 1968): 118–22.

26. See Lynn, *Mark Twain and Southwestern Humor*, 19; Lynn, "Huck and Jim," 426.

27. Opdahl, "'You'll Be Sorry,'" 617.

28. Blair, *Mark Twain and Huck Finn*, 313, 214–15; Coplin, "John and Sam Clemens," 4.

29. See, as well, other father–daughter scenes: the family of daughters' tragic loss of Peter Wilks and Jim's touching story about mistakenly striking his daughter, which later becomes his impersonation of King Lear. When it came to his own father, Clemens would often say that he could remember seeing his father be affectionate on only one occasion: when on his deathbed he gave his daughter a kiss and bade her, and no one else, farewell (*Autobiography*, 99; cf. Wecter, *Sam Clemens*, 115–16). Perhaps this experience accounts for the pathetic scene of Boggs's death in the arms of his daughter.

30. "Huck Finn the Red-Handed," as he is called in *Tom Sawyer*, guiltily watches events at graveside in the opening of that novel but was not caught and found out. Clemens, likewise, was not caught redhanded when, as a child, he spied on his father's post mortem; nonetheless, he felt guilty about having done so.

Dixon Wecter has pieced together this event which Clemens kept secret long into his adulthood and which was apparently among the most traumatic of his childhood. Several days after his father's death, out of curiosity and with permission, the town doctor performed a post mortem on the wasted body of John Clemens. Twelve-year-old Sam witnessed the procedure through a keyhole. As Wecter reasonably speculates, this moment likely had a profound effect "upon this sensitive child, so long intimidated by the stern man upon whose corpse this last indignity had fallen" (*Sam Clemens*, 116–17).

This episode may lie behind and account for the intensity of scenes in the St. Petersburg books in which a body is discovered: from the murderous reprisal at the grave robbing that begins *Tom Sawyer*; through the early pages of *Huckleberry Finn*, with its dizzy floodtime and the discovery of a naked corpse in the floating house; to the atmospheric pyrotechnics at Peter Wilks's cemetery plot, where

Huck is "caught" as the body is exhumed. As we have observed, Huck's placing the bag of gold on the corpse of Peter Wilks seems, for various reasons, like a "guilt offering."

Whenever he speaks of his father in his *Autobiography,* Clemens stresses his father's finances: the man's penury, financial reverses, poor investments and loans, and especially wild-eyed speculation in the "Tennessee land." At the same time, these fiduciary reports are often linked with funereal circumstances; so, for example, Clemens says, "[Events] ruined my father, sent him poor to his grave and condemned his heirs to a long and discouraging struggle with the world for a livelihood. But my father would brighten up and gather heart, even upon his deathbed, when he thought of the Tennessee land. He said that it would soon make us all rich and happy. And so believing, he died" (*Autobiography,* 23–24). These associations may explain why the Peter Wilks episode is a mix of gold and death, cash and corpse.

31. See Michael Paul Rogin, *Fathers and Children: Andrew Jackson and the Subjugation of the American Indian* (New York: Knopf, 1975), 24.

32. Ibid., 54.

33. Samuel Clemens, "The Czar's Soliloquy," in *Life as I Find It,* ed. Charles Neider (Garden City, N.Y.: Hanover House, 1961), 27.

34. See Simon O. Lesser, "The Image of the Father in 'My Kinsman, Major Molineux,'" *Partisan Review* (1955): 372–90; Roy Harvey Pearce, "Hawthorne and the Sense of the Past Or, The Immortality of Major Molineux," *ELH* 21 (1954): 327–40; Peter Shaw, "Fathers, Sons and the Ambiguities of Revolution in 'My Kinsman, Major Molineux,'" *New England Quarterly* (1976): 559–76.

35. See Solomon, "*Huckleberry Finn* Once More," 177; and Martin, "Genie in the Bottle," 63.

36. Robert Penn Warren, "Mark Twain," *Southern Review* (1972): 483.

37. See Samuel Clemens, "The Story of the Bad Little Boy," in *Mark Twain's Sketches, New and Old* (Hartford, Conn.: American Publishing, 1875), 51–55.

3. *REBECCA OF SUNNYBROOK FARM*

1. Mark Twain found *Rebecca of Sunnybrook Farm* "beautiful and moving and satisfying," according to Nora Archibald Smith, *Kate Douglas Wiggin. As Her Sister Knew Her* (Boston: Houghton Mifflin, 1925), 314. Jack London sent Wiggin a letter from the headquarters of the Japanese army in Manchuria in which he wrote "Rebecca won my heart," according to Kate Douglas Wiggin, *My Garden of Memory* (Boston: Houghton Mifflin, 1923), 353. Jack Kerouac called the novel his favorite childhood book (cited in *Attacks of Taste,* ed. Evelyn B. Bryne and Otto M. Penzler [New York: Gotham Book Mart, 1971], 28). Wiggin's editor at the Riverside Press once asked, "Did it ever strike you that Rebecca, of all your books,

appealed more to men than women?" (quoted in Smith, *As Her Sister Knew Her*, 316).

2. Kate Douglas Wiggin, *Rebecca of Sunnybrook Farm* (New York: Airmont, 1967), 15. Subsequent references to pages of this work appear in parentheses.

3. Wiggin appears to dally with the idea of the child bride in an incident in *The New Chronicles of Rebecca* (Boston: Houghton Mifflin, 1907), 211–12. Rebecca needs a wedding ring so that an impoverished couple can marry and innocently asks Ladd to provide one:

"I need a wedding ring dreadfully."

Adam Ladd's eyes flashed with surprise and he smiled with pleasure. "I thought it was perfectly understood between us," he said, "that if you could ever contrive to grow up and I were willing to wait, that I was to ride up to the brick house . . . put a golden circlet on your lily white finger, draw you up behind me on my [horse]"—

"And Emma Jane, too," Rebecca interrupted. . . . "The ring isn't for *me!*" she explained carefully. "You know very well that Emma Jane and I can't be married till we're through Quackenbos's Grammar, Greenleaf's Arithmetic, and big enough to wear long trails and run a sewing machine."

4. Vladmir Nabokov, *Lolita* (New York: Berkley, 1966), 18–19.

5. Ibid., 22.

6. Smith, *As Her Sister Knew Her*, 323.

7. The few facts that can be gathered about Wiggin's life do not offer enough material for extensive and ponderous psychoanalysis, but what is there offers some intimations of the origin of these oedipal themes. Wiggin's own father died when she was three. As she herself acknowledged, his death had an effect on her that was surprising (given her age) and enduring: "What is [strange], perhaps, is my conscious sense of close kinship with my father. It did not haunt me in childhood, but began when I myself began to 'do things.' I have often finished a book and thought: 'My father would have liked that!' or 'My father would have done this, in something this way, only better'" (*My Garden*, 4).

Other incidents offer hints of something similar. Among the anecdotes Wiggin found memorable enough to relate to her biographers are a number that feature a connection with fatherly men and work (often of a literary kind). For example, when she was six years old, Wiggin happened to meet Charles Dickens on a train, and she lectured her favorite author about the boring parts of his novels while he chuckled and took notes. Wiggin first took up her pen, she pointed out, when she was seventeen and her beloved stepfather died and she was obliged to help her impoverished family. When she was twenty-two, she met and spent time with her white-haired hero, Ralph Waldo Emerson, and, encouraged by him, she went on to become a famous educator and pioneer in the kindergarten movement who established the first kindergarten in the West in a San Francisco slum.

See, for example, Wiggin, *My Garden*, 38–150 and passim. Cf. Helen Frances Benner, *Kate Douglas Wiggin's Country of Childhood* (Orono: University of

Maine Press, 1956); Edna Boutwell, "Kate Douglas Wiggin—The Lady with the Golden Key," in *The Hewins Lectures, 1947–1962,* ed. Siri Andrews (Boston: Horn Book, 1963), 296–319; Lucy Ward Stebbens, "Kate Douglas Wiggin as a Child Knew Her," *Horn Book* 26, no.6 (November–December 1950): 447–54; Roderick Stebbens, "Kate Douglas Wiggin as I Knew Her," *Bookman* 59 (June 1924): 405–12; Kate Douglas Wiggin, "What Shall Children Read?" *Cosmopolitan* 7, no.4 (August 1889): 355–60; Calvin Winter, "Representative American Story Tellers," *Bookman* 32 (1910): 237–43; Francelia Butler, Preface to *Rebecca of Sunnybrook Farm,* by Kate Douglas Wiggin, Garland Series: Classics of Children's Literature 1621–1932 (New York: Garland Press, 1976), v–viii.

8. Louisa May Alcott, *Little Women* (New York: Penguin, 1983), 13.

9. Ibid., 265.

10. See, for example, Carol Gay, "The Philosopher and His Daughter: Amos Bronson Alcott and Louisa," *Essays in Literature* 2 (1975): 181–91; Martha Saxton, *Louisa May* (Boston: Houghton Mifflin, 1977).

11. Quoted in Sarah Elbert, *A Hunger for Home* (New Brunswick, N.J.: Rutgers University Press, 1987), 83.

12. Karen Horney, *Feminine Psychology* (New York: Norton, 1967), 66.

4. *LITTLE LORD FAUNTLEROY*

1. See Robert Lee White, "Little Lord Fauntleroy as Hero," in *Challenges in American Culture,* ed. Ray Browne et al. (Bowling Green, Ohio: Bowling Green University Press, 1970), 209–16. Cf. Phyllis Bixler, "Idealizations of Child and Childhood in Frances Hodgson Burnett's *Little Lord Fauntleroy* and Mark Twain's *Tom Sawyer,*" in *Research About Nineteenth-Century Children and Books: Portrait Studies,* ed. Selma K. Richardson (Urbana: Graduate School of Library Science, University of Illinois, 1980), 85–96; Bixler, "Continuity and Change in Popular Entertainment," in *Children's Novels and the Movies,* ed. Douglas Street (New York: Ungar, 1983), 69–80; Frances Hodgson Burnett, "How *Fauntleroy* Occurred," in *Piccino and Other Child Stories* (New York: Scribner, 1894), 113–60; Tom McCarthy, "The Real Little Lord Fauntleroy," *American Heritage* 21 (February 1970): 50–55, 82–85; Anne Thwaite, *Waiting for the Party* (New York: Scribner, 1974), 117; Mark Spilka, "Victorian Keys to the Early Hemingway: Part II—*Fauntleroy* and *Finn,*" *Journal of Modern Literature* 10, no.2 (June 1983): 289–310; Spilka, "Hemingway and Fauntleroy: An Androgynous Pursuit," in *American Novelists Revisited: Essays in Feminist Criticism,* ed. Fritz Fleischmann (Boston: Hall, 1982), 339–70.

Burnett's novel fell from favor, it is argued, because boys wished to run around like Huck, barefoot and in tatters. They did not like their parents dressing them in the fashionable "Fauntleroy suit"—velvet tunic and knickerbockers, Vandyke collar and cuffs of lace, complemented by long hair in curly love locks.

This symbolic juxtaposition may explain why Burnett's book has languished in obscurity for the last two generations and has only recently reappeared in print; according to a recent *Books in Print, Little Lord Fauntleroy* is now available from the following American publishers: Dell (1986), Penguin (1985), and Buccaneer Books (1981).

The situation was very different in the half century immediately following its publication. The statistics would make an accountant at a publishing firm dizzy with ecstasy. By the end of the century, *Fauntleroy's* sales were measured in millions of copies. It seemed as if everyone who *could* read *had* read the book. And it was still popular in 1936, when movie mogul David O. Selznick had a plaque erected on a house in Washington, D.C.: "ON THIS SITE FIFTY YEARS AGO THE DEATHLESS CLASSIC *LITTLE LORD FAUNTLEROY* WAS WRITTEN."

The novel seemed more mortal, however, in the postwar years, when it was a victim of the vagaries of couture and happenstance. The *fin de siècle* vogue of the Fauntleroy suit (the juvenile equivalent of the *dandyisme* of Oscar Wilde) seemed dated to twentieth-century Americans. Moreover, the novel had acquired a reputation of effeminacy, since many longhaired actresses (notably, Mary Pickford) had played the Little Lord on stage and screen.

2. See George Forgie, *Patricide in the House Divided* (New York: Norton, 1979); Christopher Looby, "'The Affairs of the Revolution Occasion'd the Interruption': Writing, Revolution, and Conciliation in Franklin's *Autobiography*," *American Quarterly* 38 (1986): 72–96; Michael Grossberg, *Governing the Hearth: Law and Family in Nineteenth-Century America* (Chapel Hill: University of North Carolina Press, 1985), 7; Philip Greven, *The Protestant Temperament: Patterns of Child-Rearing, Religious Experience, and the Self in Early America* (New York: Meridian, 1979); Norman O. Brown, *Love's Body* (New York: Random House, 1966), 3–31; Winthrop D. Jordan, "Familial Politics: Thomas Paine and the Killing of the King, 1776," *Journal of American History* 60 (September 1973): 294–308; Peter Shaw, *American Patriots and the Rituals of Revolution* (Cambridge, Mass.: Harvard University Press, 1981), 177–203 and passim; Edwin G. Burrows and Michael Wallace, "The American Revolution: The Ideology and Psychology of National Liberation," *Perspectives in American History* 6 (1972): 167–308.

3. Looby, "'The Affairs of the Revolution,'" 74.

4. See Forgie, *Patricide in the House Divided,* 109.

5. Samuel Osgood, "Books for Our Children," *Atlantic Monthly,* December 1865, 724.

6. Quoted in Catherine Morris Wright, *Lady of the Silver Skates: The Life and Correspondence of Mary Mapes Dodge* (Jamestown, R.I.: Clingstone Press, 1979), 141–42.

7. Quoted in William Wallace Whitelock, "Frances Hodgson Burnett in England," in *Women Authors of Our Day in Their Homes,* ed. Frances Whiting Halsey (New York: Pott, 1903), 76.

8. Thwaite, *Waiting for the Party,* 107–8.

9. Frances Hodgson Burnett, *Little Lord Fauntleroy* (New York: Penguin, 1981), 8. Subsequent references to pages of this work appear in parentheses.

10. Phyllis Bixler, in *Frances Hodgson Burnett* (Boston: Twayne, 1984), 51–56, suggests that the prototype is "Cinderella." See also Bixler, "Tradition and Individual Talent of Frances Hodgson Burnett: A Generic Analysis of *Little Lord Fauntleroy, A Little Princess,* and *The Secret Garden," Children's Literature* 7 (1978): 191–207.

11. Thwaite, *Waiting for the Party,* 90.

12. Brown, *Love's Body,* 5.

13. R. W. B. Lewis, *The American Adam* (Chicago: University of Chicago Press, 1955), 5–26 and passim.

5. *TARZAN OF THE APES*

1. See Jerry Griswold, "Young [Ronald] Reagan's Reading," *New York Times Book Review,* 30 August 1981, 1, 21; Leslie Fiedler, "Lord of the Absolute Elsewhere," *New York Times Book Review,* 9 June 1974, 10, 12, 14, 17; Arthur C. Clarke's remarks in Bernice Cullinan and M. Jerry Weiss, eds., *Books I Read When I Was Young* (New York: Avon, 1980), 32; Gore Vidal, "Tarzan Revisited," *Esquire,* October 1973, 281–83, 484–85.

2. Clarke, in Cullinan and Weiss, *Books I Read When I Was Young,* 50–51.

3. Erling B. Holtsmark, Preface in *Edgar Rice Burroughs* (Boston: Twayne, 1986), unpaged.

4. Fiedler, "Lord of the Absolute Elsewhere," 10.

5. Russel Nye, *The Unembarrassed Muse* (New York: Dial Press, 1970), 272. See also Derral Cheatwood, "The Tarzan Films: An Analysis of Determinants of Maintenance and Change in Conventions," *Journal of Popular Culture* 16, no.2 (Fall 1982): 127–42; Robert J. Rubanowice, "The Tarzan Series: A Twentieth-Century Case Against Civilization," in *Proceedings of the Sixth National Convention of the Popular Culture Association,* ed. Michael T. Marsden (Bowling Green, Ohio: Bowling Green University Press, 1976), 563–80; John Hollow, "Rereading *Tarzan of the Apes;* Or 'What Is It,' Lady Alice Whispered, 'A Man?'" *Dalhousie Review* 56 (1976): 83–92; James R. Nesteby, "The Tenuous Vine of *Tarzan of the Apes," Journal of Popular Culture* 13 (1980): 483–87; "12-Year-Old Human Monkey Found by Hunters/ JUNGLE GIRL IS RAISED BY APES/ Child Talks in Sign Language and Scampers on All Fours," *Weekly World News,* 29 November 1983, 1.

6. Edgar Rice Burroughs, *Tarzan of the Apes* (New York: Ballantine, 1974), 52. Subsequent references to pages of this work appear in parentheses.

7. George Santayana, *Scepticism and Animal Faith* (New York: Dover, 1955), 1–5.

8. Irwin Porges, *Edgar Rice Burroughs* (Provo, Utah: Brigham Young University Press, 1975), 366.

9. Edgar Rice Burroughs, "The Tarzan Theme," *Writer's Digest* 12 (June 1932): 29–30.

10. Quoted in David Cowart, "The Tarzan Myth and Jung's Genesis of the Self," *Journal of American Culture* 2 (n.d.): 220.

11. Robert W. Fenton, *The Big Swingers* (Englewood Cliffs, N.J.: Prentice-Hall, 1967), 88.

12. Marcus Cunliffe, Afterword to *The Jungle Books,* by Rudyard Kipling (New York: New American Library, 1961), 330.

13. Burroughs, "Tarzan Theme," 31.

14. Edgar Rice Burroughs, *The Warlord of Mars* (New York: Ballantine, 1980), 131.

15. Otto Rank, "The Myth of the Birth of the Hero," trans. F. Robbins and Smith Ely Jeliffe, in *The Myth of the Birth of the Hero and Other Writings,* ed. Philip Freund (New York: Random House, 1964), 91.

16. Ibid., 92.

17. Sigmund Freud, *Civilization and Its Discontents,* trans. and ed. James Strachey (New York: Norton, 1962).

18. Porges, *Edgar Rice Burroughs,* 368.

19. Charles Darwin, *The Descent of Man* (New York: Appleton, 1897), 142.

6. *THE PRINCE AND THE PAUPER*

1. Peter Brunette, "Faces in the Mirror: Twain's Prince, Warner's Pauper," in *The Classic American Novel and the Movies,* ed. Gerald Pearcy and Roger Shatzin (New York: Ungar, 1977), 106.

2. Victor Fischer, Foreword to *The Prince and the Pauper,* by Mark Twain (Berkeley: University of California, 1983), xv. References to pages of this work appear in parentheses.

3. "My idea is to afford a realizing sense of the severity of the laws of that day by inflicting some of their penalties upon the king himself, and allowing him a chance to see the rest of them applied to others; all of which is to account for a certain mildness which distinguished Edward VI's reign from those that precede it and follow it" (Clemens to Howells, quoted in Albert Bigelow Paine, "The Prince and the Pauper," *Mentor* 16 [December 1928]: 9).

4. Ibid.

5. While other critics talk about "the burden of history" and about authors' feeling of obligation to be original, it is interesting in this novel to note the works

that influenced it, since the book is so concerned with dangers of usurpation and the need for historical succession. See Howard G. Baetzhold, "Mark Twain's *The Prince and the Pauper*," *Notes and Queries* 1 (September 1954): 401–3; Leon T. Dickinson, "The Sources of *The Prince and the Pauper*," *Modern Language Notes* 64 (February 1949): 103–6; Robert L. Gale, *"The Prince and the Pauper* and *King Lear*," *Mark Twain Journal* 12 (Spring 1963): 14–17.

6. J. D. Stahl, "American Myth in European Disguise: Fathers and Sons in *The Prince and the Pauper*," *American Literature* 58, no.2 (May 1986): 203–5. Cf. Arthur Lawrence Vogelback, *"The Prince and the Pauper:* A Study in Critical Standards," *American Literature* 14 (March 1942): 48–54; Albert Stone, *The Innocent Eye* (New Haven, Conn.: Yale University Press, 1961), 91–120; Marcus Cunliffe, "Mark Twain and His 'English' Novels," *Times Literary Supplement*, 25 December 1981, 1503–4; Tom H. Towers, *"The Prince and the Pauper:* Mark Twain's Once and Future King," *Studies in American Fiction* 6, no.2 (Autumn 1978): 193–202.

7. For comparisons of *Adventures of Huckleberry Finn* and *The Prince and the Pauper*, see Walter Blair, *Mark Twain and Huck Finn* (Berkeley: University of California Press, 1967) 190 and passim; Robert J. Coard, "Huck Finn and Two Sixteenth Century Lads," *Midwest Quarterly* 23, no.4 (Summer 1982): 437–46.

8. Samuel Clemens, *Selected Mark Twain–Howells Letters, 1872–1910*, ed. Frederick Anderson, William M. Gibson, and Henry Nash Smith (Cambridge, Mass.: Harvard University Press, 1967), 160.

9. Otto Rank, "The Myth of the Birth of the Hero," trans. F. Robbins and Smith Ely Jeliffe, in *The Myth of the Birth of the Hero and Other Writings*, ed. Philip Freund (New York: Random House, 1964), 66, 68.

10. See, for example, two works by Pauline Rose Clance and Suzanne Ament Imes: "The Imposter Phenomenon in High-Achieving Women: Dynamics and Therapeutic Intervention," *Psychotherapy: Theory, Research and Practice* 15, no.3 (Fall 1978): 241–47; and "Treatment of the Imposter Phenomenon in High-Achieving Women," in *Women Therapists Working with Women*, ed. Claire M. Brody (New York: Springer, 1984), 74–75.

Bells of recognition apparently sounded when the "impostor phenomenon" was delineated, because discussion soon leaped from scholarly circles into the arena of pop psychology. *Time* ran an article on the subject (Janice Castro, "Fearing the Mask May Slip," *Time*, 12 August 1985, 60), and bookstores began to stock titles like Joan C. Harvey's *If I'm So Successful, Why Do I Feel Like a Fake?* (New York: Pocket Books, 1986). Despite the publicity of discovery, therapists indicate that this worry of being disingenuous is a bona fide problem and can be a debilitating anxiety.

11. Samuel Clemens, *The Autobiography of Mark Twain*, ed. Charles Neider (New York: Harper and Brothers, 1959), 21.

12. Ibid., 28–29.

13. See Susan Gilman, *Dark Twins: Imposture and Identity in Mark Twain's*

America (Chicago: University of Chicago Press, 1989). Cf. Kenneth S. Lynn, Afterword to *The Prince and the Pauper,* by Mark Twain (New York: New American Library, 1964), 213–19.

14. Phyllis Greenacre, "The Relation of the Impostor to the Artist," *Psychoanalytic Study of the Child* 13 (1958): 521.

15. Ibid., 521–40. See also Phyllis Greenacre, "The Impostor," *Psychoanalytic Quarterly* 28 (1958): 359–82; Lionel Finkelstein, "The Impostor: Aspects of His Development," *Psychoanalytic Quarterly* 43 (1974): 85–114.

16. Quoted in Fischer, Foreword, xvi.

17. Howells to Clemens, 13 December 1880, in Clemens, *Selected Mark Twain–Howells Letters,* 160.

18. Whippings appear frequently in *The Prince and the Pauper.* Edward is saved from one. Tom is regularly beaten by his father. The other boy who has a considerable but minor role in the book, and is the same age as the prince and the pauper, is Humphrey Marlow, the Whipping Boy.

Whippings seem to be associated with fathers or patriarchalism, which recalls, of course, the way Huck suffers at the hands of Pap. It is also notable that, despite their many conspicuous differences, Tom and Edward do notice that they have one thing in common when Edward says, "Fathers be alike, mayhap. Mine hath not a doll's temper. He smiteth with a heavy hand" (15). According to Paine, when Clemens's daughters were enacting *The Prince and the Pauper* as a play for their Nook Farm neighbors, this line most amused the gathered adults ("Prince and the Pauper," 9).

In a deleted passage in *Following the Equator,* Clemens pictured his father whipping a slave boy. In that regard, it is notable how often Clemens himself identified with slaves—for example, "I was a playmate to all the niggers, preferring their society to that of the elect" (quoted in Dixon Wecter, *Sam Clemens of Hannibal* [Boston: Houghton Mifflin, 1952], 75).

Finally, it is worth remarking that fantasy seems a compensatory reaction to punishment: "Many a night, . . . smarting from a thrashing [Tom] unleased his imagination and soon forgot his aches and pains in delicious picturings to himself of a charmed life of a petted prince in a regal palace" (6).

19. Greenacre, "Relation of the Impostor to the Artist," 525.

20. "A Boy's Adventure" first appeared in the *Bazar Budget* (Hartford) 4 June 1880, 1–2, reprinted in Kenneth R. Andrews, *Nook Farm: Mark Twain's Hartford Circle* (Cambridge, Mass.: Harvard University Press, 1950), 243–46.

21. Greenacre, "Impostor," 362. Cf. Finkelstein, "Impostor," 86–87.

22. Rank, "Myth of the Birth of the Hero," 94–96. Jay Martin explores a related topic in his examination of identity disorders that appear in literature and in modern-day assassins in *Who Am I This Time? Uncovering the Fictive Personality* (New York: Norton, 1988).

23. These themes are also echoed in the Miles Hendon subplot, in which, again, the issues are identity, imposture, succession, legitimacy, and the ability or

inability to recognize others. When Miles presents himself at Hendon Hall to make his claim and assume his rightful place, his evil brother, Hugh, arranges to have others pretend not to recognize him. Thinking of his own situation, Edward consoles him: "There be others in the world whose identity is denied, and whose claims are derided" (217). Still, Miles is anxious to prove "I am no impostor" and relies on Edith, his childhood sweetheart and now Hugh's wife, to remember him. But, blackmailed by her husband, Edith lies and denies knowing him; in a passage that recalls Tom's denial of his own mother, Edith says, "I know him not!" (219). Fortunately for him, some pages later, denial is replaced by remembrance when an old family servant comes to jail and indicates that he recognizes Miles.

24. Tom has, however, at least one occasion to make good use of *true* memory. When a criminal is brought before him who is accused of poisoning a man, Tom pardons him because he recalls seeing the man in an entirely different part of London at the time the crime is supposed to have taken place. This species of true memory, however, might compromise Tom's charade if he were to reveal it openly, so he contrives a way to conceal it and pardon the man for other reasons.

25. William Dean Howells, Review of *The Prince and the Pauper, New York Tribune,* 26 October 1881, 6, quoted in Everett Emerson, *The Authentic Mark Twain: A Literary Biography of Samuel L. Clemens* (Philadelphia: University of Pennsylvania Press, 1984), 110.

26. In *The Prince and the Pauper,* for example, some mention is made of Edward's intention to supplant his father by substituting a "law of mercy" for a "law of blood" (169).

27. Edward's father, Henry VIII, dies of natural causes. The other "pap" simply disappears: "Tom Canty's father was never heard of again" (287).

28. See Douglas Woodruff, *The Tichborne Claimant* (London: Hollis and Carter, 1957); Michael Gilbert, *The Claimant* (London: Constable, 1957).

7. *THE ADVENTURES OF TOM SAWYER*

1. Humphrey Carpenter, *Secret Gardens* (Boston: Houghton Mifflin, 1985).

2. See Samuel F. Pickering, Jr., *John Locke and Children's Books in Eighteenth-Century England* (Knoxville: University of Tennessee Press, 1981).

3. *A New Gift for Children* (Boston: D. Fowle, ca. 1750). "Mary Home-bred" makes use of Locke's famous notion of the child as tabula rasa in her Introduction. Information regarding these early works will be found in Jerry Griswold, "Early American Children's Literature: A Bibliographic Primer," *Early American Literature* 18 (1983–1984): 119–26.

4. *The Grateful Return* (Lansingburgh, Pa.: Luther Pratt, 1796), 23.

5. Anne Scott McLeod, *A Moral Tale: Children's Fiction and American Culture 1820–1860* (Hamden, Conn.: Archon Books, 1975), 42–43.

6. Quoted in Charles Welsh, "The Early History of Children's Books in New England," *New England Magazine* 26 (April 1899): 149–50.

7. Samuel Clemens, "The Story of the Bad Little Boy," in *Mark Twain's Sketches, New and Old* (Hartford, Conn.: American Publishing, 1875), 51–55; see also "The Story of a Good Little Boy," 56–61.

8. Other critics have noticed this parody and said as much. See Leslie Fiedler, *Love and Death in the American Novel* (New York: Dell, 1966), 259–90; John Hinz, "Huck and Pluck: 'Bad' Boys in American Fiction," *South Atlantic Quarterly* 51 (January 1952): 120–29; Jim Hunter, "Mark Twain and the Boy Book in 19th Century America," *College English* 24 (March 1963): 430–38; Albert Stone, *The Innocent Eye* (New Haven, Conn.: Yale University Press, 1961), 58–90; Judith Fetterley, "The Sanctioned Rebel," *Studies in the Novel* 3 (Fall 1971): 293–304; Anne Trensky, "The Bad Boy in Nineteenth-Century Fiction," *Georgia Review* 27 (1973): 503–17. Cf. Walter Blair, "On the Structure of *Tom Sawyer*," *Modern Philology* 37 (1939): 75–88; John Seelye, "Sounding the Depths of *Tom Sawyer*," *Sewanee Review* 90, no. 3 (Summer 1982): 408–29; Cynthia Griffin Wolff, "*The Adventures of Tom Sawyer:* A Nightmare Vision of American Boyhood," *Massachusetts Review* 21 (1980): 637–52.

9. By the middle of the nineteenth century, the Pathetic Child had become the pitiable juvenile of sentimental fiction in children's books by America's "lachrymose ladies": Susan Warner, who, with copious tears and liberal doses of Christianity, offered *The Wide, Wide World* (1850) and its account of Ellen Montgomery, a poor girl victimized by uncaring adults and an indifferent world; Maria Susanna Cumins, who told in *The Lamplighter* (1854) the Dickensian story of young Gerty adrift in the streets of Boston; and Martha Finley, who presented an American Jane Eyre in her vision of the aggrieved but pious *Elsie Dinsmore* (1867).

10. Oliver Wendell Holmes, *The Professor at the Breakfast-Table,* vol. 2 of *The Writings of Oliver Wendell Holmes* (Cambridge, Mass.: Riverside Press, 1895), 193–95.

11. Mark Twain, *The Adventures of Tom Sawyer* (Los Angeles: University of California Press, 1980), 22. Subsequent references to pages of this work appear in parentheses.

12. This scene closely resembles one in the *Adventures of Huckleberry Finn,* in which Huck is missing and Jim concludes that the boy has been swept off the raft and drowned. Like Aunt Polly, Jim mourns the boy's passing. Both adults are angry when they learn they have been tricked and are hurt when they believe the boys have fooled them in order to laugh at them. But here the resemblance ends. A series of convoluted events follow in *Tom Sawyer* that may be summarized in this fashion: Tom explains to Aunt Polly that he did not return to spy on her and laugh at her, but to give her a kiss and leave a note indicating that he was alive and she should not worry; Aunt Polly denounces him for lying; but then, in his absence, she rummages through his jacket pocket and finds the note; as a result, all her previous misgivings about the boy now seem shabby and wrongheaded, and Aunt Polly is once more full of remorse. The opposite is seen in *Huckleberry Finn:* Jim makes clear that *he* has been the victim of a low joke and—in one of the most

famous scenes in the novel—*Huck* is smitten with guilt and apologizes. This scene is a turning point not only in the novel but also in Clemens's amused treatment of childish self-indulgence when it results in emotional pain for others. And it marks a shift away from the recurring theme in *Tom Sawyer* of "remorse and regrets." As Huck says about having apologized, "I warn't ever sorry for it afterwards" (105).

13. There are a few moments in the novel in which these feelings are treated in a touching or sentimental way. For example, when Muff Potter is languishing in jail and praises the boys of the town who have been so good to him, Tom (who has said nothing to the authorities about Potter's innocence) is genuinely conscience-stricken. When Tom and Becky are hopelessly lost in the cave, they reproach themselves for taking the wrong paths and leaving the company of others, and then pour out their "unavailing regrets, and the far echoes turned them all into jeering laughter" (226). Despite his own reputation for jeering laughter, Clemens himself often felt misgivings and was a writer acutely sensitive to the particular emotions he described, a man especially haunted by regrets—the things he might have done, for example, to prevent the death of his brother Henry or the death of his infant son Langdon. He always wept when he heard the old song with the line "over the hills and far away." See Edward Wagenknecht, *Mark Twain: The Man and His Work* (Norman: University of Oklahoma Press, 1967), 86–87. Nonetheless, while the novel is ablaze with contrition, the genuinely pathetic has only a minor role in *Tom Sawyer*.

8. *LITTLE WOMEN*

1. Madeline B. Stern, Introduction to *The Selected Letters of Louisa May Alcott,* ed. Joel Myerson, Daniel Shealy, and Madeline B. Stern (Boston: Little, Brown, 1987), xlii.

2. Meyerson, Shealy, and Stern, *Selected Letters,* 300, 194.

3. Ibid., 125.

4. See Madeline Stern, ed., *Behind the Mask: The Unknown Thrillers of Louisa May Alcott* (New York: Morrow, 1975). Cf. Angela M. Estes and Kathleen Margaret Lane, "Dismembering the Text: The Horror of Louisa May Alcott's *Little Women,*" *Children's Literature* 17 (1989): 98–123; Judith Fetterley, "Impersonating 'Little Women': The Radicalism of Alcott's *Behind the Mask,*" *Women's Studies* 10 (1983): 1–14.

5. Quoted in Martha Saxton, *Louisa May* (Boston: Houghton Mifflin, 1977), 270.

6. Louisa May Alcott, *Little Women* (New York: Penguin, 1983), 11. Subsequent references to pages of this work appear in parentheses.

7. See Madelon Bedell, Introduction to *Little Women,* by Louisa May Alcott (New York: Modern Library, 1983), xxxiii.

8. Ibid., xxi.

9. Jo's act is a bundle of various, conflicting motives:

- She aims to spite Aunt March, who will provide the family with a loan but will accompany it, as the old woman often does, with a lecture about the family's improvidence.

- She does it out of love for her father, sacrificing her hair or sexuality to him or for him in what Bedell calls (giving a nod to the novel's oedipal themes) "a delicious father–daughter fantasy."

- She does it because it makes her more "boyish" (211).

- But doing it also makes her more feminine; her father notes on his return that "the shearing sobered our black sheep" and emasculated the tomboy: "In spite of the curly crop, I don't see the 'son Jo' whom I left a year ago. . . . I see a young lady who pins her collar straight, laces her boots neatly, and neither whistles, talks slang, nor lies on the rug like she used to do. . . . She doesn't bounce, but moves quietly, and takes care of a certain little person in a motherly way which delights me. I rather miss my wild girl; but [in her place I begin to see] a strong, helpful, tender-hearted woman" (286).

- But her haircut is also a gesture of defiance against that maturity her father credits her with; Jo does not wish to grow up if that means minding her hair and become a primping young woman like Meg, with her long tresses (13).

- All the same, she makes her sacrifice because she *has* matured, a condition Jo measures by financial independence; "I didn't beg, borrow, or steal it," she says about the money, "I earned it" (211).

- Jo's act, then, is an act of self-assertion; when she lays down the roll of bills before her mother, she insists, "That's *my* contribution to making father comfortable, and bringing him home" (211).

- At the same time, however, it is an act of self-denial; she rationalizes: "It will be good for my vanity; I was getting too proud of my wig" (211).

As this panoply of interpretations suggests, the scene is a bundle of conflicting impulses—and a cameo of the welter of impulses throughout *Little Women*. Alcott does not try to resolve the conflicts. She presents them *in statu quo*. See Bedell, Introduction, xxi, xxxiii; Elizabeth Langland, "Female Stories of Experience: Alcott's *Little Women* in Light of *Work*," in *The Voyage In: Fictions of Female Development*, ed. Elizabeth Abel, Marianne Hirsch, and Elizabeth Langland (Hanover, N.H.: University Press of New England for Dartmouth College, 1983), 122–23.

10. Bedell, Introduction, xxxiii.

11. Georg Wilhelm Friedrich Hegel, "The Contrite Consciousness," trans. Josiah Royce, in *Hegel Selections,* ed. Jacob Loewenberg (New York: Scribner, 1957), 79–97.

12. I have been unable to discover where I first encountered this quote.

13. Henry James, Review of *Moods,* by Louisa May Alcott, *North American Review* 101 (July 1865), reprinted in *Critical Essays on Louisa May Alcott,* ed. Madeline B. Stern (Boston: Hall, 1984), 73.

14. Secularized, this *mentalité* can be said to be embodied in the story of Cinderella, a tale that was important to Alcott. Perrault's Ash Girl, it should be remembered, is not forced to sit in the ashes of the hearth, but chooses to do so. She is unusually kind to her stepsisters—dressing their hair and readying them for the ball—all the while knowing she will only be mistreated in return. She asks to borrow a dress, knowing she will be refused. She asks to go to the ball, knowing she will not be permitted to. She asks to try on the glass slipper, knowing that this request from a cinder-wench will be met with jeers. Cinderella welcomes her mistreatment, even provokes it. If "the last shall be first," Cinderella is intent to be last.

Alcott improvised on this tale in her story "A Modern Cinderella," which appeared in the *Atlantic Monthly* (October 1860, 425–41) and which was, in many ways, a rehearsal for *Little Women*. A number of details in the novel also seem to recall the tale: the shoes by the fire remind the girls of Marmee (15); like Cinderella, Beth often creeps off to the hearth (18 and passim); Meg attends the Gardiners' ball, has problems with her shoe, and is given a ride home in a carriage by Laurie, a prince of a fellow; at the Moffats' party, Meg undergoes a sparkling transformation with the help of a borrowed dress and seems like "Cinderella" (122); and so on.

15. Quoted in Roland H. Bainton, *The Age of the Reformation* (Princeton, N.J.: Van Nostrand, 1956), 95.

16. Ruth MacDonald has explained how Alcott made use of Bunyan's moral allegory *The Pilgrim's Progress* in "The Progress of Pilgrims in *Little Women*," in *Proceedings of the Seventh Annual Conference of the Children's Literature Association*, ed. Priscilla Ord (New Rochelle, N.Y.: Iona College, 1982), 114–19. By secularizing this work, however, Alcott ran the risk that comes with putting new wine in old wineskins.

That is precisely what the Old Guard did not like. When the book appeared, one cranky reviewer wrote:

We dislike the disspiritualizing in it of Bunyan's great Allegory.
. . . The fight with Apollyon [in Bunyan's book] is reduced to a
conflict with an evil temper, and [Bunyan's] the Palace Beautiful and
Vanity Fair are made to be ordinary virtues or temptations. We cannot
commend the book as its quality merits. It is without Christ, and hence
perilous in proportion to its assimilation of Christian forms. Don't put
it in the Sunday School Library. (quoted in C. Waller Barrett, "Little
Women Forever," in *Bibliophile in the Nursery*, ed. William Targ
[Cleveland: World, 1957], 384)

17. Kate Ellis, "Life with Marmee: Three Versions," in *The Classic American Novel and the Movies*, ed. Gerald Pearcy and Roger Shatzin (New York: Ungar, 1977), 63. Ellis's suggestion seems apropos, in light not only of the capitalization of "Father" in the text but of certain comments by the characters: "learn to feel the strength and tenderness of your Heavenly Father as you do that of your earthly one" (112); "trusting in God and mother" (243); and so on.

9. *TOBY TYLER*

1. James Otis Kaler [James Otis, pseud.], *Toby Tyler, or Ten Weeks with a Circus* (New York: Grosset and Dunlap, 1967), 3. Subsequent references to pages of this work appear in parentheses.

2. See Bernard Wishy, *The Child and the Republic* (Philadelphia: University of Pennsylvania Press, 1968), 34–41. For the twentieth century, consider an Associated Press wire story of September 22, 1986 (dateline: Windsor, Maine), regarding Maine farmers who nine years ago created an alternative to the circus: "You can't find Ferris wheels, ox-pulling contests or junk-food stands at the Common Ground Country Fair. . . . The food stands featured all-natural snacks and additive-free fruit juices and teas. The organic popcorn was cooked in safflower oil and flavored with sea salt, and the pizza had a whole-wheat crust. There were also ginger carrots, corn bread, brown rice, organic salads, lamb barbecue and maple milkshakes."

3. "Kaler, James Otis," in *Something About the Author,* ed. Anne Commire (Detroit: Gale, 1979), 15: 151–55.

4. Kirk Munroe, Foreword to *Toby Tyler, or Ten Weeks with a Circus,* by James Otis (New York: Harper and Brothers, 1930), ix–xiii.

5. Bruno Bettelheim, *The Uses of Enchantment* (New York: Knopf, 1976), 159–66.

6. Ibid., 159.

7. John Seelye, Preface to *Toby Tyler,* by James Otis, Garland Series: Classics of Children's Literature, 1621–1932 (New York: Garland Press, 1977), v–vi.

10. *HANS BRINKER*

1. Mary Mapes Dodge, *Hans Brinker; or, The Silver Skates* (New York: Airmont, 1966). Subsequent references to pages of this work appear in parentheses.

2. Catherine Morris Wright, *Lady of the Silver Skates* (Jamestown, R.I.: Clingstone Press, 1979), 158.

3. Ibid., 32.

4. Raff Brinker's actual condition defies medical description. It might be referred to as amnesia or the "Rip Van Winkle Syndrome," since for ten years he remained alive but with a diminished mental capacity and loss of memory. His amnesia, incidentally, might be contrasted to the prodigious memories of Dodge's juveniles when—in this book meant both to delight and to teach—they provide unusually long chronicles of Dutch history and customs.

The role of memory in this book might be compared with its importance in *The Prince and the Pauper.* As we have observed, in discussing the third of "The Three Lives of the Child-Hero," some recognition has to be reached that the youth has previously led two lives—first with the biological family, and then in circumstances apart from it. What is important in the Third Life is some recognition of continuity. Tom Canty, in his intoxication with his royal Second Life, runs the danger of forgetting who he was; but, finally, he remembers. Edward Tudor, in contrast, has a prodigious memory, never forgets who he is, and (in the conclusion of this memorious or historical novel) remembers where he hid the Great Seal; his succession is assured.

In *Hans Brinker* fathers, not sons, have problems with continuity. During Hans's childhood, Raff Brinker was a kind and loving man. After "the accident," during Hans's adolescence, Raff became an "angry" father and a hysterical madman—a reflection, perhaps, of the projection of oedipal feelings. One result of this change was Raff's loss of memory, his inability to recognize his family or remember where he buried the family's savings, which had once made them prosperous. After Hans grows older and saves his father by getting him needed medical attention, Raff recovers his memory and remembers where the treasure is buried, and the family is reunited. Or, again, since oedipal problems are worked through, antagonism is no longer an issue and the family can be "restored"—hence the motifs of the lost being found and (with the recovery of the buried guilders) the return of the vanished happy times.

These motifs are echoed in the Dr. Boekman subplot. Dr. Boekman was a kind father to Laurens. Then came a "misunderstanding" that resulted in a separation between the two, during which Dr. Boekman became the "crossest" man in Holland. Finally, continuity is restored when Raff recovers his memory and the Brinkers puzzle out the identity of the owner of the "lost" watch he was given. By this means, Dr. Boekman's "lost" son Laurens is found, a rapprochement occurs, and another family is memorably restored.

5. Denis de Rougemont, *Love in the Western World,* trans. Montgomery Belgion (Greenwich, Conn.: Fawcett, 1966), 15–58 and passim.

11. *THE SECRET GARDEN*

1. See Madelon S. Gohlke, "Re-reading *The Secret Garden,*" *College English* 41 (April 1980): 894–902; see also the response by Susan H. McLeod, *College English* 42 (December 1980): 423–25. Cf. Rosemary Threadgold, *"The Secret Garden:* An Appreciation of Frances Hodgson Burnett as a Novelist for Children," *Children's Literature in Education* 10, no. 3 (Fall 1979): 113–19; Virginia L. Wolf, "Psychology and Magic: Evocative Blend or Melodramatic Patchwork?" in *Children's Novels and the Movies,* ed. Douglas Street (New York: Ungar, 1983), 121–30; Sarah Smedman, "Springs of Hope: Recovery of Primordial Time in 'Mythic' Novels for Young Readers," *Children's Literature* 16 (1988): 91–107. First serialized by the *American Magazine* in 1910, and then published as a book in 1911, *The Secret Garden*'s popularity has been perennial. Surveys indicate that

women, particularly, remember it among their favorite childhood books; only *Little Women* is chosen more often. See Sarah Crichton, "What We Read as Youngsters: Top Editors Recall Their Favorite Childhood Books," *Publishers Weekly*, 26 February 1982, 121–24; an unpublished survey conducted in 1977 by the Public Library of Mobile, Alabama; Bernice Cullinan and M. Jerry Weiss, eds., *Books I Read When I Was Young: The Favorite Books of Famous People* (New York: Avon, 1980); Evelyn B. Byrne and Otto M. Penzler, eds., *Attacks of Taste* (New York: Gotham Book Mart, 1971); Jerry Griswold, "Young [Ronald] Reagan's Reading," *New York Times Book Review*, 30 August 1981, 11, 21; Jerry Griswold and Amy Wallace, "What Famous People Read," *Parade Magazine*, 13 March 1983, 21–25.

2. Frances Hodgson Burnett, *The Secret Garden* (New York: Dell, 1962), 282. Subsequent references to pages of this work appear in parentheses.

3. While in some cases Burnett seems to assign characters names for no particular reason or to pick those that might be common to Yorkshire, in other cases they seem to have some significance. The housekeeper who has keys to all the rooms is Mrs. Medlock. The grisly gardener who works in rain or shine is Ben Weatherstaff. And Mary's maid is Martha—a combination of names that seems biblical. Perhaps the most significant, however, is Craven, which connotes weak-kneed and simpering. In a sense, Colin must overcome the legacy of that name and become assertive. In the latter parts of the book, he becomes, to everyone's approval, a magisterial boy "rajah"—a character type Mary remembers from her days in India and described to him.

Mary's association with the nursery rhyme also seems significant. When Burnett began to compose *The Secret Garden*, she took up a manuscript titled *Mistress Mary* that she had abandoned some years before. Given the allusion to the nursery rhyme, it may be assumed that this work dealt with "contrariness." As Elizabeth Keyser has noted, *The Secret Garden* gives appearances of having been started as a novel meant to condemn contrariness as an undesirable attribute of spoiled and petulant children like Mary and Colin, but somewhere along the way Burnett ended up writing a hymn of praise to contrariness as a form of spunk. See Elizabeth Lennox Keyser, "Quite Contrary: Frances Hodgson Burnett's *The Secret Garden*," *Children's Literature* 11 (1983): 1–13. Mary is able to help Colin because she is just as contrary as he is. When she confronts him in the midst of his tantrum and scolds him, she does what no "nice" child would ever do; but by violating convention, by being willful and contrary, she sets the boy straight. Likewise, when Colin tries to walk for the first time in his life, he does so out of contrariness because he wants to spite the patronizing old gardener who calls him a cripple.

4. A number of scholars have pointed out the influence of *The Secret Garden* on T. S. Eliot's "The Four Quartets," especially in the opening section, where he recalls his own childhood and compares it with what happens in Burnett's book:

Footfalls echo in the memory
Down the passage we did not take

Towards the door we never opened
Into the rose garden [. . .]
Quick, said the bird, find them find them. [. . .]
Go, said the bird, for the leaves were full of children,
Hidden excitedly, containing laughter.

See Alison White, "Tap-Roots into a Rose Garden," *The Great Excluded: Critical Essays on Children's Literature* 1 (1972): 74–76; Stephen D. Roxburgh, "'Our First World': Form and Meaning in *The Secret Garden,*" *Children's Literature in Education* 10, no. 3 (Fall 1979): 120–30; Ruth Barton, "T. S. Eliot's Secret Garden," *Notes and Queries* 31 (December 1984): 512–14.

In terms of deep symbolism, the garden was sealed when Mrs. Craven died and no one has entered it since. Akin to the impotent kingfisher in Eliot's wasteland, Mr. Craven buries his key. But like Dorothy's Toto, the promiscuously curious robin points out what is hidden. Mary finds the key and then the hidden door, and the wasteland once more becomes a fertile place, Kansas becomes Oz.

5. This particular sound seems to play an important part in the book. During the cholera outbreak, Mary was frightened by the sound of distant crying and hurrying feet. Since coming to Misselthwaite Manor, Mary has been bothered by the very same sound. In the last pages of the book, however, Mr. Craven hears laughter and the sound of hurrying feet as the children play in the garden.

6. A 1983 newspaper story suggests that there was a curse with which Burnett may have been familiar—though it is not associated with hereditary hunchbacks, but with promiscuity and premature deaths:

The 7th Earl of Craven—who lived in fear of a curse that reputedly causes all the males of his family to die young—has killed himself at age 26. . . . None of Craven's ancestors going back to the 17th century reached the age of 60. . . . The reputed curse says that all the boys of the Craven family, which traces its lineage back to William the Conqueror, will die before their mothers. Residents in the earl's village of Hampstead Marshall, Berkshire, said it was uttered by a village mother whose daughter was made pregnant by a Craven ancestor. ("Ancient Family Curse Recalled by Death of British Earl," *Los Angeles Times* [25 October 1983], sec. 1, p. 10)

7. This issue of secrecy is notable. As the days pass, Colin concludes "that the mystery surrounding the garden was one of its greatest charms. Nothing must spoil that. No one must ever suspect that they had a secret" (204).

Gillian Adams begins a wonderful essay on secrecy in *The Secret Garden* with a quote from Carl Jung: "The maintenance of secrets acts like a psychic poison, which alienates the possessor from the community. In small doses, [however,] this poison may actually be a priceless remedy, an essential preliminary to the differentiation of the individual." Adams argues that Mary and Colin move from being secrets themselves (their existence is concealed by their parents, and this results in physical and emotional ill health) to those who are empowered because they possess secrets they can share or not share with others. The possession of these secrets isolates them from the adult world, but it also allows them to differentiate, to nurture themselves as individuals. Once they have done so, they rejoin the community and share secrets with adults (Gillian Adams, "Secrets and Healing Magic in *The Secret Garden*," in *Triumphs of the Spirit in Children's Literature,* ed. Francelia Butler and Richard Rotert [Hamden, Conn.: Library Professional Publications, 1986], 42–54. Cf. Roderick McGillis, "Secrets and 'Sequence' in Children's Stories," *Studies in the Literary Imagination* 18, no. 2 [Fall 1985]: 35–46).

We can say, in other words, that the children do something similar to indigenous people who retreat to ancestral hiding places where, in secret, for purposes of curing and empowerment, they handle their totemic objects. In *The Secret Garden,* however, the place itself is totemic; the retreat is not from the tribe, but from adults; the results are not only health and power, but childhood maturation.

8. Anne Thwaite, *Waiting for the Party* (New York: Scribner, 1974), 218; Vivian Burnett, *Romantick Lady* (New York: Scribner, 1927), 376–77.

9. While most heroes in children's books are (in one way or another) lovable, the two main characters of this book, Mary and later Colin, are spoiled and repugnant when they are introduced. It is as if Burnett had learned from her experience some thirty years earlier with *Little Lord Fauntleroy.* In that book, Burnett had presented a child who was a paragon of virtues and (at least in the novel) universally loved. A number of readers, however, found the little lord "an insufferable mollycoddle, even a prig" (Thwaite, *Waiting for the Party,* 91). While that may be an inaccurate description of Fauntleroy, it is the perfect one for both Mary and Colin. Instead of the ideal child who unwittingly provoked repugnance, then, Burnett presents in this book two juveniles who are already repugnant and then shows their transformation.

Dickon presents another type of ideal child. When he is first seen, his resemblance to Pan is almost too obvious: he is playing pan-pipes, has the satyr's goatlike nose, and (like the guardian of woodland creatures) is surrounded by a bevy of animals. In *Secret Gardens* (Boston: Houghton Mifflin, 1985), Humphrey Carpenter has discussed how British Children's Literature of the Golden Age, looking for an alternative to Christianity, embraced a romanticized version of nature worship. Pan (including Peter Pan) and Nature Boys (from Bevis to Mowgli) became the new version of the ideal child. Likewise, Children's Literature came to be associated with the pastoral, with the domesticated English countryside of Beatrix Potter and Kate Greenaway. All these motifs reached an apex in Kenneth Grahame's *Wind in the Willows* (1908), the central scene of which is an apparition of Pan in a passage distinctly echoed by Burnett in Chapter 21 of her own novel.

10. Frances Hodgson Burnett, *The One I Knew Best of All* (New York: Scribner, 1893), 254–60. Burnett's interest in gardening became an obsession in her later life (between 1899 and 1907), when she rented a home in England and there befriended a robin much like the one in *The Secret Garden.* Her son Vivian describes that period:

The taking of Maytham Hall began a new era in her life, and introduced a new and consuming interest. Here began what might be called her Pastoral period; here entered the Passionate Gardener. She had always been keenly interested in flowers, but the joy of planning a garden and personally supervising the planting of bulbs and the setting out of plants had never been hers. The leasing of Maytham provided the opportunity. . . . The Rose Garden became a most important feature of Maytham Hall, for it served as Mrs. Burnett's outdoor workroom, and in it large portions of many of her later books were written. Enclosed by high brick walls, Mrs. Burnett found an old orchard, reverted to wilderness.

Burnett's son goes on to speculate that *The Secret Garden* was inspired by this garden and written out of her regret when she heard, years later, that her flower garden at Maytham had been converted to a vegetable garden. See Burnett, *Romantick Lady,* 286, 293, 327. Cf. Frances Hodgson Burnett, *In the Garden* (Boston and New York: Medici Society of America, 1925); *My Robin* (New York: Stokes, 1912); and *The One I Knew Best of All,* especially chaps. 3 and 14.

11. See Phyllis Bixler, *Frances Hodgson Burnett* (Boston: Twayne, 1984), 95. See also Bixler, "Formula Fiction and Children's Literature: Thornton Waldo Burgess and Frances Hodgson Burnett," *Children's Literature in Education* 15, no. 2 (Summer 1984): 63–71; "The Oral-Formulaic Training of a Popular Fiction Writer: Frances Hodgson Burnett," *Journal of Popular Culture* 154 (Spring 1982): 42–52; "Tradition and the Individual Talent of Frances Hodgson Burnett: A Generic Analysis of *Little Lord Fauntleroy, A Little Princess,* and *The Secret Garden,*" *Children's Literature* 7 (1978): 191–207.

The enclosed and forgotten rose garden also recalls the Grimms' tale "Briar Rose"; as Mary observes, being in the Secret Garden "seemed like being shut out of the world in some fairy place. The few books she had read and liked had been fairy-story books, and she had read of secret gardens in some of the stories. Sometimes people went to sleep in them for a hundred years, which she had thought must be rather stupid. She had no intention of going to sleep, and, in fact, she was becoming more awake every day" (83).

In the Grimm tale, the Sleeping Beauty falls into a century-long slumber behind castle walls that are soon overgrown with roses—all because someone forgot to invite the thirteenth fairy to the child's christening. P. L. Travers muses on this uninvited fairy and unintentionally offers what might be taken as a particularly apt description of the circumstances of the children in *The Secret Garden:* "Down in its dungeon it plots and plans, waiting, like the unloved child, the day of its revenge. What it needs, like the unloved child, is to be recognized, not disclaimed; given its place and proper birthright" (*About the Sleeping Beauty* [New York: McGraw-Hill, 1976], 56–57).

But there are differences as well. Mary stresses how her own circumstances differ from those of the tale. She thinks of herself as the Waking Beauty, since she is shrugging off her cranky listlessness. Moreover, an arriving prince does not awaken her. Instead, Mary brings the bedridden Colin out of his torpor.

12. There are, of course, exceptions. A French example of the advocacy of positive thinking might be found, to mention one, in Jean de Brunhoff's *Babar the King,* in which the elephant regnant is troubled by a dream of demonic bad thoughts fighting with angelic good thoughts; the point, the Old Lady says, is not to get discouraged. A Swiss example might be found in Johanna Spyri's *Heidi,* in which the child hypochondriac Clara Sesemann is encouraged and cured.

12. *POLLYANNA*

1. In 1987, Dell reissued a paperback edition of the book. Cf. James D. Hart, *The Popular Book* (Berkeley: University of California Press, 1963), 21–23; Frank Luther Mott, *Golden Multitudes* (New York: Bowker, 1947), 222.

2. "Pollyanna Whittier," in Margery Fisher, *Who's Who in Children's Literature* (London: Weidenfeld and Nicholson, 1975), 288. Cf. Marcia E. Allentuck, "Old Books: *Pollyanna* by Eleanor H. Porter," *Georgia Review* 14 (Winter 1960): 447–49.

3. Grant Overton, "Eleanor Porter," in *The Women Who Make Our Novels* (Freeport, N.Y.: Books for Libraries Press, 1967), 263.

4. Robert Shankland, "She was glad, Glad, GLAD!" *Good Housekeeping,* July 1947, 185.

5. *Boston Transcript,* 24 April 1913, 9.

6. Shankland, "She was glad," 185.

7. Eleanor Porter, *Pollyanna* (London: Penguin, 1969), 81. Subsequent references to pages of this work appear in parentheses.

8. Shankland, "She was glad," 185.

9. See Gladiola, "The Screen," *Commonweal,* 3 June 1960, 257; *Time,* 9 May 1960, 88; "The Brighter Side," *Newsweek,* 16 May 1960, 110–11. A reviewer in *America* (28 May 1960, 320–21) wrote that Disney "has taken out most of the saccharine . . . and replaced it with muscle and sinew and a saving flavor of lightness and humor. An unmixed blessing in bringing off this feat is the performance in the title role of young Hayley Mills, surely the most winning adolescent actress within recent memory." Hayley Mills, *People Weekly* indelicately suggested, also had a hard time living down the curse of Pollyanna. She had not been allowed to take the lead in the movie *Lolita* because the Disney people had wanted to protect her image: "A few years later, just possibly to put her mentors in their place, she upstaged Nabokov's nymphet. Hayley, at a virginal 19, moved in with a thrice-wed 52-year-old Humbert, British filmmaker Roy Boulting" (Fred Hauptfuhrer, "Pollyanna Never Had It So Happy," *People,* 14 April 1975, 62).

10. Leonard Maltin, *The Disney Films* (New York: Popular Library, 1978), 321.

11. Quoted in Overton, "Eleanor Porter," 262.

12. Mary Cadogan and Patricia Craig, *You're a Brick, Angela! A New Look at Girls' Fiction from 1839 to 1975* (London: Gollancz, 1976), 89, 94, 99. Cf. Perry Nodelman, "Progressive Utopia: Or, How to Grow Up Without Growing Up," in *Proceedings of the Sixth Annual Conference of the Children's Literature Association,* ed. Priscilla Ord (Villanova, Pa.: Villanova University, 1980), 146–54; Louise Hart Strecker, "Child Heroines in Popular American Fiction: 1900–1920" (M.A. thesis, San Diego State University, 1984), 124–60; Gillian Avery, "Porter, Eleanor H.," in *Twentieth-Century Children's Writers,* ed. D. L. Kirkpatrick (New York: St. Martin's Press, 1978), 622–23; two essays by Jacqueline Berke: "'Mother, I Can Do It Myself!': The Self-sufficient Heroine in Popular Girls' Fiction," *Women's Studies* 6 (1979): 187–203, and "Eleanor Hodgman Porter," in *American Women Writers,* ed. Lina Mainiero (New York: Ungar, 1981), 400–402.

13. *New York Sun,* 8 March 1913, 3.

14. Grace Isabel Colbron, "The Popularity of *Pollyanna,*" *Bookman* (May 1915): 298.

15. For example, *Rebecca* and *Pollyanna* also begin in similar ways: Pollyanna's nonstop chatter in the buggy on the way to her aunt's home makes Nancy (the maid) dizzy; this scene recalls a similar volubility on the part of Rebecca when she travels by stagecoach to her aunts' home and makes Jerry Cobb (the driver) feel the same way. When Pollyanna's arrival is imminent, the gardener wonders how the aunt will do with a child in the house, but the more sympathetic maid wonders how the child will do with Miss Polly in the house—just as Aunt Miranda wonders how she and her sister will endure Rebecca, and the more sympathetic Aunt Jane wonders how the girl will endure them.

16. Shirley Marchalonis, "Eleanor H. Porter," *American Novelists, 1910–1945,* vol. 2 of *Dictonary of Literary Biography,* ed. James J. Martine (Detroit: Gale, 1981), 294.

17. While *Pollyanna*'s Pietà might be used as an illustration of change in American Children's Literature (when compared with the pietàs of the eighteenth century), another episode might serve as well because it employs and modifies a typos that appeared in the early nineteenth century—the Sunday school story. In Porter's hands, the traditional good-child/bad-child anecdote is not used as an exemplum to be considered by youths, but becomes instead a lesson for adults in recommended child-raising practices.

This anecdote appears in a story within a story, a magazine article that is quoted at some length within the novel. To understand it, we first have to understand its frame. Late in the novel, Pollyanna aids the dejected Reverend Ford. The minister is depressed by his backbiting congregation and, in the countryside outside town, prays for guidance. Like Hawthorne's Dimmesdale, he throws himself on the ground, but instead of the elf-child Pearl, along comes an angel in the form of Pollyanna. Reverend Ford had been contemplating a fire-and-brimstone sermon to chastise his congregation. Pollyanna reorients his thinking by telling him of the Glad Game and explaining that when her own minister father had found himself in similar circumstances, he had remembered and constructed sermons around the 800 "rejoicing texts" found in the Bible: "rejoice greatly," "Be glad in the Lord," and so on.

A few paragraphs later, Pollyanna's point is rephrased in more secular terms in the story within the story when Reverend Ford returns to town and reads a magazine article. It tells of a boy named Tom who fills his mother's woodbox because, when his father makes the request, he assumes that the boy will be glad to do so. That woodbox would not have been filled, the article continues, if the father had said to Tom that he was ashamed the boy had not yet completed the task. The moral of this story concerns positive reinforcement:

> What men and women need is encouragement. . . . Instead of always harping on a man's faults, tell him of his virtues. . . . The influence of a beautiful, helpful, hopeful character is contagious, and may revolutionize a whole town. . . . When you look for the bad, expecting it, you will get it. When you *know* you will find the good—you will get that. . . . Tell your son Tom you *know* he'll be glad to fill that woodbox—then watch him start, alert and interested! (152)

This magazine story, of course, presents a synoptic description of Pollyanna and her enterprise. Equally revealing is the progress from a religious sermon (delivered by the daughter of a minister) to a secular lecture found in a magazine; instead of lessons in spiritual improvement, in other words, the magazine's moral is phrased in terms of secular psychology and preferred patterns of child raising. Finally, while it resembles the Sunday school story, the magazine article does not present what is typical of this genre: the hoary bearded elder who points to a lesson for children in the example of some youthful miscreant or virtuous ephebe. Instead, we have a lesson (ostensibly coming from a child) that is directed *to adults*. What is advocated, in other words, is not the reformation of a child, but the reformation of adults and their notion of childhood. Instead of religion, we are offered evangelical pediatrics.

18. R. W. B. Lewis, *The American Adam* (Chicago: University of Chicago Press, 1955).

19. Carol Weston, "Are You a Pollyanna or a Pessimist?" *Seventeen*, January 1986, 45. Cf. Ethel Marbach, "Will the Real POLLYANNA Please Stand Up?" *Farm Journal*, November 1965, 101.

20. Similar to the scene of whitewashing is another in which Tom explains to Aunt Polly why he gave the medicine Painkiller (which Tom decribes as "fire in a liquid form") to the family cat—an act that turns the pet into a woolly comet that streaks around the room and then sails out the window:

> "I done it out of pity for him—because he hadn't any aunt."
> ". . . Because if he'd a had one she'd a burnt him out herself! She'd a roasted his bowels out of him 'thout any more feeling than if he was human!"

Aunt Polly felt a sudden pang of remorse. This was putting things
in a new light; what was cruelty to a cat *might* be cruelty to a boy, too.
She began to soften; she felt sorry. . . .
"I was meaning for the best, Tom." (94–96)

Tom is surprised by how quickly opinions change when matters appear "in a
new light." When they become rich, children who have been thought insignifi-
cant suddenly become sages whose statements are carefully listened to by adults.
When Tom identifies the true murderer at the trial and the innocent Muff Potter is
let off the hook, "the fickle, unreasoning world took Muff Potter to its bosom and
fondled him as lavishly as it had abused him before," (173).

Moods are changeable in *Tom Sawyer*. When the boys are camping out on
Jackson's Island, they are high-spirited; but when a thunderstorm breaks, the
mood grows solemn as the boys wonder whether they are ready to meet their
maker. Likewise, Clemens knew how humor puts things "in a new light," how the
tedium of a school recital can easily be changed to amusement when a cat is
lowered from the attic and seizes the teacher's wig.

Clemens stresses the importance of subjectivity. As the whitewashing episode indicates, the way an activity is imaginatively conceived is what determines
whether it is a chore or fun. For this reason, Tom has incredible difficulty mem-
orizing his passages from the Bible for Sunday school, but he knows by heart his
book on Robin Hood. He is slow doing his chores but incredibly fast when it
comes to escaping them.

Clemens also employs the whitewashing episode's distinction between "play"
and "work" to discriminate between children and adults. Tom and Huck are on a
lark when they find hidden treasure in an empty house; a few days later "every
'haunted' house in St. Petersburg and the neighboring villages was dissected,
plank by plank, and its foundations dug up and ransacked for hidden treasure—
and not by boys, but men—pretty grave, unromantic men, too" (254). When
they reenact the story of Robin Hood, Tom Sawyer and Joe Harper play at being
outlaws, quarreling, and killing; a few chapters later, their senior counterparts
engage in grim work—the grave robbing occurs, and the outlaw Injun Joe quar-
rels·with Doc Robinson and kills him. What difference is there, Clemens asks,
between kids and grown-ups? The difference is the light in which they see things.

21. Ihab Hassan, *Radical Innocence: Studies in the Contemporary American
Novel* (Princeton, N.J.: Princeton University Press, 1961).

22. Quoted in ibid., 40. In an elaborate psychological study of American
culture—reported in a book they chose to title *The Pollyanna Principle* (Cambridge, Mass.: Schenkman Books, 1979)—Margaret Matlin and David Strang
concluded that "to a considerable extent we are *all* Pollyannas. Our studies, and
those of others, yield the following generalizations": people take longer to recognize unpleasant stimuli, and they communicate good news faster than bad news;
pleasant words are used more frequently in the English language than unpleasant
ones; we commonly ask "how good" something (a book, movie, restaurant) is

rather than "how bad" it is; pleasant events are judged more likely to occur than unpleasant ones; pleasant objects are judged larger than unpleasant ones; and so on. Also excerpted in "The Pollyanna Principle: Inherent Optimism in Humans," *Psychology Today,* March 1978, 56–58.

AFTERWORD

1. See Steven Kanfer, "A Lively, Profitable World of Kid Lit," *Time,* 29 December 1980, 62–65; Leslie Barker, "Kids'-book Sales Aren't Kid Stuff," *Dallas Morning News,* wire story in *The Times Advocate* (Escondido, Calif.), 20 November 1990, C1, C2.

2. Information from the U.S. Bureau of Census. See "Fertility of American Women: June 1987," Series P-20, no. 427; "Population Aged 35 to 44 Growing the Fastest" (press release [CB90–38], 2 March 1990).

3. Mary Jarrell, Note to recording of Randall Jarrell reading *The Bat-Poet,* Caedmon TV1364. See Jerry Griswold, *The Children's Books of Randall Jarrell* (Athens: University of Georgia Press, 1988), 52–53, 61–63.

4. Russell Hoban, "Thoughts on a Shirtless Cyclist, Robin Hood, Johann Sebastian Bach, and One or Two Other Things," *Children's Literature in Education* 4 (March 1971): 23.

5. Leslie Fiedler, *Love and Death in the American Novel* (New York: Dell, 1966), 24.

6. This attitude lingers in some quarters. The most recent attempt to compose a new standard history of American literature is Emory Elliott et al., eds., *Columbia Literary History of the United States* (New York: Columbia University Press, 1988). What is unique about this work is its acknowledgment of arguments that the literary canon must be widened and its open-minded attitude toward previously unacceptable genres and authors; science fiction and detective fiction, for example, are now regarded with a new seriousness and acceptability, as are (to mention just two other examples) works by women and Asian Americans. Nonetheless, the one great omission, a lacuna so large you could drive a Mack truck through it, is this standard work's lack of coverage of Children's Literature. A reader can search high and wide in its index (which includes, for example, references to Raymond Chandler, Zora Neale Hurston, and Pearl Buck) and still not find (to mention just two notable omissions) Frank Baum's *The Wizard of Oz* and E. B. White's *Charlotte's Web.* Alas, a lack.

✦ ✦ ✦ ✦ ✦ ✦ ✦
Index

FOR THE BEST IN PAPERBACKS, LOOK FOR THE

In every corner of the world, on every subject under the sun, Penguin represents quality and variety—the very best in publishing today.

For complete information about books available from Penguin—including Puffins, Penguin Classics, and Arkana—and how to order them, write to us at the appropriate address below. Please note that for copyright reasons the selection of books varies from country to country.

In the United Kingdom: Please write to *Dept. JC, Penguin Books Ltd, FREEPOST, West Drayton, Middlesex UB7 0BR*.

If you have any difficulty in obtaining a title, please send your order with the correct money, plus ten percent for postage and packaging, to *P.O. Box No. 11, West Drayton, Middlesex UB7 0BR*

In the United States: Please write to *Consumer Sales, Penguin USA, P.O. Box 999, Dept. 17109, Bergenfield, New Jersey 07621-0120.* VISA and MasterCard holders call 1-800-253-6476 to order all Penguin titles

In Canada: Please write to *Penguin Books Canada Ltd, 10 Alcorn Avenue, Suite 300, Toronto, Ontario M4V 3B2*

In Australia: Please write to *Penguin Books Australia Ltd, P.O. Box 257, Ringwood, Victoria 3134*

In New Zealand: Please write to *Penguin Books (NZ) Ltd, Private Bag 102902, North Shore Mail Centre, Auckland 10*

In India: Please write to *Penguin Books India Pvt Ltd, 706 Eros Apartments, 56 Nehru Place, New Delhi 110 019*

In the Netherlands: Please write to *Penguin Books Netherlands bv, Postbus 3507, NL-1001 AH Amsterdam*

In Germany: Please write to *Penguin Books Deutschland GmbH, Metzlerstrasse 26, 60594 Frankfurt am Main*

In Spain: Please write to *Penguin Books S. A., Bravo Murillo 19, 1° B, 28015 Madrid*

In Italy: Please write to *Penguin Italia s.r.l., Via Felice Casati 20, I-20124 Milano*

In France: Please write to *Penguin France S. A., 17 rue Lejeune, F-31000 Toulouse*

In Japan: Please write to *Penguin Books Japan, Ishikiribashi Building, 2–5–4, Suido, Bunkyo-ku, Tokyo 112*

In Greece: Please write to *Penguin Hellas Ltd, Dimocritou 3, GR-106 71 Athens*

In South Africa: Please write to *Longman Penguin Southern Africa (Pty) Ltd, Private Bag X08, Bertsham 2013*